# PUBLIC RELATIONS FOR THE DESIGN PROFESSIONAL

## Gerre Jones

McGRAW-HILL BOOK COMPANY

New York   St. Louis   San Francisco   Auckland   Bogotá
Düsseldorf   Johannesburg   London   Madrid   Mexico
Montreal   New Delhi   Panama   Paris   São Paulo
Singapore   Sydney   Tokyo   Toronto

Parts of Chapter 8, "Audiovisuals,"
appeared as a series in the newsletter
*Professional Marketing Report* (December 1976, p. 3;
January 1977, p. 4; and February 1977, p. 3).

Library of Congress Cataloging in Publication Data

Jones, Gerre L, date.
  Public relations for the design professional.

  Bibliography: p.
  Includes index.
    1.   Architectural firms—Public relations.   2.   Archi-
tectural services marketing.   3.   Consulting engineers—
Public relations.   4.   Engineering services marketing.
I.   Title.
NA1966.J665        659.2'9'72        79-14088
ISBN 0-07-032815-3

The editors for this book were Jeremy Robinson and
Tobia L. Worth, the designer was Richard R. Roth,
and the production supervisor was Sally Fliess.
It was set in Palatino and Avant Garde Bold
by University Graphics, Inc.

Printed and bound by Von Hoffmann Press, Inc.

# CONTENTS

Wherein the mind does these three things; first it
chooses a certain number [of specific ideas]; secondly,
it gives them connection, and makes them into one
idea; thirdly, it ties them together by a name. Men
form such ideas for the convenience of
communication.[1]

# PREFACE

*P*ublic Relations for the Design Professional
might be viewed as the third installment in a series of "how-to" marketing
reference books. I hesitate to characterize it as the last volume in a marketing
trilogy, since there may remain at least one or two related subjects worthy of
book-length coverage.

The initial contribution, *How to Market Professional Design Services*, was
published by McGraw-Hill in 1973 and has gone through a number of print-
ings. The next installment was *How to Prepare Professional Design Brochures*,
also from McGraw-Hill and published in 1976. All three books were written
in response to expressed professional needs and perceived voids in the literature, as determined and interpreted by the author.

In *How to Market Professional Design Services* I pointed out:

> Public relations, publicity, advertising, and sales promotion are all basic parts
> of the successful marketing techniques of American business. . . .
> Public relations for the architect, engineer, or planner means getting to be
> known, liked, trusted, respected, and preferred—while developing and uphold-
> ing professional dignity. Public relations is not witchcraft; it cannot make some-
> thing out of nothing. It merely points out the deserving person to the public.
> The public cannot be blinded to nefarious deeds by anyone or any organization,
> nor can fine words substitute for honest acts.[2]

Over the past half-dozen years I have conducted or served on the faculty
of an average of two workshops a month. The majority of these workshops
involved the general aspects of marketing; others were more specialized—
covering such subjects as brochure design and production, writing, public
relations, presentations, and telephone qualification techniques. The workshops have been held in every major U.S. and Canadian city (plus a few
minor ones). In addition to accumulating several hundred thousand travel
miles in the process, it has been a stimulating, thoroughly interesting, and
highly educational personal experience to meet and discuss marketing techniques with the thousands of participants in the workshops. As I indicated
above, out of these sessions grew many of the ideas for the triad of books on
marketing principles and tools.

---

[1]John Locke, *Essay Concerning Human Understanding* (1690).
[2]Gerre Jones, *How to Market Professional Design Services,* McGraw-Hill Book Company, New
York, 1973, pp. 283–284.

The prefaces of my first two books referred to a number of years of personal experience and involvement with the subjects covered. I now find that expressing my experience in terms of quarter centuries or decades is personally somewhat unsettling. (I can't have been doing this for more than 30 years!) So I will simply state here that my qualifications for writing on the subject of public relations are pretty good by most standards.

Throughout the remainder of this volume we'll be looking at the origins and early history of public relations, its practice in modern society, and some of the more popular, proven, and productive processes and techniques used by contemporary practitioners. One chapter is given over to an exploration of the ideal and actual roles of public relations counselors. Another chapter discusses the various publics to whom a successful program must relate. Two other chapters cover the varied and wondrous tools and techniques available to public relations people and their clients. The staging and coverage of special events receives in-depth attention in Chapter 7.

The production and proper use of audiovisuals I believe deserves a full chapter, as do writing, press releases, and photography. Several types of promotional publications are covered in Chapter 12, while Chapter 13 is about measuring the results of public relations efforts (very difficult to do, as you'll see). Chapter 14 explores the relation of advertising to public relations and to the overall professional marketing program.

It would be difficult to write a serious book about public relations without some discussion of lobbying and its many ramifications. Somewhat related is the chapter dealing with certain of the legal problems to be encountered and solved along the way.

In the final chapter an attempt is made to help the reader arrive at some conclusions on the subject of public relations and its role, function, and place in a world oversaturated by communications. What I hope to be one of the most complete bibliographies ever compiled on the subject of public relations follows the last chapter, with the final entry an exhaustive index. (The indexer was exhausted at any rate.)

If the reader takes away nothing else of value from this book, we hope these two points will be remembered:

1. Experience is a tough teacher who insists on giving the test before the lesson.
2. Real knowledge is knowing where to find it.

GERRE JONES

# PUBLIC RELATIONS FOR THE DESIGN PROFESSIONAL

# PART
## 1

Change has been modified by the combined forces of technology, education, mobility, and especially communication. Widespread literacy is less than 500 years old; and well into the Twentieth Century the only media of communication were speech and print. Then in quick succession came the motion picture, recordings, radio, television, and other electronic media. The explosion of communications led to an implosion of the once vast and remote world. Suddenly it is all there to see, to experience, to judge; a person's scope of awareness and judgement has been multiplied thousands of times. Diverse, instant communication has changed the world of man much more than man has changed his institutions for living in that world.[1]

# CHAPTER 1
# Introduction

**T**HE EXPLOSION IN communications is a reflection of the information explosion. Consider that it took about 1750 years—from the birth of Christ to the industrial revolution—to double knowledge the first time. From late in the eighteenth century up to 1950 or so, knowledge doubled about every 50 years. Seventy-five percent of all the information available to humankind has been developed over the last 2 decades and, at the present rate of growth, the world's total knowledge now doubles about every 2 years. As Gerald Snyder, in *1994: The World of Tomorrow*, pointed out: "Each *minute*, technical reports, seminar proceedings, trade journals, documents, and books add 500,000 pages to the existing store of man's knowledge."[2] That translates into three-quarters of a billion pages every 24 hours!

## PRESENT SHOCK

By compressing the entire history of human evolution into a 50-year time span, we get another example of the constantly accelerating flow of knowledge and information. It took humans 49 years of the 50 in our compressed time line to get over being nomads and settle down into established communities. Only 6 months ago we learned to read and write. A couple of weeks ago the first printing press was built. And only in the last 3 or 4 days have we learned to use electricity.

3

Yesterday was a very busy day. We developed radio, television, diesel power, rayon, nylon, motion pictures, and high-octane gasoline. Since breakfast this morning we've released atomic energy, built jet planes, and produced several new antibiotics. A few minutes ago we sent a man to the moon. Less than a minute has elapsed since the Viking spacecraft landed on Mars. On this time scale—or even on a normal, noncompressed scale—who can (or would want to) predict what will happen this afternoon?

With all of this information to be communicated, credibility and confidence have become scarce commodities in many areas and among many people. Today most of us *want* information, answers, and solutions—but we prefer the knowledge to be transmitted as quietly and as simply as possible. The needs of humans are not met with bombast, hyperbole, and commands.

## FUTURE SHOCK

Alvin Toffler, in *Future Shock*, observed: '' . . . there are discoverable limits to the amount of change that the human organism can absorb, and that by endlessly accelerating change without first determining these limits, we may submit masses of men to demands they simply cannot tolerate. We run the high risk of throwing them into that particular state I have called future shock.''[3]

Toffler is concerned that beset individuals will blow a fuse in reaction to an overload of inputs (future shock), and simply refuse to take in new information by building up mental barriers. When the barriers finally are breached, he predicts the result will be a series of widespread personal catastrophes.

Toffler also noted: "There is . . . less time for extended, peaceful attention to one problem or one situation at a time. This is what lies behind the vague feeling . . . that 'Things are moving faster.' They are. Around us. And through us.''[4] A few statistics of past, present, and future shock:

- Ninety percent of all scientists who ever lived are alive today.
- Almost three-quarters of a century after the first flight of the Wright brothers, 70 percent of Americans have yet to take their first plane ride. More than 80 percent of us have never been outside the continental limits of the United States.
- Ninety percent of all wonder drugs have been developed since 1953.
- Only one-fourth of our present population can remember the Great Depression.
- Twenty-five percent of all our population who ever lived are alive today.
- Seventy percent of the U.S. population lives on one percent of the land. By the year 2000 the entire population will live on about nine percent of the land.
- By the end of this century 3.2 billion persons—half the world's population—will live in cities.
- Sixty percent of the population is eligible to vote, compared with two percent in Colonial times.

• Modern man is subjected to more information from all sources in 1 day than the medieval peasant was exposed to in an entire lifetime.

## THE OMNIPRESENT MEDIA

The fight for our attention by news and information media has risen to a continuous roar. Television wakes us up in the morning and puts us to sleep at night—literally, in many cases. Radio helps to fill in some of the potentially silent periods during the rest of the day; especially the time used in going to and returning from work.

Someone or something, it seems, is constantly trying to give us a message. Bumper stickers, stenciled advertisements on the sidewalks and streets— even T-shirts and sidewalk trash cans have been subverted into message-carrying media!

Once in the office we must scale, skim, and assimilate the information in the daily mountain of correspondence, direct mail, and press releases. Memos to and from colleagues flow from desk to desk, office to office, branch to branch, in a never-ending stream. At lunch, tent cards on the restaurant table advertise wine, charity campaigns, and today's Blue Plate Special. Less than halfway through the day our eyes and ears have been assaulted by hundreds of messages from dozens of media, all competing for the attention of an increasingly jaded public. Either human tolerance must expand until indifference results, or else our collective mental resistance will rise to the point where we slip into some approximation of Toffler's future shock.

"Communication will save the world!" the experts shout, while much of the world's literate population sits increasingly unresponsive, uncomprehending, and tuned out—catatonic victims of media and communications overkill. Many members of the so-called advanced societies are perilously close to becoming desensitized to all forms of communication.

In spite of the conditions just described, the information explosion in many areas of the globe might be characterized as muffled. About 70 percent of the world's population still falls below the minimum standards established by the United Nations Educational, Scientific and Cultural Organization (UNESCO) for mass media availability: ten newspapers, five radios, two television sets, and two movie house seats per 100 persons. (In early 1977 there were an estimated 120 million TV sets in U.S. homes—a ratio of better than one set for every two Americans. And radios outnumber people in this country by almost two to one!) So, while it is still possible to avoid some of the worst effects of the communications overkill, it is doubtful that many would opt for the alternative.

## LAND OF ILLITERATE COMMUNICATORS?

In late 1975 a U.S. Office of Education study concluded that almost 35 million American adults were unable to calculate comparative costs of the same goods in different sized packages.

A few other startling statistics from the same report: 86 million American adults could not accurately compute their car's gasoline mileage; 52 million were unable to read and interpret a classified help wanted ad well enough to determine if they qualified for a job listed (the relentless miniaturization of classified ad type size and the ever-shrinking column widths in many metropolitan newspapers may bear some of the blame here). Almost as many of us (48 million) could not figure out how much change we should get back from a purchase in a store. And 39 million people couldn't find the social security deduction figure on their paycheck stub.

The Office of Education report classified these millions as "functional illiterates." Up to one-half of the U.S. population thus must be considered as incapable of comprehending a relatively simple written or printed message.

Even more disheartening, if possible, were the results of a similar study among Maryland seventh and eleventh grade students in 1975–1976. One-third of the seventh graders and one-fifth of the high school juniors tested out as functionally illiterate; unable to read with any practical degree of comprehension such items as telephone directories, job applications, cooking recipes, first-aid instructions, dictionaries, and grocery ads.

The real significance of the study results was highlighted by a public relations executive:

> What . . . does this [Office of Education report] tell us? It tells us, I think, that as public relations practitioners, we had better rethink our love affair with the printed word; especially our historic belief that well-written leaflets, pamphlets, booklets and institutional ads will get our corporate or non-profit message across to the broad general public.[5]

Like Johnny, the broad general public can't read!

In October 1977 Florida high school juniors began taking a state-mandated functional literacy test. Students who fail the two-part exam—117 questions on reading, writing, and arithmetic at about the eighth-grade level—receive "certificates of attendance" instead of high school diplomas for their 12 years of primary and secondary school work.

Students have three chances to pass both the math and communications sections of the test with at least a 70 percent correct score. In the first round in Florida 8 percent failed the communications part and 36 percent failed math.

Try these sample questions, based on the actual test questions prepared by Educational Testing Service for the Florida literacy exam.

## Mathematics

1. The Army had a special 30-month recruitment program. Pat joined the Army on October 1, 1977. When will Pat be discharged?
   A. April 30, 1979
   B. February 28, 1980
   C. March 31, 1980
   D. April 30, 1980

2. Mr. Jones maps out a route from Miami to Pensacola. The distance is about 685 miles. If Mr. Jones drives this distance in about 14 hours, his average driving speed was about how many miles per hour?

A. 40     B. 45     C. 50     D. 55

3. A package of 8 hamburger buns costs 65 cents. A package of 12 buns costs 95 cents. You need to buy four dozen buns. What would you save if you bought packages of 12 instead of packages of 8?

A. 10¢     C. Nothing. Cost is the same,

B. 30¢     D. Nothing. You would lose money.

4. You are baking brownies in a 9- by 12-inch pan. How many brownies will you have if you cut them into 3-inch squares?

A. 9     C. 27

B. 12     D. 36

## Communications

Two tourists to the Miami area, Bob Greene and Victor Hayes of New Jersey, suffered serious injury when their Ford van, driven by Greene, collided with a Chevrolet driven by Miami resident May Herndon. The accident occurred at 11 a.m. Saturday at West Dixie Highway and 25th Street.

The cause of the accident is under investigation and neither driver has been charged as of this report. Witnesses have stated that the van was out of control. At least one witness believes the driver of the van was "on something." Mechanical failure is another possibility.

Greene is listed in critical condition at Jackson Hospital. Hayes is listed as serious but stable. Herndon was treated for injuries and released last night. The investigation will continue.

5. Which of the following sentences is fact?
   A. Bob Greene was charged with reckless driving.
   B. Mechanical failure caused the accident.
   C. The investigation has been completed.
   D. Three people were injured.

6. Which of the following sentences is opinion?
   A. Bob Greene and Victor Hayes are visitors.
   B. The accident happened in the morning.
   C. The driver of the van was "on something."
   D. There are witnesses to the accident.

Answers to the six questions are below, with the percent of Florida high school juniors who missed each question in parentheses:

1. C (64 percent)     4. B (53 percent)
2. C (16 percent)     5. D (18 percent)
3. A (57 percent)     6. C (18 percent)

In mid-1977 television viewers were tested with the oculometer, a device developed to monitor eye movements of our astronauts. The study revealed that viewers' attention spans are shorter than scientists previously had believed. One advertising executive suggested the test proved that a camera shot of as long as 4 seconds on one image was a waste of time.

If the public can't, or won't, read, and has no appreciable attention span for such audiovisual media as television, what's a serious communicator to do?

## VIVE LA COMMUNICATION GAP

"Communication" is one of the ten or twelve most overworked (and least understood) words in the English language. Of those in reasonably complete possession of their senses of sight and hearing, who has not heard and read ad nauseam of the "communication problem," caused by various and sundry "communication gaps"?

I am often tempted to throw in with Edwin Newman, perhaps the best known of the self-appointed curmudgeons-in-residence in charge of saving the English language as some of us know it, use it, and love it. In his book, *Strictly Speaking*, Newman observed:

> The notion that the trouble between generations is caused by a failure in communication may have some merit, but it makes a large and not necessarily justified assumption that there should be communication and that if there is, things will be better. I am not so sure. It may be that we have entered a time when some groups would do better to ignore each other than to communicate with each other. Not communicating saves energy; it keeps people from worrying about things they cannot do anything about; and it eliminates an enormous amount of useless talk.[6]

What, one might ask at this point, is the connection between these disheartening statistics about the information explosion, functional illiteracy, and communication gaps and overkill—and our subject of public relations? Simply that the art, profession, trade, business, craft—or whatever you will—of modern public relations deserves a fair share of the credit for the dissonance, pap, and garbage which spews on us from the media. Many of the definitions for public relations, as we shall see in Chapter 2, turn around the word "communication." For example: "Public relations; The communication and interpretation of information and ideas . . ."; and "Public relations is planned, persuasive communication . . ."

Among other things, this book will be a plea to turn down the volume, at least ever so slightly. Shouting *is* a form of communication, but so is whispering. Slang, jargon, and obscenities afford a certain level of communication, but so also does the use of good, clear English in writing and speaking.

## THE MUTED APPROACH

John E. Marston, professor of advertising and journalism at Michigan State University, makes a good case for understatement and understanding in the practice of public relations. Pointing out that "public relations efforts are frequently too much argument, too much special pleading, too much defense, too much transparent persuasion—and too little information upon which both sender and receiver might possibly agree," he suggests:

> Public relations communication is not debate. It is not advertising in which something *must* be said to convert someone because something must be sold. Public relations ideas do not have to be sold—they must be *bought*. Public relations is . . . the discovery and exposition of facts that are to the common interest of two or more parties. It is information, credible to everyone, fundamental. Without it, an honest case cannot be made. . . .
>
> The best role for public relations communication in these days of fact-shortage and incredulity clearly seems to bring information upon which mutual understanding may be established. There is no need to rush around taking positions. Conclusions develop from facts and are best achieved when seen by the reader himself. Psychologists say that, especially for less well-informed readers, conclusions need to be stated, but this can be done modestly and in terms of mutual benefit. In the end it is not what the speaker wants, but what the hearer wants that will be remembered.[7]

## LINCOLN ON PUBLIC RELATIONS

At least one writer has observed that President Lincoln's commanding position in his party in 1860 was due "not to his policies, not to his course of action, but to his way of saying things. In every revolution there is a moment when a man who can phrase it can lead it."[8]

Lincoln put his own feelings about public opinion on the record during one of his debates with Stephen Douglas in 1858: "Public sentiment is everything. With public sentiment nothing can fail; without it nothing can succeed. . . ." No one, Lincoln might have added, should take sentiment (public opinion) for granted, or assume that good performance and strength alone automatically result in public recognition, understanding, and support.

Lincoln also understood the values of understatement, simplicity, and the soft-sell approach in human and public relations. All but 70 of the 271 words he immortalized at Gettysburg were one-syllable words. (The fledgling Associated Press gained instant membership in the "Nobody's Perfect Club" when it reported Lincoln's Gettysburg Address in four words: "The President also spoke." This is not the type of understatement we recommend.)

## A BACKWARD LOOK

On occasion, a look into a subject's past will help one to better understand the present and, of even greater import, to comprehend at least some of the future directions and developments.

A few writers and other experts on public relations have attempted to make the case that deliberate efforts to win approval through communication predate human ability to communicate. It seems possible that at least some of the effort expended on finding historical antecedents for the practice of public relations is designed to put the craft on a more equal footing with other, better known professions—or even to legitimize its somewhat sordid beginnings.

One author suggests that advisory bulletins to farmers on how to harvest crops, issued around 1800 B.C. by the Iraqi equivalent of the U.S. Department of Agriculture, were among the earliest recorded efforts at governmental public relations.

Another writer settles on ancient Rome as the birthplace of the art of public relations. "When the Roman statesman Cato the Elder, long before the birth of Christ, ended each of his Senate speeches with the words, 'Also, I think Carthage should be utterly destroyed,' he was practicing public relations by reiterating an idea to attract public interest and support. So, centuries later, were the French revolutionaries who seized on the unfortunate phrase, 'Let them eat cake,' and by publicizing it as a symbol of the monarchy's irresponsibility, made it a tool in the overthrowing of the Bourbons."[9]

An historical aside: "Let them eat cake" first appeared in Jean-Jacques Rousseau's *Confessions,* written in 1767, about an incident that occurred in Lyons around 1740. Marie Antoinette was born in 1755 and the French Revolution started in 1789, so if she ever said "Let them eat cake," she was plagiarizing Rousseau.

In the event anyone believes otherwise, historians Allan Nevins and Henry Steele Commager went on record in *A Pocket History of the United States,* stating that the American Revolution "was not a vast spontaneous movement . . . it was carefully planned by shrewd men and laboriously and sagaciously executed by some of the most active spirits on the continent. *It could never have succeeded if it had been left unorganized.*"[10] [Emphasis added.]

Some communications cynics, probably including this author, would question the spontaneity of practically any successful movement—revolutionary or otherwise.

## EARLY U.S. PUBLIC RELATIONS PRACTITIONERS

While Nevins and Commager predictably stopped short of calling the American Revolution an early exercise in public relations, other authors have not. Samuel Adams, Thomas Paine, Alexander Hamilton, Benjamin Franklin, and Thomas Jefferson—among others—have been singled out as originators of American-style public relations.

> Using events, voice, pen, and organization, [they] had a tremendous impact on the public opinion of their time. They knew, intuitively, how to mold and manipulate opinions. They circulated pamphlets by the thousands, filled the few newspapers of the time with essays and articles, usually unsigned, and spread their ideas of revolt by public meetings and by word of mouth. Their methods can be found in use today.[11]

Because of his efforts in staging the Boston Tea Party, Samuel Adams is regarded as "a direct ancestor of today's PR practitioner" and the Tea Party itself as a demonstration of "the value of created events to dramatize a point of view or a situation."[12] Both theses may have some validity; we will discuss staged events and created news as a useful publicity technique in a later chapter.

## First Presidential Press Secretary

Whatever the true genesis of public relations in the United States, or its progenitors, there is pretty general agreement that the first U.S. president to employ a press secretary or representative was Andrew Jackson. Amos Kendall, a one-time newspaper editor from Kentucky, served President Jackson in many areas of public affairs—as a speech and article writer, as an advisor on strategy and policy, and as one who sounded out opinion among influential publics. Kendall had no impressive title, such as presidential secretary, in Jackson's first term; he was carried on the federal rolls as an auditor in the Treasury Department.

Jackson came to rely on Kendall and the other members of his Kitchen Cabinet (many of whom were also former newsmen) to create events upon demand, as well as to shape and direct public opinion with the events. Kendall's skill as a communicator and political organizer served Jackson well. In his second term Jackson appointed Kendall Postmaster General, setting up that office as a top political plum for generations to come.

## The First Press Agent

Almost 20 years before Jackson took office for his first term as president, Phineas Taylor Barnum, press agent *summa cum laude,* was born in Bethel, Connecticut. Barnum's entry into show business, when he was 25 years old, came 2 years before the end of Jackson's second term when the young showman paid $1000 for Joice Heth, his first exhibit. Ms. Heth claimed to be 161 years old and the former slave-nurse of George Washington. Later successful Barnum promotions included the midget, General Tom Thumb, and singer Jenny Lind.

Barnum pioneered the technique of getting free publicity for admittedly commercial ventures. Every press agent who followed him built on the foundation Barnum laid, wherein results counted for more than the methods used to get publicity for clients.

It is safe to say that, regardless of immediate motives or ultimate goals, most of the public relations pioneers shared at least three common characteristics:

> a recognition of the immense power held (and wielded) by the public
> an ability to persuade publics by communicating ideas
> a pervasive singleness of purpose

A direct relationship seems to exist between the intermittent growth of public relations and periods of struggle for power among intensely competitive elements of society.

## PR IN THE TWENTIETH CENTURY

The first full-time university public relations effort came in 1904, when the University of Wisconsin hired W. G. Bleyer to set up a press bureau. In 1908 Ivy Lee (regarded by many as the father of modern public relations) went to work for the Pennsylvania Railroad.

World War I brought the Committee on Public Information into being, under the leadership of George Creel. Woodrow Wilson, who in less hectic times had written, "Publicity is one of the purifying elements of politics," took full credit for the Committee on Public Information. In *Exploring Journalism*, Wolseley and Campbell opined that the committee's collection of "newspapermen, scholars and experts on public opinion . . . probably shortened the war by several months"[13]—an eminently unprovable statement.

Edward L. Bernays, an active member of the Creel Committee and a nephew of Sigmund Freud, is supposed to have said, post-hostilities, that "it was the war which opened the eyes of the enlightened few to the possibilities of regimenting the public." It was the same Bernays who, a few years later, wrote the first book about public relations, *Crystallizing Public Opinion;*[14] taught the first course in public relations; and originated the lofty-sounding term, "public relations counsel."

### The Unnoticeable Blip

A few years ago one of the profession's eminent practitioners suggested that "organized public relations is a creature of the last 30 years. On the timeline of the 5,000 years of mankind's recorded history, public relations is not even a noticeable blip, because public relations is very recent."[15]

Following the 1929 stock market crash, the debunkers of capitalism and business took the limelight. Some large corporations hired journalists to fight what they considered unwarranted attacks by President Roosevelt on big business. But many historians date the real growth of public relations in this country from World War II, when the military services literally created the public relations industry by training thousands of information officers. In addition, a number of postwar public relations people came out of World War II intelligence services.

### A Capsular History

An internal memo on new business development prepared for a large PR firm in New York City carried this condensed history of modern public relations:

> The [PR] business generally achieved stature during the 30s by equipping business to face the sometimes frightening challenges of booming unionism and mushrooming government; in the 40s by supporting the war effort; in the 50s by working the expanding new products market against post-war hungers, and in the 60s by building a climate for corporate mergers and coming to terms with the new media.

It is admittedly a little early to try to characterize the seventies in relation to the development of public relations, but it may well be the decade described as the one in which everything that came before went right out of the window. Up to now, it has been the decade of the activist and the investigative reporter. Activists quickly learned how to manipulate and direct the media through created and staged events and by gaining access to and selectively leaking official documents. Reporters and newspapers have won Pulitzer prizes for outstanding journalism just by being in the right place at the right time to serve as receivers of such documents—your property and mine, if you will.

## THE NUMBERS GAME

Public relations firm listings in the Manhattan telephone directory have been used as one measurement of the growth of the business. I'm not sure how significant it is, but in 1910 not a single public relations counselor was listed in the Manhattan directory. In 1935 there were about a dozen. By 1962 the listing took up more than seven columns, with some 700 names, and in 1972 almost 900 practitioners were listed.

We trust that the 1977 Manhattan Yellow Pages, with just slightly over 600 entries for public relations counselors, were more of a comment on the faltering state of the economy than a statement about the public relations business. Interestingly, there were almost exactly as many listings for Manhattan architectural firms.

## PRESS AGENTS AS FILTERS

Press agentry, as we've seen, dates back to Andrew Jackson's days in the White House. That particular form of the art had a much earlier and faster growth rate than pure public relations.

> Shortly before [World War I] the newspapers of New York took a census of the press agents who were regularly employed and regularly accredited and found that there were about twelve hundred of them. How many there are now [in 1919] I do not pretend to know, but what I do know is that many of the direct channels to news have closed and the information for the public is first filtered through publicity agents. The great corporations have them, the banks have them, all the organizations of business and of social and political activity have them, and they are the media through which the news comes. Even statements have them.[16]

In 1936, of the three hundred largest companies in the United States, only six had full-fledged public relations departments; today the ratio is better than three out of four. General Motors did not have a PR department until 1931; Standard Oil of New Jersey had none until 1942.

There is no record of which design firm first employed a public relations counsel, but it seems a safe bet that it did not happen until the late forties or early fifties. Obviously, many early practitioners served as their own public relations consultants. H. H. Richardson or Frank Lloyd Wright, for example, could have taught many things to some of today's PR consultants.

In "The Role of Public Relations in Marketing Architectural and Engineering Services," a 1974 master's thesis by public relations counsel Diane Creel, eleven of the firms responding to a questionnaire had had a public relations staff for more than 20 years—which lends some credence to our estimate above.

Another of the interesting statistics turned up in the Creel report was that 86 percent of the responding firms reported public relations budgets equivalent to from 1 to 6 percent of their total spending. Throughout the remainder of this book, one of our goals will be to help you get full measure from dollars allocated to public relations, and to show the close working relationship among public relations, publicity, advertising, sales, and marketing.

## References

[1] Philip Lesly, ed., *Lesly's Public Relations Handbook,* Prentice-Hall, Inc., Englewood Cliffs, N.J., 1971, p. 1.

[2] Gerald Snyder, *1994: The World of Tomorrow,* Copyright 1973 U.S. News & World Report, Inc., Washington, D. C., p. 146.

[3] Alvin Toffler, *Future Shock,* Random House, Inc., New York, 1970, p. 326.

[4] Ibid., p. 34.

[5] Romney Wheeler, Vice President for Public Relations, Consumers Power Company, in a July 24, 1975, speech to the North Texas Chapter of the Public Relations Society of America, in Dallas, Texas.

[6] Edwin Newman, *Strictly Speaking,* Bobbs-Merrill Company, Inc., New York, 1974, p. 10.

[7] John E. Marston, "A Strategy for Public Relations Communication," *Public Relations Journal,* September 1975, p. 10.

[8] Gerre Jones, *How to Prepare Professional Design Brochures,* McGraw-Hill Book Company, New York, 1976, p. 109.

[9] Alexander B. Adams, *Handbook of Practical Public Relations,* Thomas Y. Crowell Company, New York, 1965, p. 1.

[10] Allan Nevins and Henry Steele Commager, *A Pocket History of the United States,* 6th ed. rev. and enl., Pocket Books, New York, p. 71.

[11] Scott M. Cutlip and Allen H. Center, *Effective Public Relations,* 4th ed., Prentice-Hall, Inc., Englewood Cliffs, N.J., 1971, p. 37.

[12] Ibid., p. 37.

[13] Ronald E. Wolseley and Laurence R. Campbell, *Exploring Journalism,* Prentice-Hall, Englewood Cliffs, N.J., 1957, p. 470.

[14] Edward L. Bernays, *Crystallizing Public Opinion,* Boni Liveright, New York, 1923.

[15] Kalman B. Druck, in a speech to the Fourteenth Annual Institute of the Public Relations Society of America, loc. cit.

[16] Frank Cobb, in an address to the Women's City Club of New York, Dec. 11, 1919.

The hard fact is, despite its seventy years as an identifiable vocation, public relations remains a nasty word to some administrators, a confused concept to others. It is also an inescapable fact that the work of many practitioners is based on the outmoded practices of the 1920s.[1]

# CHAPTER 2
# Public Relations Today

**A** 1975 SURVEY, FUNDED by a grant from the Public Relations Society of America (PRSA) Foundation, found that public relations is taught in one form or another in well over 300 U.S. colleges and universities. More than three-fourths of the responding schools offer public relations in their journalism schools or departments, while another 10 percent cover the subject within the business curriculum. Slightly more than 7 percent have separate departments of public relations.

Among all of these offerings, in mid-1977 only fifteen schools had public relations sequences accredited by the American Council on Education for Journalism. They were:

Boston University
University of Florida (Gainesville)
University of Georgia
Kent State (Ohio)
University of Maryland
Northern Illinois University
Ohio State University
Ohio University

Oklahoma University
Oregon University
San Jose State (California)
South Florida University
University of Southern California
University of Texas (Austin)
University of Wisconsin (Madison)

Journalism schools generally began offering majors and minors in public relations right after the end of World War II. Since some surveys show more than a third of the informational content of all news media originating with public relations people, it is difficult to quarrel with the premise that a good background in news writing is desirable, if not essential.

But news training is spotty—even faddish—in some schools of journalism and the later arrivals, "schools of communications." A fair number of public relations executives, including the author, have had the experience of interviewing job applicants (some with master's degrees) from a famous Boston school of communications, and learning that the new graduates were never required to write a news story in all their years of communications higher education.

Most college-level students of public relations spend about three-fourths of their class time in liberal arts courses, the PRSA Foundation survey found. Supplemental trade school courses usually include reporting, writing, editing, story placement, promotion, and programming for public relations.

## PR DEFINITIONS

As we said in *How to Market Professional Design Services*, "Formal and informal definitions of public relations run the gamut from idealistic to gutsy, from the sublime to the ridiculous." Eleven definitions of public relations followed, including two negative ones (what public relations isn't).

Creating a definitive definition of public relations has long occupied some of the great (and a few of the small) minds of those who practice or observe the craft. Like marketing, public relations is anything but an exact science, but this has not seemed to deter a legion of speakers, writers, and theoreticians—both in and out of the business—from periodically redefining the undefinable.

Since it is *de rigueur*—or at least a tradition of sorts—to set out various definitions of PR in any book on the subject, we furnish the following for the edification and amusement of readers who are interested. These are in addition to the definitions found in *How to Market Professional Design Services*.

- Public relations means all the things done (or not done) that affect public opinion (whether favorably or unfavorably).[2]
- Public relations is planned, persuasive communications designed to influence significant publics.[3]

- [Public relations] consists of
  Making the right impression
  On the right audience
  For the right objective.[4]
- Public relations is the planned effort of a business organization, or other institution, to integrate itself into the society in which it exists. In this concept, public relations becomes much more than publicity or promotion, and it implies also that any organization must adapt itself to the objectives, the needs and the standards of our democratic society.[5]

In an earlier edition (1952) of *Effective Public Relations,* authors Cutlip and Center included these formal and informal definitions of public relations:

- PUBLIC RELATIONS: The communication and interpretation of information and ideas from an institution TO its publics and the communication of information, ideas and opinions FROM those publics to the institution, in a sincere effort to establish a mutuality of interest and thus achieve the harmonious adjustment of an institution to its community.
- Public relations consists of ninety percent doing the right thing and ten percent in telling about it.
- Good conduct coupled with good reporting.
- The common aim of all that is labeled PR is to influence public opinion, one way or another, by fair means or foul.

A few others of possible interest:

- Public relations may be looked on as the art, science or skill of projecting a company's reputation or image to the greatest number of people who will be favorably influenced or will favorably influence others.[6]
- Public relations has sometimes been described as publicity or press agentry with a conscience.[7]
- Public relations—the state of mutual understanding between an organization or individual and any groups of persons or organizations, and the extent and quality of the reputation which results. PR Practice—the planned effort to establish and improve the degree of mutual understanding between an organization or individual and any groups of persons or organization or individual to deserve, acquire and retain a good reputation.[8]

And, finally, some new definitions of what public relations is *not:*

- Professional public relations does not consist of turning a negative impression into a positive one by misrepresenting the facts in order to alter the image. Nor is it simply the ability to write intelligent press releases in an acceptable journalistic style. It is a mixture of knowledge, experience, sensitivity, and judgement in dealing with information that can affect the lives of others. But it is especially a fundamental understanding that in all communications, honesty and candor must prevail.[9]

## PUBLIC RELATIONS MASQUERADERS

If you should be in the market for a public relations counsel, you may select from a diverse assortment of "exes"—ex-Congressmen, ex-diplomats, ex-admirals, ex-fighters, ex-generals, ex-football players, ex–Capitol Hill secretaries, and ex-actors—all of whom have set up public relations firms. The unfortunate fact is that there is little regulation of public relations practitioners outside of the financial field. Anyone with $10 or so for 500 business cards can become an instant public relations counsel.

Fred Stitt commented on this point in *Guidelines Architectural Letter:*

> Some architects have fallen into bad company in their choices of public relations consultants. Totally unqualified ex-politicians and socialites offer such services. So do bureaucrat influence peddlers, press agents and others with supposed "contacts" to sell.
>
> Sometimes these people will hook a client. Most often they offer open ended expense demands and hot prospects who remain eternally "just about to bite." Some have caused extreme embarrassment to their architects. Some have caused legal problems.
>
> There are plenty of reputable PR firms around—why the bad choices? One explanation: some architects have a low opinion of PR, even when they use such services. They assume some degree of shadiness or razzle dazzle is requisite for the trade.
>
> Professional PR services are anything but razzle dazzle. A solid PR consulting firm will usually make a detailed assessment of public relations needs and goals. Then they'll work out policy and a logical program of action based on agreed-upon goals.[10]

A quick sampling of classified ads for public relations people underscores the general confusion about what is (and isn't) public relations. A few examples:

---

**PUBLIC RELATIONS HOSTESS**
To work for No. Va. builder. Real estate lic. not nec., Excel. salary and/or comm. Call _____ _____ .

---

**TEXTBOOKS**
Deg. + desire for future in sales/mgmt. or editorial. Sell textbooks to coll. $10K salary, co. car, bonus, expense. FEE PAID. Call _____ .

---

**Public Relations**—Company doing $2 million in sales needs presentable personnel to set up key appointments in Md. communities. Average earnings $500/wk. commission. Competitive draw provided. Call _____ .

---

**Public Relations**—Sales-Host for exciting new private discotheque opening in Georgetown. We seek attractive, agressive people with contacts or mailing list to aid in marketing, promotion or hosting of our sophisticated disco. Call _____ .

---

**PUBLIC RELATIONS**
**Part Time—Eves. & Sats**
Positions are available in Public Relations Dept. of a national firm. Working Eves. and Sats. SALARY PLUS an EXCELLENT opportunity to supplement your income. Car and neat appearance necessary. Contact _____ .

---

All these ads are from the classified section of the *Washington Post,* whose
editors presumably know the difference between public relations and selling
textbooks—or between public relations and portrait photography.

A final classified example from the columns of the *Los Angeles Times*—a
sort of West Coast counterpart of the *Post:*

In November of 1976 a Federal Trade Commission (FTC) administrative
law judge found that Grolier, Inc., used unfair and deceptive means to
recruit door-to-door sales personnel. Grolier publications include *Encyclopedia Americana, New Book of Knowledge, World's Greatest Classics,* and *Harvard
Classics.* Among the FTC judge's findings:

- In seeking to attract applicants for sales work, Grolier used blind advertisements which were deceptive in that they did not disclose the nature of the
position offered, i.e., door-to-door or in-home selling, the name of the employ-
ing company, or the product involved.
- Frequently, these . . . advertisements misrepresented that the positions
offered were non-selling in nature, such as public relations work, linear programming, and conducting interviews and opinion poll surveys.
- The firm used fictitious or unauthorized endorsements, including an
implied representation that its *American Peoples Encyclopedia* was endorsed by
Pope Paul.[11]

## PUBLIC RELATIONS SOCIETY OF AMERICA

While, as we've noted, there are presently no legal restrictions on who can
call themselves public relations counsels, there does exist a professional
organization for PR people. The Public Relations Society of America (PRSA)

was founded in 1948. Another group, the American Public Relations Association, merged with PRSA in 1961.

Membership figures for the surviving PRSA are sometimes difficult to pin down, but the director of PRSA's membership department advises that there were 8713 members in 1977. Edward L. Bernays, in an article for the *Public Relations Journal* in December 1976, estimated that 60,000 people were engaged in public relations. Others have suggested the total is much closer to 100,000.

## Ethical Boundaries

PRSA has a Code of Professional Standards with fourteen articles and an accreditation program for members. The code used to have seventeen articles, but under pressure from the Federal Trade Commission in 1977, the organization deleted articles banning encroachment, contingency fees, and derogatory practices toward non clients. (The PRSA Code of Professional Standards appears as Appendix I.)

The membership accreditation program was instituted in the mid-1960s. Something less than half of PRSA members have passed the oral and written accreditation tests. Of the 366 members of the Washington, D.C., National Capital PRSA Chapter, for example, only 98 (25 percent) were accredited in May 1977.

## THE PUBLIC RELATIONS PROCESS

A brief look at the process of public relations is in order at this point; brief because the remainder of the book consists of detailed considerations of the elements that make up the total PR process.

The staff of a professional public relations firm consists of counselors experienced in research techniques, analysis, communication, and mass persuasion. This experience is brought to bear on specific short- and long-range requirements of the firm's clients. As with design firms, some PR counselors specialize in one or a few areas of practice: corporate and financial relations, government, education, the arts, associations, publishing, and a number of other specialties.

In one sense, public relations is the practice of *evaluating* a firm's services in relation to the public's needs and wants, *identifying* and matching the firm's services with those needs and wants, and then *communicating* the resultant ideas to the pertinent publics. Evaluation, identification, and communication—any purposive public relations program can be measured against those three considerations.

Evaluation includes an analysis of what services a firm is prepared and qualified to offer, as well as what additional services it should prepare itself to offer to meet new public needs or demands.

At any given point in time a design firm possesses certain resources in the form of material, technological, and financial assets. But more important, a firm also has certain human and professional skills in the form of its staff—staff members who, as the result of the firm's past experience, training, and hiring procedures, have the professional expertise to design and manage certain kinds of jobs, but not others. A truly objective inventory of the firm's resources and capabilities is a necessary first step in the establishment of a workable, productive public relations program.

Identification is the key to the success of any public relations program. Properly applied, the results of the analysis can be converted into ideas for speeches, articles, news releases, feature photographs, brochures, and presentations—all of which should serve to relate the firm's work to public needs.

The publics (audiences) important to the success of your operation must be clearly identified. They might include

> The general public
> Direct representatives of clients
> Employees
> Competitors
> Government—at all levels
> Suppliers
> The news media
> Consultants
> Educators
> Shareholders (when the firm is publicly held)
> The financial community

Communication is achieved when a message is transmitted in terms known to the receivers, and within their areas of general interest and experience. When a common frequency is established, the public relations counsel must choose the appropriate media—publicity, civic activities, radio or television appearances, in-house activities, and so on—for each message. A keen sense of timing, knowledge of relevant issues, and familiarity with the personalities involved are some of the considerations for choosing the most productive medium or combination of media.

Properly utilized, public relations will increase the efficiency of any sales force. A large part of a salesperson's time is used to explain his or her company to the prospect. If a prospective client can be informed in advance about the company, the salesperson can move quickly into selling the product or service.

Some years ago an advertisement appeared in many publications. It was titled "A Tough Purchasing Agent," and staring out of the page was an unfriendly gent. He was saying:

> "I don't know who you are."
> "I don't know your company."
> "I don't know your company's services."
> "I don't know what your company stands for."

"I don't know your company's clients."
"I don't know your company's record."
"I don't know your company's reputation."
"Now—what is it you want to sell me?"

Public relations should start long *before* salespeople make their first call.

PR practitioner Milton Fairman once described the public relations process as three-phased, consisting of analysis, prescription, and action.

> In analysis, you proceed from a clear definition of the objective to assembling and evaluating all data pertinent to it. A fact-finding exercise, it calls for interviews, for review of available source material, for the use of research techniques. It embraces both the organization and the public involved, and results in a solid factual basis for subsequent steps.
>
> In prescription, you recommend a decision, policy or action based on the analysis. Before taking this step you consider alternate courses, costs vs. anticipated values, prospects of success or failure, and risks—should any be indicated. And the prescription may be for no action. (There is an adage in surgery that wisdom is knowing when not to cut.)
>
> If, however, the prescription calls for action and is accepted, you take the final step, mustering the necessary resources and carrying out the action yourself or by coordinating the efforts of others.[12]

We've seen the public relations process outlined as "evaluating, identifying, and communicating," and as "analysis, prescription, and action." Public relations counsel Robert Clay describes it as a four-step process: research, planning, communicating, and evaluation.

> 1. *Research.* All of the necessary information must be obtained to really understand the client, to determine what qualities make the client unique, to ferret out whatever problems the client may have, and to establish which groups of people—or publics, as they are called in public relations—are important to the client. This stage should also include opinion research to determine what these publics think of the client.
>
> 2. *Planning.* The research material should be studied, with the significant information used to create a public relations program that outlines the problems, the goals, the publics to be reached, and the messages to be communicated.
>
> 3. *Communicating.* Messages are aimed at the selected publics in a number of ways.
>
> The most frequent way is to utilize existing communications media—newspapers, magazines and radio and television stations—to communicate via publicity. If you want your story to be told in the media in your words, with no editing, you must use corporate advertising, which may either be institutional (image building) or reportorial (telling your side of a situation in your own words).
>
> However, even if you tell your story in your words in the media of your choice, there is little possibility that the majority of the people within your target area will see it. They might not read that publication or may miss a specific issue or program. While the shotgun approach is helpful, it also is necessary to zero in your message on specific targets. You need direct communication which goes right to the individual.

Direct communication may be periodic: newsletters, house organs, annual reports, etc., or it may be occasional: brochures, special mailings, mass-distributed movies, etc. Direct communication may be presented personally in a slide show, display, or graphic presentation. Or it may be an oral presentation in the form of a speech, panel, or meeting. It might also be a special event, such as an open house, a press day, a series of lessons, or a unique, specially created program.

4. *Evaluation.* Because much of public relations repeats the same functions, one has the opportunity to improve their effectiveness each time. Hindsight is helpful; each effort should be analyzed to determine how it may be improved. At the same time, one should monitor the success of the program in terms of its accomplishing changes in attitudes or opinions. This can be done in an informal way—keeping tab on mail and grapevine comments—and formally—by various types of opinion research.[13]

## AIDA

This AIDA has nothing to do with opera—it's an action-oriented model for promotion. In *Basic Marketing* Professor E. J. McCarthy defines the AIDA process as "four fundamental and interrelated promotion tasks which have been recognized for many years: (1) to get *attention,* (2) to hold *interest,* (3) to arouse *desire,* and (4) to obtain *action.*"[14]

The Air Force recruiting service drills the AIDA concept into its recruiters. A senior recruiting officer once explained AIDA in this fashion:

A = Attention. Get it.
I = Interest. Awaken it (ask questions a prospect has to answer with a "yes").
D = Desire. Arouse it.
A = Action. Sell or close.

## References

[1]Scott M. Cutlip and Allen H. Center, *Effective Public Relations,* 4th ed., Prentice-Hall, Inc., Englewood Cliffs, N.J., 1971, p. 4.

[2]Lawrence W. Nolte, *Fundamentals of Public Relations,* Pergamon Press, New York, 1974, p. 5.

[3]John E. Marston, *The Nature of Public Relations,* McGraw-Hill Book Company, New York, 1963, p. 3.

[4]Alexander B. Adams, *Handbook of Practical Public Relations,* Thomas Y. Crowell Company, New York, 1965, p. 289.

[5]J. Carroll Bateman, *Public Relations Journal,* September 1972, p. 34.

[6]*TWA Public Relations Handbook,* 1960, p. 5.

[7]Ibid., p. 6.

[8]Working definition adopted by The British Institute of Public Relations, *International Public Relations Review,* cited in *PRSA National Newsletter,* April 1975, p. 6.

[9]Letter from William S. Story, PRSA executive vice president, to Mary Louise Smith, chairwoman of the Republican National Committee, December 20, 1975.

[10]Fred Stitt, *The Guidelines Architectural Letter,* Orinda, Calif., June 1975, p. 3.

[11]Federal Trade Commission, *FTC News Summary,* Washington, Nov. 5, 1976, p. 1.

[12]Milton Fairman, "The Practice of Public Relations," speech given at the Fifteenth Annual Institute of the Public Relations Society of America, University of Texas, Austin, June 1973.

[13]Robert Clay, "Bridging the Credibility Gap," *Orange County (CA) Business,* 4th Quarter, 1972, p. 36.

[14]M. S. Heidingsfield and A. B. Blankenship, *Marketing,* Barnes & Noble, Inc., New York, 1957, p. 149.

As a researcher, the public relations man delves into reasons and causes; as a communicator he tells about them: but as an activator he is a man of affairs who knows the thrill of setting up events and gambling on their success or failure, of making policy, and of personifying organizations by their deeds.[1]

# CHAPTER 3
# Role of a Public Relations Counsel

**U**NLESS YOURS IS a fairly large firm—one with 100 or so technical employees—chances are that you won't yet have an internal public relations staff. If you've implemented any formal public relations program at all, it is probably accomplished through an outside consulting firm. Diane Creel's master's thesis research, cited in Chapter 1, showed that 31 percent of the responding firms made use of outside public relations consultants, with slightly less than 10 percent relying entirely on their external advisers.

## WHY USE CONSULTANTS?

It is not practical for modern executives to keep up with the ever-increasing number of professional skills and proliferating disciplines in the public relations field. Neither is it feasible to maintain qualified people on the payroll who might someday be needed to advise on one or more of the emerging specialty areas of public relations.

In most cases, practicalities dictate that advisers and consultants will be hired from the outside, with results, as one writer put it, "that fall fairly evenly along the spectrum from triumph to disaster." We hope to show you how to stay closer to the triumphal end of this particular scale.

## HOW TO USE CONSULTANTS

Here are some pointers on finding, hiring, and making the best use of a public relations consultant. Some of these principles are based loosely on a list developed by Antony Jay for an article in the July–August 1977 issue of the *Harvard Business Review*. As you might have guessed, many of the procedures, concerns, and considerations parallel those of clients looking for architectural or engineering consultants.

• Don't feel that your problems are necessarily unique. Within the general business world most problems have arisen many times in a number of places under a variety of circumstances—and there is bound to be some body of knowledge in existence somewhere. One of the things to expect from consultants is that they know—or have the ability to find out—what's already been done in the field, and that they have the related ability to apply their knowledge to specific situations.

• If you are going to the trouble of finding a good consultant and spending the money to hire him or her, be sure you have the budget, internal staff, and intent to put into effect what may be required. When you have developed confidence in a consultant, be prepared to let his or her recommendations inspire equal confidence. This is not to say that one must ever blindly accept every point in a report or program. That would verge on the abdication of good management principles and personal judgment. But don't waste corporate funds on consultants by paying for studies, reports, surveys, and programs—and then ignoring them.

• Get advice from friends and other professionals, particularly from those who seem to have a good public relations program underway. But always go beyond references from clients, who are not always or necessarily in a position to make informed comparisons or judgments. Think of the individuals and organizations who might have had direct experience with public relations consultants, and are knowledgeable about the skills they should have. Newspaper editors and reporters, television and radio program directors and newspeople, other public relations consultants not under consideration, and even printers are some of the possibilities.

• Pick a consulting firm with a size relative to your own. If yours is a small design firm in Colorado, you should not journey to New York City to retain one of the large public relations firms who normally deal with IBM, General Motors, and other corporate conglomerates. Even if one of these consulting giants agreed to take your account, it is doubtful that you could expect much in the way of priority treatment and top-level attention—which you can expect and get from a smaller, local consultant.

• Naturally, you'll try to find someone who is already familiar with the design profession, unless you are attracted by the idea of running a training school for public relations executives. If the consultants are knowledgeable about your profession, there is a good possibility they will already have a network of useful contacts in the media and elsewhere.

• If a particular account executive from a public relations firm makes an early, positive impression on you, establish how much she or he will be involved with your account. The extent of personal service might be made a part of the contract.

Here again we see a close relationship to any client's interests in selecting a design consultant. Most clients are not interested in a heavy selling job by the superstar architect or engineer, who, they can be reasonably certain, will not be checking shop drawings or writing specs for their project. If consultants who call on you say they will not be personally involved, insist on interviewing the people who will be.

• Get the consultant to put as much as possible of the agreement in writing. As a minimum you should have a letter or memo of agreement setting out the agreed-upon objectives, responsibilities (mutual and individual), time schedules for meeting the objectives, dates of regular review meetings, and every detail of payment.

Some public relations firms, for example, add on a percentage fee to all purchases of materials and services they make on behalf of clients. This is perfectly ethical and legal, but some clients are in a position to make such purchases directly, saving themselves the consultant's override. Have a definite understanding about all such matters in advance.

As do most consultants, public relations advisers have various methods of setting fees, all of which naturally have a relation to hourly personnel costs, overhead factors, and profit goals. Long-term associations often involve a set monthly retainer fee, against which consulting fees and other charges may or may not be credited. If yours is simply a single public relations project—perhaps to handle a groundbreaking event—a lump sum or "not-to-exceed" fee may be established. Whatever the arrangement for payment will be, make certain you understand it—and that it's clearly written out.

• Be candid about everything with a public relations consultant. If a particular public relations activity actually is a smokescreen to divert attention from a potentially more serious situation, don't keep your adviser in the dark.

• Since initial decisions are often the most expensive—especially in a large undertaking—bring in public relations consultants at the earliest possible time. All too often decisions are made and funds committed, and then outside expertise and advice is sought. Since the consultant's input involves a fee anyway, make certain the advice is available in advance of significant decisions.

• Always communicate with a public relations consultant on common ground. Professionals tend to use their own jargon, which should cause no real problems among members of the same profession—but you are not a public relations expert. Antony Jay suggests that in such situations "Honest ignorance is a hundred times better than simulated understanding." Communicate with each other in a common vocabulary; never hesitate to ask for clarification.

• Scope the problem as fully as possible *before* calling in a consultant. When clients fail to clearly define requirements beforehand, the consultant is tasked with finding the problem *and* the solution.

## WHAT TO ASK

A baker's dozen of the basic questions to get answers to in selecting a public relations consultant:

1. What is the general professional competence and background of the principals in the consulting firm?

2. Are the principals accredited members of the Public Relations Society of America? If so, was accreditation achieved through the grandfather clause or by examination?

3. Are the principals active members of the Counselors Section, PRSA?

4. Do the principals hold memberships in local, regional, and national press clubs?

5. What direct experience has the potential account executive (the staff person who would be in charge of your account) had with design professionals or the construction field?

6. What is the general reputation of the firm in the community? Does it appear to endorse and subscribe to PRSA's Code of Ethics? Are the integrity and professional standing of the consulting organization above reproach?

7. Who are some of the present clients of the firm? How long have they been clients?

8. What is the rate of client turnover? What is the current work load of the firm?

9. Who among the principals and staff of the counseling firm would work on your account? What are their qualifications, general background, and special training as related to your identified needs?

10. Is it a full-service firm?

11. Do the samples of products shown to you produced by the firm (brochures, press releases, slide shows, photographs) indicate a passionate attention to detail by everyone concerned?

12. Do references furnished check out positively? Are referents still clients of the public relations firm?

13. Are answers to all questions about fees and other potential charges candid and clear? Do you understand exactly what costs you may incur?

### What Some of the Answers Should Be

A few comments on the suggested questions and the possible answers:

1. Just as for the client selecting a design firm, a full and complete answer to this question must come from a variety of sources—and the final answer will be subjective in varying degrees.

2. In an earlier chapter we mentioned PRSA's accreditation program. When it was instituted in the mid-1960s, a large group of senior PRSA members was accredited automatically by the Society. Since that time accreditation must be earned by passing a fairly difficult oral and written examination.

3. PRSA has a number of special interest sections for its members. The Counselors Section includes principals and staff of private counseling firms.

4. Since a considerable part of the servicing of your account will involve contact with the media—at least in the initial stages—active membership and participation in press clubs can be helpful to public relations counselors and their clients. Many press clubs are also local chapters of the national journalism fraternity, The Society of Professional Journalists, Sigma Delta Chi. The National Press Club in Washington and the New York City–based Overseas Press Club of America are usually considered the "elite" of such organizations. Membership in one of the major press clubs ordinarily carries visiting privileges in other clubs around the country and overseas. (The author's memberships in the New York City, Philadelphia, and Kansas City Press Clubs, plus a long-time affiliation with the Overseas Press Club, have proved to be quite helpful over the years in a variety of media contacts around the world.)

5. The reason for this question should be obvious. The more direct experience with your type of business, including past and present clients in the design, construction, and related fields, the less time will be lost in the beginning in educating the consultant. And during the time you are sponsoring the consultant's education, he or she will not be very productive on your behalf.

6. Just as there are good and bad apples and good and bad (ill-trained, uncaring, and unethical) architects and engineers, there are good and bad public relations consulting firms. PRSA has procedures for disciplining its members, but cannot deny them the right to practice outside the organization. One old-line consulting firm, which presently has almost three dozen PRSA members on its staff (eighteen of them accredited), was severely censured some years ago for its activities in setting up dummy or front companies to promote the interests of one segment of the transportation industry. So it pays to ask a lot of questions in many quarters before settling on a public relations consultant.

7. Don't be awed by the names of large corporate clients, particularly if they have no connection with your own field. Be aware of the fact that some companies retain several PR consulting firms, each of which advises on separate corporate interests or problems. And a record of long relationships with clients *may* be the result of lethargy rather than outstanding service.

8. Turnover rates are worth inquiring about, but a prospective client should look much deeper into a consultant's operation than this one factor. Overcommitting staff, for whatever reason, is one of the deadly sins often committed by consulting firms. Avoid situations where you must compete constantly for staff time and attention.

9. Know whom and what you're buying. Let them sell you.

10. Full-service firms normally provide counseling on research (opinion and market), publicity, brochures, direct mail, reports, newsletters, audiovisual presentations, special events (created news), and stockholder, consumer, and employee relations. If you don't believe you require all these

services, then look into more restricted or specialized public relations operations.

11. If you retain the consulting firm, presumably they will be advising you on some or all of the products and services mentioned in number 10. If the examples of past work shown bother your sense of ethics, propriety, aesthetics or graphic design approach in any way, look further.

12. The selection of a consultant, as was suggested earlier in this chapter, is an imperfect science at best. The human chemistry between consultant and client is important, but performance is more so. Check out a reasonable number of references, Visit two or three if possible.

13. Review the recommendations of a few paragraphs back about getting it in writing. Equivocation at this stage is an ominous sign.

## And for Good Measure

For a really thorough investigation here are five more questions (with comments about the possible answers) for your consideration:

1. In addition to press club memberships, does the candidate PR counselor belong to other technical and professional organizations and associations that are related to or might be potentially helpful to your interests?

Such organizations might include the National Association of Science Writers, International Radio and Television Society, Alpha Delta Sigma (the professional advertising fraternity)—even the International Association of Chiefs of Police.

2. Is she or he listed in any of the major business directories and directories of public relations consultants?

Two examples—*Who's Who in Finance and Industry* and Barbour's *Who's Who in Public Relations—International.*

3. Do they publish regularly, aside from placement of client articles, articles in professional journals, books, and the like?

There are several publications open to public relations counselors; PRSA's *Journal,* Sigma Delta Chi's *Quill,* and others. Because writing is an expected skill of those in the field, many public relations practitioners have written books about their profession.

4. What is their experience in international public relations?

Not really a requisite, but a helpful factor in evaluating the overall experience of a PR man or woman. Most foreign correspondents of American media are the highest caliber of reporters and writers, and to have successfully dealt with them for any appreciable length of time is one measure of the skill of a public relations practitioner.

5. Do they lecture, or have they lectured in the recent past, on public relations or marketing at the college level?

This question is not really related to the old saw, "To know a subject, one must teach it," but the saying has some validity. More important, perhaps, is the professional recognition implied.

## QUALITIES TO LOOK FOR

Academic backgrounds, especially in younger public relations counselors, should be considered. Has she or he had courses in public relations, English composition, news writing, graphics, advertising, creative writing, photography, radio and television writing and production, marketing, psychology, economics, political science, research, and sociology? Nothing can really beat years of experience in professional public relations, consulting with a variety of clients, but academic courses can be a satisfactory substitute at times.

One public relations practitioner has a list of eleven qualities he looks for in prospective employees for his firm. The first six are of prime and equal importance: detail-mindedness, imagination, intelligence, and the abilities to plan, organize, and write. Only slightly behind these six qualities are an acceptable appearance, extroverted qualities, a positive attitude, sensitivity to people, and an ability to verbalize.

"Imagination" is one of the qualities that seems to make all such lists. Paul F. Vey, writing in the *Connecticut Architect*, noted: "Imagination is one of the most important ingredients in effective publicity, but too much may backfire. Imaginative ideas should be executed with dignity and simplicity."[2]

Another consultant suggests that "public relations is really common sense, with a dash of imagination." While in general agreement with the idea that imagination plays a key role in effective public relations, we cannot really endorse such a simplistic definition. An ability to write clearly, with concision, and in an interesting style is our primary test of the worthiness of a public relations adviser.

The outspoken L. L. L. Golden, a frequent commentator on the practice of public relations, made some interesting and pertinent observations on how *not* to select an internal PR director in his book, *Only by Public Consent*. Most of Golden's comments apply equally well to the selection of outside consultants.

> There are many examples of corporate chiefs, their recruiting officers, or executive search firms looking for a public relations department head without knowing what his qualifications should be. Here we can have the case of a blind executive recruiter leading a blind corporation. In one case, a medium-sized corporation, together with the executive recruiting firm, drew a profile for a public relations director who had to have these qualifications: He had to be between thirty-eight and forty-two years old; tall, preferably over six feet; well-built, with a good overall appearance; a graduate of an Eastern college, preferably Ivy League; soft-spoken; with a liking for people and a willingness to relocate.
>
> The qualifications here listed for their man had nothing to do with how he might perform his job. A good public relations director can no more be measured by age, college, height, size of smile, timbre of voice, and fondness for people than a good history professor can be chosen by the number of hairs on his head.
>
> Actually no one can specify the "right" background for a good public relations man. Good ones have come from a wide variety of work. They have been high

school teachers, newspaper reporters, magazine writers, sales promotion men, opinion pollsters, radio and television broadcasters, and fund raisers. Some have gone directly from college into corporations and learned the trade by watching, listening, and above all by doing. Some have been men with advanced degrees; others have not finished high school. There is then no special background from which to choose a potentially good public relations man. . . .

It is certainly pleasant to have a public relations man "like people." In fact it is pleasant to have anyone like people. But liking people has little more to do with performance in public relations than liking mashed potatoes. A public relations man deals only with a tiny part of the public in person. A man may love people to death and still not understand what motivates them or how they will respond to certain actions at various times.[3]

## THE CORPORATE APPROACH

Several years ago the faculty of the Department of Communications at the University of South Dakota asked public relations directors of over 100 of the largest U.S. corporations for a list of the skills and qualities they looked for in hiring new staff people.

The results of the study were reported in the *Public Relations Journal* of September 1972. Nearly 90 percent of the corporate PR directors said writing was the most important skill. One executive pointed out: "Just about everything we do in public relations ends with someone putting words on paper. Therefore the common-denominator skill required by public relations men and women is the ability to write in a clear, understandable, believable manner—letters, scripts, speeches, news stories, feature articles, booklets, reports."

The next most important skill is a knowledge of the graphic arts—"the ability to carry a project through from concept to printed-paper-in-the-mailbox." The public relations director for a railroad commented, "Many projects cost too much or are delayed because the fellow who wrote the brochure knew nothing at all about getting it printed."

The other skills, in order of importance:

- Ability to organize
- Ability to verbalize
- Ability to get along with people
- Knowledge of economics and finance
- A "news sense"

Regarding the requirement of familiarity with economics and finance, PR veteran John Hill pointed out in a 1973 talk:

Forty years ago, early polls on the subject showed that most people in America thought that the average level of business profits was 25 percent, whereas the real bottom line figure was, and is, closer to 5 percent. Many people rose up to combat this wild notion and after four decades of combined public relations effort on the part of countless organizations and companies, the good people of

America no longer have the monstrous belief that business earns 25 percent—they now think the figure is 28 percent.

So the corporate PR executives' point seems well taken.

## HOW A PR COUNSEL CAN HELP

Here are some of the ways in which public relations consultants can assist their clients:

- Guide opinion research.
- Set up an action program or program of work. This is the road map ·or umbrella for practically all other public relations services.
- Generate third-party endorsements.
- Research, write, and place news and feature articles in the trade, business, and general media—local and national.
- Establish your firm as a principal source of information.
- Set up press conferences.
- Supervise preparation of exhibits and design award entries.
- Design, write, and produce newsletters—both internal and external.
- Develop corporate identity and graphics standards programs.
- Set up speaking appearances.
- Write speeches.
- Design and produce general capability and special brochures.
- Set up meetings, seminars, and workshops.
- Set up special events—open houses, dedications, office open houses, and the like.
- Produce audiovisual presentations.
- Supervise photo taking, selection and placement.

## FEES

A 1976 survey among public relations counselors turned up several significant points about the subject of fees.* For the survey, firms with annual billings of up to $250,000 were categorized as "small." The staff of small firms averaged four people. Median billings of the larger firms (over $250,000 in annual billings) were $1 million, and they averaged 60 employees.

Service charges fall into four basic types (and certain combinations of the four methods). Almost 30 percent of all firms in the survey charge a monthly retainer. Another 25 percent charge a retainer plus an hourly fee for actual staff time put in on the account. A monthly service fee for services performed (no retainers) is the billing method used by 12.5 percent. Some 33 percent

---

*Survey was taken among PR counselors at an April 1976 conference of Public Relations Society of America members in Hilton Head, S.C. Survey results were reported by Anthony M. Franco in the *Public Relations Journal* for August 1976 under the title "Counseling Fees: It's a Matter of Cost Consciousness," pp. 28–29, 36.

operate on a straight hourly charge. Most firms, small and large, have a minimum monthly retainer or service fee for all accounts. This minimum can range from a few hundred to several thousand dollars a month.

For the majority of the survey respondents (78 percent), hourly charges are based on a multiplier of from 2.5 to 3 times salary.

Most public relations firms prefer open-end contracts over more binding arrangements such as 1-year renewable contracts. Some form of a 60-day cancellation notice appears in most contracts, but this can range from 30 to 90 days. Since most public relations counseling falls into a highly personal adviser-client relationship, it is understandable that professional practitioners have little interest in tying their firms to long-term contracts.

A few pages back, mention was made of the practice of adding a handling fee or mark-up to purchases of materials and services on behalf of clients. Of the small firms in the survey, 40 percent gave their mark-up as the trade standard of 17.65 percent, another 40 percent said they do not add an override, and the rest use a range of mark-up figures. Less than one-third of the large firms forgo all such mark-ups, 58 percent add the 17.65 percent, and about one in ten uses lesser or greater add-on percentages.

## References

[1]John E. Marston, *The Nature of Public Relations,* McGraw-Hill Book Company, New York, 1963, p. 166.

[2]Paul F. Vey, "Putting Your Best Foot Forward," *Connecticut Architect,* November–December 1974, pp. 8–9.

[3]L. L. L. Golden, *Only by Public Consent,* Hawthorn Books, Inc., New York, 1968, pp. 346–347.

*The* public, in its broadest sense, is all mankind. *A* public is any particular group of these people distinguished from other people by one or more factors common among those who belong to the group.[1]

# CHAPTER 4
# Who Are Your Publics?

**D**URING THE PLANNING of a public relations program of work there will be much discussion of the client's "publics." A few moments reflection at this point should show readers that every individual is a member of an almost infinite number of publics and subpublics. This realization should help the lay person understand some of the problems of a public relations practitioner.

A typical design professional might belong to as many as a hundred identifiable publics—plus a larger number considerably more difficult to isolate and define. As engineers, for example, we belong to that large homogeneous group of fellow professionals. If one specializes in acoustic engineering, he or she then belongs to a smaller public-within-a-public.

Women naturally come under the umbrella grouping of females, subdivided, perhaps, into the over-20, under-30 age group; further subdivided into marrieds or unmarrieds (and divorced, still married, or widowed); university graduates or high school dropouts; with or without children; homeowners or renters; bicycle riders or walkers; and so on.

Every organization to which people belong adds another dimension to their personal group of publics: the American Consulting Engineers Council, the American Institute of Architects, Rotary, the Catholic Church, PTA, American Legion, a homeowners association, the National Association of

Science Writers, the Book-of-the-Month Club, and the Republican party, to name a few examples.

Antiwar groups, citizen's band operators (CBers), Boy Scouts and Girl Scouts, and subscribers to any and all newspapers, magazines, and newsletters are a few more possibilities.

The "publics" of public relations concern are similar to the "universes" of prospects for direct mail selling operations. Before starting up a newsletter, for example, the potential publisher will usually want to be satisfied that there is an identifiable universe of at least 30,000 names—potential subscribers for which mailing lists, in most cases, are readily available. This is based on the fact that it is extremely difficult to ever sign up more than 10 percent of the potential universe through direct mail promotion. A well-heeled small universe might be canvassed, based on a high proposed unit subscription cost. One hundred subscriptions at an annual rate of $2000 each would enable most newsletter entrepreneurs to at least break even.

The multiplicity of publics to be reached and influenced can be both a blessing and a curse to a public relations consultant, in that certain channels exist for reaching most identifiable publics, and the more media in number and variety available, the better are one's chances of getting acceptable placement of publicity materials. The potential disadvantage is that unnecessary and unwanted duplication of coverage can occur, as publics inevitably begin to overlap.

## THE DESIGN PROFESSIONAL'S PUBLICS

In laying the groundwork for a public relations program for an engineering or architectural firm, who are the publics we should be immediately aware of?

Internally are management, staff (administrative and production), and, if it's a publicly-held company, the stockholders. And never overlook the spouses of employees. Other internal publics are suppliers and consultants.

External publics could include:

- clients (lost, past, and present)
- prospective clients
- banks and other financial institutions
- attorneys
- unions
- minority groups
- consumer groups
- environmental groups
- historic preservation groups
- conservation groups
- planning commissions
- zoning boards
- governments (local, county, state, provincial, national)

- political parties
- the media
- peers and competitors, including professional associations

Most readers should be able to add several more publics to this basic list.

## CHANGING PUBLICS

A public, once established and identified, does not necessarily become a permanent entity. The public of 14 or 15 million service personnel from World War II, through discharge, separation, retirement, and death, has become almost extinct. Amoeba-like, that particular public has become many publics: veterans—both able and disabled, college students (through the GI Bill), and dozens of other groupings. Those veterans who were college students in the late forties and early fifties are now members of various graduate publics, including alumni groups.

## TAKING AIM AT PUBLICS

In public relations, as in selling, the importance of the rifle approach over shotgunning cannot be overstated. As one PR counselor put it, "Shooting a gun without aiming at a target results in some noise, a waste of ammunition, and no results except sporadic, lucky hits."[2]

One of the first steps in mapping a public relations campaign is to list all of the publics who might be important to reach in achieving the campaign goal or goals. Ideally, a public relations campaign would call for individual contact with each member of every public of potential importance. As a practical matter, this is not possible. One therefore targets on the most important publics in the total list.

One piece of bad advice often given principals of architectural and engineering firms by their public relations consultant is not to waste time and money by trying to place articles in the design "trades"—publications for the professional such as *Architectural Record, Engineering News-Record, Progressive Architecture, Building Design and Construction,* and *Consulting Engineer.* The usual rationale for ignoring such magazines is that it isn't productive "to talk to ourselves."

What the PR consultant in such cases apparently does not know is that a small but very important public is hidden among the readership of these publications. The majority of those in charge of interviewing and selecting design consultants for corporations and government agencies regularly read (and clip) the architectural and engineering trades. Never forget that most of those representing public and private clients are themselves registered design professionals.

When American Airlines opened its new terminal building at Boston's Logan Airport a few years ago, several preopening affairs were scheduled. The receptions were for the usual publics—government officials, the news media, other airline management personnel—with one interesting exception. A familiarization tour of the terminal, followed by a beer-and-sandwiches party, was held for local taxi drivers. Measuring specific returns from the cab drivers' bash would be difficult, but the word-of-mouth publicity to the captive audience of arriving and departing passengers which resulted has to be considered a PR asset.

Another example of targeting a public was the decision by public relations counsel Lynn Fischer about the placement of an article about Harvard's Advanced Management Program. One of the principals in her engineering client firm was a recent graduate of the Harvard course, and a story for one of the airline magazines was written. It appeared in *PACE*, the in-flight magazine of Piedmont Airlines, and Lynn Fischer explains why:

> Piedmont operates in the areas my client is interested in penetrating. United Airlines said they would use the article, and at first I was tempted to place it with the better known, more prestigious airline, but it wouldn't have been as effective. United's operations are in areas we couldn't have responded to, even if clients were interested. *PACE* was more appropriate since my marketing plan was to achieve greater recognition in an area where we already had strength.[3]

Why would a regional airline be interested in a story—no matter how well written or interesting—about a management course at Harvard? A slight local angle is part of the answer, but a paragraph halfway down the third column of the article gives us more of the answer.

> There are two long weekend breaks appropriately spaced during each session, with the executives all rushing to airports to fly home and to take care of company business and spend the weekend with their families. It is not untypical to see an airline terminal full of middle-aged book-carrying executives, their name tags still on, sometimes with a friend in tow to come home with them.[4]

## CRISIS PR

Crisis or disaster PR usually involves several of an organization's publics. In extreme cases, as in a national disaster, it can involve practically every public in one way or another.

Planning before the fact about how to handle a plant explosion, strikes, riots, the accidental death of a construction worker—even the assassination of a president—is at the same time a negative and necessary activity for a well-organized public relations operation.

Earlier in this century the rule of thumb in the construction industry was one worker killed for each story of a building. That sorry safety record has been vastly improved, but accidents—some fatal—still occur on large projects, both during and following construction. To wait for the first call from the news media before deciding how to handle, say, a pedestrian crushed to death by a load of falling steel pipe from the forty-second floor level, is to court disaster in several forms.

The curious saga of the breaking windows in the John Hancock building in

Boston is an example of a continuing public relations nightmare. The John Hancock case will be discussed in some detail in the final chapter.

Several years ago the Blue Cross–Blue Shield agency in a large midwestern city was on the verge of announcing a large rate increase to its subscribers. The increase was to be publicly blamed on rapidly increasing hospital charges to the agency.

About a month before the rate increase announcement was scheduled to be made, someone in management remembered that Blue Cross was a creature of the hospitals—and the planned action was somewhat akin to children accusing their parents of profligacy because they had just received a long-demanded increase in their allowance.

A local public relations firm was called in at this late hour; not an unusual occurrence. The consultants had about three weeks to plan, implement, and complete an educational campaign to explain why hospital rates were escalating so fast, so that the Blue Cross rate increase would be more palatable to all concerned.

As the account executive for that exercise, my recollection of the ensuing three weeks is little more than a blur. The 18-hour days were the short ones, as every possible activity was activated on a crash basis. Brochures and full-page advertisements were designed, written, produced, and distributed in 36 hours; hospital open houses were scheduled, publicized, and held; speakers drawn from all medical specialties and hospital administrative fields were drafted, briefed, and sent out to speak to all manner of groups; articles were written and placed in every publication within a 100-mile radius; patients and former patients were interviewed and reinterviewed.

The final cost of the campaign reflected the long hours of the consultants and the premium production costs. The client, who had well-founded and reasonable doubts that it could be done, was overjoyed at the results. And any thoughts of a continuing public relations campaign, to avoid similar problems in the future, were apparently never entertained.

Public relations, just as marketing, should never be reactive. Proper planning for crises and disasters can avoid many problems. And the few truly unpredictable situations that arise will seem easier to handle because internal thinking has been periodically directed to the general considerations of crisis public relations.

## References

[1]Herbert M. Baus, *Public Relations at Work*, Harper & Brothers, New York, 1948, p. 19.

[2]Ibid., p. 19.

[3]Lynn Fischer, "The School for Presidents," *PACE*, March–April 1975, pp. 34–35.

[4]Ibid.

# PART
## 2

Any marketing of professional design services should be of the low key, soft sell—even understated—variety. One could hardly expect to inspire confidence among prospective clients through the strident, hard sell hucksterism often used to promote consumer products.[1]

# CHAPTER 5
# Tools and Techniques: Basic

**W**HILE PRACTICALLY EVERYONE would agree that budgets are important to all aspects of business—and no less so in the public relations function—it has been difficult, if not impossible, for most principals and marketing directors to find substantive guidance in setting up a PR budget.

## BUDGETS

Anthony N. Mavis, in an otherwise helpful article about public relations in the August 1976 *Consulting Engineer*, after pointing out the importance of establishing a budget before undertaking a public relations program, backed away from the brink:

> Since public relations and marketing are so closely related in a professional design firm, it is difficult to define clearly what belongs in a public relations budget and what belongs in the marketing budget. Generally, a marketing budget incorporates the public relations activities related to marketing. . . . Because the major thrust of public relations is marketing oriented in most firms, we will limit our discussion to establishing a marketing budget.[2]

Several marketing consultants have developed recommendations and guidelines for establishing an overall marketing budget. As a practical matter, both the marketing and public relations budgets should have some

### TABLE 5-1. Marketing Budgets*

| Annual billings | Percent range | Budget range |
|---|---|---|
| $ 100,000 | 8–12 | $ 8,000–12,000 |
| 250,000 | 7–10 | 17,500–25,000 |
| 500,000 | 6–9 | 30,000–45,000 |
| 750,000 | 5–8 | 37,500–60,000 |
| 1,000,000 | 4–7 | 40,000–70,000 |
| 2,000,000 and over | 3–5 | 60,000–? |

*These figures represent the experience of several hundred design firms, as compiled and averaged over the past six years.

SOURCE: "Marketing for Design Professionals," *Professional Marketing Report*, Washington, April 1977, p. 1.

relation to the amount of expected or projected billings during the budget period. Table 5-1 gives guidelines for acceptable marketing budget ranges based on annual billings (gross income). These figures are for a growth situation.

The American Institute of Architects suggests these marketing budget rules of thumb, based on annual gross income:

Gross income under $100,000 ........................ 10–15 percent
Gross income $100,000–250,000 ...................... 7–10 percent
Gross income $250,000–500,000 ........................ 5–7 percent
Gross income above $500,000 ......................... 5 percent

## An Alternate Approach

Another budget rule-of-thumb approach is to take 3 percent of the average annual fee income (based on at least 3 years' experience), then add 7 to 8 percent of any projected increase in gross billings desired over the next 3 years.

For example, if your firm's present annual gross income averages $500,000, and you want to achieve $750,000 annual gross income in 3 years, the budget would be 3 percent of $500,000 ($15,000) plus 7 to 8 percent of the increase of $250,000 ($17,500 to $20,000). This would result in a total annual marketing budget of $32,500 to $35,000 for each of the next 3 years—or a 3-year total of $97,500 to $105,000.

Use the $97,500 figure. Budget from it perhaps $49,500 for the first year and $24,000 for each of the remaining 2 years. After a heavier initial cost to build momentum in the first year, less money will be required to keep it going.

Diane Creel's masters degree thesis, cited in Chapter 1, is one of the few sources of dependable information about public relations budgets. Of 100 firms responding to a questionnaire, 52 said they allotted between 1 and 3 percent of their operating budget to public relations. A third said they spent between 4 and 6 percent of their total budget for PR, and 12 of the firms claimed public relations expenditures of 7 to 12 percent.

Most firms, as Tony Mavis pointed out, will have a problem differentiating between items belonging in the public relations budget and those more properly charged against marketing. The public relations budget probably should include direct expenses such as photography, printing, dues, travel and entertainment, meetings, telephone, subscriptions, and office supplies. Internal labor costs and consultants' fees are also charged against the public relations budget. Printing and reproduction would include brochures, newsletters, and announcements.

It would seem reasonable, practical, and pretty close to usual practices for firms to allot between 20 and 30 percent of their total marketing budget to direct and indirect public relations costs.

## BROCHURES

Since I have written a book of almost 300 pages on the design, production, and use of brochures (*How to Prepare Professional Design Brochures*, McGraw-Hill Book Company, 1976), it might be assumed that I have little more to say on the subject. And that would be a safe assumption had I not been involved in conducting a number of brochure design workshops and in individual consulting assignments since completing the manuscript for *How to Prepare Professional Design Brochures.*

In reviewing hundreds of brochures over the past couple of years these bothersome points and criticisms kept bobbing up:

### Layout and Format

• When loose sheets (for projects and key personnel) are incorporated into a brochure, make certain that each sheet carries the firm's name and address.

• Too many designers still make insufficient and improper use of white space. Use it as a design element—and use plenty of it.

• Spreads (each set of two facing pages) *must* be designed as an entity; too many are not.

### Typography

• Too many typefaces are used, often mixed indiscriminately on one page.

• Reverses are often used improperly. If they are unreadable, they are bad reverses.

• Typelines (often headlines) are run at an angle or vertically on a page. Never sacrifice legibility for what seems to be design.

• Try to use familiar, legible typefaces—in sizes large enough to be read comfortably by older readers.

### Illustrations

• Photographs are too small; too full of detail; not used as a design element.

- Don't be afraid to go big with illustrations on occasion—jump gutters; bleed four sides. Crop closely. Get the most out of all illustrations. Use closeups and microphotography for a change of pace.
- Don't get carried away with photomechanical effects—but don't ignore their possibilities, either.
- Use people for interest and to establish scale.
- In too many brochures the photo quality is inconsistent from page to page—and even on the same page.
- Too many graphic designers are still using obituary or "wanted" type photos of principals and staff.

## Color

- Four-color work is generally not up to acceptable standards; registration of colors is off, unbelievably so in some cases.

## Covers

- Blind embosses on front covers are sometimes placed so as to disturb, interfere with, or even negate the layout of the inside front cover.
- Not enough attention is given to cover design. The cover has to (1) stop prospects and (2) get them into the brochure.

## Headlines

- Too wordy; not pertinent or appropriate to the text.

## Ink

- We see too much bad ink coverage of the page.
- Odd colors are used in combination; often clashingly.
- The effect of overprinting two or more colors in screens and solids is not checked out before final press runs.
- Ink colors or hues are too light for darker paper stocks. Text and photographs disappear into the page.

## Copy

- Keep it to the minimum and keep it simple.
- There is still too much ego-tripping, back-patting, and executive salve getting into copy.
- Edit, rewrite, edit, rewrite, edit, rewrite.

## Key Person Writeups

- Avoid the use of nicknames.

- Don't include useless or unnecessary information.
- Don't overdo listings of individual state professional registrations.

## In General

- There is still a lack of flexibility evident in many brochure formats.
- Don't head statements of philosophy "Statement of Philosophy." If it must appear, try to bury it somewhere.
- It is amazing to see the number of brochures that fail to carry the firm's name, address, and telephone number.
- Far too many brochure writers still insist on capitalizing such generic terms as architect, engineer, firm, and principal. If the habit cannot be broken in any other manner, remove the capital shift key from your typewriter.

## REPRINTS

Reprints are the end product of some of the public relations writing and placement activities discussed in Chapters 9 and 10, but since reprints are definitely a basic PR tool we'll take up their use here.

In a recent talk, David Finn, chairman of the New York–based public relations firm of Ruder & Finn, Inc., pointed out:

> An old adage of public relations is that half of the job is getting the article in print; the other half is what you do with it once it's published. How you merchandise that article can be more important than having it published in the first place. This rule is going to become more important than ever as specialized media proliferate.

Sending out reprints of articles to special lists of clients, prospects, and opinion leaders is the equivalent of transforming a shotgun into a rifle. Prompt distribution of reprints to appropriate recipients must be considered the final step in what David Finn calls "merchandising" an article.

Reprints, in addition to being sent out as mailers to various direct mail lists (almost always with a brief transmittal note or letter), have other public relations uses:

- In brochures, reproduced in printed form as pages of the publication or as loose sheets carried in a cover pocket flap.
- John Portman & Associates uses reprints of articles about its projects as the firm's brochure. Visitors are given a folder filled with reprints from publications such as *Fortune, Time,* and the New York *Times.* The total effect is pretty impressive.
- Bound into proposals, including Standard Form 255 (the official form used by design professionals to indicate interest in specific U.S. government projects—usually building projects).
- As handouts for in-house functions—open houses, receptions, parties, and the like.

• Displayed on a table in the office reception area, for clients and other visitors to pick up.

The public relations department will usually know that an article is scheduled for publication well in advance of its appearance in a magazine—for the simple reason that someone from the public relations staff placed the article with the publication. The exception would be in the case of spot news coverage, where no public relations input was possible.

Since there should be few such surprises, one normally has plenty of time to make arrangements with the editor and production department of the periodical for reprints in advance of publication. It is much cheaper, especially where color is involved, to extend the press run at the time the magazine is printed than to go back a few days or a few weeks later for a special press run. Most publications will arrange to package the reprint in the regular cover.

We've been talking about articles of two or more pages. If the story is a page or less in length, it may be simpler to have your own printer run off the necessary copies. In any event, be sure you ask for, and receive, the publisher's approval to reprint any material used. A credit and copyright owner line is usually carried somewhere on the reprint.

Various techniques have been developed to "punch out" (emphasize) certain sections of a reprinted page, while holding other parts back. Edith Seidel, a publications specialist, developed a screening method that fades out unwanted photos and text. (See Figure 5-1.)

## HITCHHIKING PUBLIC RELATIONS

Engineers and other consultants can usually "hitchhike" on news releases from architects; architects can often get a free ride in client releases; and all design professionals have opportunities to tag along on supplier advertisements.

When architects are prime they will ordinarily take the lead in originating publicity material about the design of a project. But no building story can be considered complete without input from at least the major consultants, and engineers should not be backward about offering assistance to the architect's PR staff.

When an engineer is prime the publicity shoe is obviously on the other foot. Project news coverage should be generated by the engineering firm, with input from the architect.

Suppliers of all sorts of building material and equipment annually spend millions of dollars to advertise their products, with a large part of their advertising budget going for four-color magazine ads. A large proportion of such ads features structures in which their products were used, and it is a rare building materials ad that does not carry full design credits. Many consulting firms make it a point to get copies of advertisements showing their projects, to use as supplementary reprint material.

## In progress

**1 Luxury development in Miami**—The first 40 units of a 300-unit luxury residential community next to Biscayne Bay in Miami have opened and 100 more should be under construction by spring. Quayside, planned and designed by Miami architect Alfred Browning Parker, has "city villa" townhouses starting at $175,000; the homes are from two to four stories, each with an elevator and underground garage. The units are brick with copper roofs. Courtyards and cloisters interrelate the built elements, which accommodate such activities as tennis, boating, bicycling, and swimming. Overall cost is $80 million—the developer is Haft-Chasen Associates, Ltd. of Miami. Architects for the upcoming units are Reiff/Fellman Associates of Miami and Dale Naegle Associates of LaJolla, Calif.

**2 Giant shopping city planned**—ArchiSystems of Van Nuys, Calif., has received a contract to plan and design a regional shopping complex which will serve as town center for Farahzad, a new community of 100,000 people northwest of Tehran. The air-conditioned megastructure will contain 1.5 million sq ft of shopping space in four department stores, plus supporting retail shops, a 600-room luxury hotel, 850-room convention hotel, automotive center, entertainment center, 750,000 sq ft of office space in two 30-story towers, community facilities, and parking for 7000 vehicles. The client is Tehran Development Organization.

**3 Architecture building at Texas A & M**—Harwood K. Smith & Partners of Dallas is architect for the new Architecture Center at Texas A & M University, College Station, Texas. The $8 million building, to be completed in July, is linked to two existing classroom structures by a covered pedestrian bridge. Overhangs and sun control devices on each elevation provide energy conservation. Harwood Smith (Class of 1936) designed the building to programming of Raymond Reed, dean of the College of Architecture and Environmental Design. The building is named for Ernest Langford, a former dean of the school.

**4 Space frame terminal**—A French-developed space-frame produced in the United States will be used for the 110,000-sq-ft roof of the Baltimore-Washington International Airport Terminal expansion. Unibat of America Inc. makes the frame, which the manufacturer said, is one of the first frames available at a reasonable cost, since the field welding usually required has been replaced by shop-assembled modules bolted together on site. The design group for the project is Friendship Associates of Baltimore, comprising Ewell, Bomhardt & Associates and Peterson & Brickbauer, both of Baltimore, and Howard, Needles, Tammen & Bergendoff of Alexandria, Va. The $64.5 million project will be completed in 1978.

**5 Damavand College**—Taliesin Associated Architects, is architect for the Damavand College of 1200 students (all women) north of Tehran. The site is 21 acres in the Alborz mountain range of which Mt. Damavand is the highest peak. Native brick is used as is the traditional Persian arch and vault. Glazed turquoise tile covers long arching roofs. Phase I includes an administration/classroom complex, library, and theater centered around an inner space. Sweeping stairs and ramps connect the buildings.

Figure 5-1. This technique for reprint pages used by Edith Seidel emphasizes the project of one firm by rescreening other sections of the page. It's a subtle—almost subliminal—process, but effective in snapping out certain areas.

If the advertiser had the project specially photographed for the ad, it is usually possible to get extra prints of the photos at little or no cost.

The last method of public relations hitchhiking is through client releases and ads. Make certain the client's PR staff has complete information about the structure, materials used, the design rationale (if any), and a full list of consultant credits. If both the client and the design firm have full-time, professional public relations staffs, then a joint publicity effort is indicated—and the results should make everyone happy.

## PUBLIC RELATIONS NEWS SERVICES

Relatively unknown to the general public are the half dozen largest public relations news wire and feature services. For a flat fee these companies become an adjunct to internal and external public relations consultants. Some, such as the Audio Network of PR Communications, Inc., specialize in servicing radio broadcasters, but most of the services cover all media. Two of the oldest and best known of the latter are Derus Media Service, Inc., of Chicago, and North American Précis Syndicate, Inc. (NAPS), with headquarters in New York City.

An inquiry to either Derus or NAPS will bring more information about their operations and services than most people want to know. The Derus "Catalogue of Communications Services," for example, points out that their news releases are regularly sent to over 6000 selected editors of weekly and daily suburban papers, with a combined circulation of more than 25 million families. A one-column by 7-inch mailing to all 6000 papers would cost around $2500, postage included. For a fee of $350, plus postage costs, Derus will send releases to 2210 "receptive" radio program directors (about half the nation's total). If your interests run more to television exposure, $375, plus postage, will get photos with up to 100 words of suggested narrative mailed to 850 TV commentators.

The pages of *DMS Editorial Pace* are open at no cost to large and frequent users of other Derus services. *Pace* is a clipsheet mailed regularly to 30,000 editors of metropolitan dailies, all weeklies, company publications, and some trade publications. News clippings and postcard reports from radio and television users are furnished clients to prove use of the mailed material.

An interesting subsidiary service is the construction and placement of crossword puzzles. If "13 Down" happens to be the name of a celebrity with a public relations consultant, don't be surprised.

Why do editors use releases with obvious points of view? Part of the answer is that a point of view must be muted and otherwise be made palatable. Derus gives these tips on preparing copy for news and feature distribution services:

• Editors prefer short, one- or two-column, illustrated features which tell the story in picture captions.
• Material should be timely but not, as a rule, dated, since editors may hold a feature for several weeks before using it.

• When you must date copy, it should be distributed at least 4 weeks in advance.

• Editors have an affinity for headlines using the word "NEW," and like short, simple headlines.

• The opening sentence or two must hold the editor's interest—so hold your soft sell for later in the story.

• The best way of assuring that your article will *not* be used is to put the name of your company or product in caps, to quote prices, or otherwise to use copy better left for advertisements.

• Write objective copy. Blatant commercial stories belong on the advertising pages, not in news columns.

• Slant stories to general interest, keeping in mind that what is interesting in big cities isn't always interesting to editors in smaller communities.

• Pictures must mean something to justify the space they occupy in your release. Editors like action shots—but they still have a weakness for cheesecake, children, and animals in their photos. All ask for maps, graphs, and line art.

NAPS, which also has a clipsheet service for its clients, tends to run more to editorials, cartoon features, signed columns, and other special news and feature treatments. Some examples of NAPS articles for clients such as the American Institute of Architects, the American Wood Preservers Institute, the American Society of Civil Engineers, and the Institute of Electrical and Electronics Engineers will be found in Figure 5-2.

A Derus clipsheet feature from Xerox is shown in Figure 5-3. This is an example of the architect hitchhiking on a client promotion effort.

## SIGNS

Job or site signs can serve as a visual reminder of the project designer's name throughout the construction phase. Sign spectaculars seem to go with the more speculative projects and builders (Houston developer Jerry Hines reportedly considers $40,000 job signs nothing out of the ordinary).

If your clients can't come up with $40,000 for site signs, work with them to make certain that what is posted will be legible, is graphically pleasing, and has the names of all designers and consultants spelled right.

## DIRECT MAIL

Until recently, the opportunities for design professionals to use direct mail as part of their total marketing program have been somewhat circumscribed by ethical codes of their professional societies. The restrictions are fast falling by the wayside in most cases.

The excellent S. D. Warren Company booklet, *Direct Mail,* has a good, brief working definition of the subject: "Direct mail can be a letter, a booklet, a folder, a catalog. You can use it to advertise, produce sales leads, offer

## BUILDING A BETTER WORLD
### LAND USE PLANNING TO ENHANCE ENVIRONMENT

Changes in the use of land are so radical and so widespread that the quality of life is affected for everyone. For some it's better, for some it's worse. How you are affected depends on where you are. Abuses of land are obvious and given wide attention. The decay of the center city, the sprawl of dumps where water fowl once nested, and all associated evils are well publicized.

But what about changes that promise a better life for man and bird alike? These too are taking place in response to diligent planning and persistent effort in developing rational land use patterns. Well intentioned professionals in and out of government are calling for coordination of the extensive planning needed for wise and balanced use of land.

One group of experts in the American Society of Civil Engineers (ASCE) has an ambitious program underway to promote and support creative land use and to correct or avoid the abuse of land resources. They are endeavoring to assure the coordination of the thousands of existing planning authorities and agencies now in operation, and to attract the support of other interested groups. While most of their work is organizational, the goal is a better environment; more recrea-

tional areas; enhanced residential, commercial, industrial use of land; preservation or restoration of natural or historic sites.

The ASCE points out that most obvious abuses have "just happened." Cities overwhelmed by wastes have created dumps in the most convenient marshland or hollow. Developers, private or public, have built housing or stadiums or industries without benefit of impact planning. And, the public loses when this happens. More needs to be done to show that improvements can be made—not just talked about, says ASCE. The probability that legislation, federal, state and local community will require such land use planning coordination is very great. With or without the compulsion of law, the coordination of planning efforts just makes good sense.

According to one civil engineer and suburban planner, if we "had a plan of this type 20 years ago, the energy problem would not be as serious as it is." Resource development is inescapably a part of land use planning. Most obvious to the energy user is what he sees: energy wasting transportation or transmission resulting from urban-suburban-exurban sprawl. But much of the threat is not so easily seen, until it has happened. Example: the development of a high cost residential community in flood zone area, where the new regional airport will become a noisy neighbor.

With optimism, civil engineers say "something" can be done about it. Coordinated land use planning is the way to go. These professionals are working away to assure the "building of a better world."

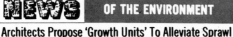

## NEWS OF THE ENVIRONMENT

# Architects Propose 'Growth Units' To Alleviate Sprawl

More and more Americans are demanding that we stop building "urban sprawl." But what can we do about the millions of acres of sprawl that already exist in our suburban areas?

The American Institute of Architects believes that the environments of many suburbs could be greatly improved by making a virtue out of one of the vices that helped create urban sprawl in the first place.

In nearly every suburban area of the nation, the 24,000-member national professional society points out, there exist scattered tracts of vacant land that have been "leapfrogged" by development. Usually, developers have avoided these sites because, for any of a number of reasons, they have been considered uneconomical to build on.

As a result, suburban growth has been "sprawled" — leaping ever further into outlying areas and leaving isolated, uncoordinated development in its wake.

To help restore some sense of order to these areas, as well as to provide many of the public amenities that they now lack, the AIA has proposed that federal, state and local governments, acting in concert, buy up vacant suburban sites — plus some that exist even in the center cities — and develop them as

catalysts for improving the overall environment. Through imaginative planning and design, says the Institute, the difficult terrain and other problems that have caused developers to overlook these sites could make for far more interesting environments then those on so-called "economical" sites.

"By taking advantage of many of these sites," says Archibald C. Rogers, FAIA, first vice-president of the Institute, "we could begin to pull our now-disjointed suburbs into some kind of rational shape. We could bring isolated subdivisions together by providing focal points that all of them could use and identify with. And at the same time, we could provide new public open space, recreational facilities, conven-

ience shopping and other community needs that so many of our suburbs don't have now."

The tool that AIA proposes for filling these gaps is the "Growth Unit," a carefully planned and designed neighborhood that would contain 500 to 3,000 residential units plus a full range of public amenities to serve its residents as well as those in nearby subdivisions.

"Growth Units," says Rogers, "have many purposes besides their use as infill for suburban gaps, but this could be one of their most valuable applications. Infill Growth Units could be catalysts for new urban transportation systems that would make travel between suburbs more convenient and economical. They could impart a real sense of place and identity to areas that are now seas of anonymity. And they could bring neighborhoods — and people — together that now have little or no relationship to each other."

And filling in the leapfrogged lands within existing suburban areas would help to relieve the pressures of development on the outer fringes of metropolitan areas, says the AIA. Thus more remote, unspoiled areas would be less likely to be affected by urban growth, which in the past has carved up millions of acres of farmland, woods and forest to succumb to the bulldozer.

## NEWS OF SCIENCE
### ENGINEERING FOR A BETTER WORLD

Your automobile is changing. As we have become concerned with pollution and safety, new devices are being added to your car. Many of these innovations have been designed by electrical engineers.

Electronically controlled windshield wipers, electronic ignition and the ability to make a diagnostic inspection of your car at your service station are some of the more recent electrical improvements that are available on many car models. Mr. Robert Hood, speaking at a recent technical session on automotive electronics sponsored by the Institute of Electrical and Electronics Engineers, noted that the "success of these...controls has been central to the advance of electronics in automobiles because they represent a transfer of trust into the automotive electronic environment."

The newest device adopted by U.S. auto manufacturers is electronic fuel injection. While previously used in some European models, it is now being utilized by

a domestic producer. First marketed in 1968, this system of electronically regulating gas flow has received increased attention because of the new federal emission standards.

Autos run on energy created by a mixture of gas and air. If there is too much gas present, hydrocarbons and carbon monoxide are emitted in the exhaust. Too much air in the mixture promotes high temperatures and excessive nitrous oxide is given off. Electronic fuel injection constantly monitors the mixture to make sure that they are in the proper proportions. While other devices can produce the same emissions standard, electronic fuel injection works more efficiently and can produce up to 10% better gas mileage.

More changes in your car can be expected in the near future. According to Mr. Hood, these devices will create a car "which is safer, more economical, and more responsive to the driver's needs."

WOOD UTILITY POLES — A KEY NATIONAL ASSET — BY PAUL D. CHRISTERSON — AMERICAN WOOD PRESERVERS INST.

### THE WHY OF WOOD

All of the nation's electrical utility companies (both public and private) use chemically-treated wood poles for more than 90% of their electricity delivery systems. The reasons: economy, easy serviceability, and good insulation.

These overhead delivery systems represent a total investment by utility companies of more than $26 billion — but that is "petty cash" compared to the $375 billion it would cost to replace this system. Individual poles have an average cost of $35.

Easy accessibility means service is up in the air in cranes—not a costly digging out process. And if there is an emergency, service can be restored without extensive delays.

Wood is known for its favorable "dialectric" properties—which means, wood is an excellent insulator. As if that weren't enough, utility poles carry porcelain or glass insulators which make "double" sure electricity won't leak out of the wires.

WOOD UTILITY POLES — A KEY NATIONAL ASSET — BY ROBERT O. HAWES — AMERICAN WOOD PRESERVERS INST.

### LOWDOWN ON OVERHEAD

One factor that has sparked America's vast success in industrialization has been the reasonable cost of electrical power. In fact, electricity rates have been decreasing since the turn of the century.

The use of overhead electric its distribution systems has helped make electricity one of the nation's biggest bargains. These overhead systems are an economical as well as highly efficient means of delivering electricity. To cut costs even further, the wood utility poles that support the wires over which electrical energy flows are chemically preserved. This means that the average pole lasts over 35 years.

If the overhead system were completely replaced, it would mean an estimated increase of $74 a month in each customer's electric bill.

Figure 5-2. Examples of NAPS clipsheet articles. NAPS clients represented are, clockwise from upper left, American Society of Civil Engineers, Institute of Electrical and Electronic Engineers, American Wood Preservers Institute, and American Institute of Architects. The AIA story is based on a speech.

# Training For Today And Tomorrow

Figure 5-3. A feature story from the *Derus Editoral Pace* clipsheet for December 1972. Xerox was the Derus client here and the architect got a free ride on the publicity generated.

A series of terrace-like buildings on the side of a hill in Loudoun County, Virginia, will be the home of Xerox Corporation's International Center for Training and Management Development when it opens in the summer of 1973. The multi-million dollar employee education facility, nestled deep within a 2,265-acre farmland site near the Potomac River, will accommodate 1,000 students and have a full-time staff of 500. The school's purpose is to train and develop worldwide Xerox people for personal growth and better service to customers. Vincent G. Kling, Philadelphia architect (center), whose firm designed the center, discusses a model with Xerox executives Willard H. Duetting, school director (left), and William F. Souders, vice president for marketing and planning.

information, raise funds, sell magazines and merchandise or solicit valuable market research data. The key is to get your message to the right people."

Commit that last sentence to memory: "The key is to get your message to the right people." With printing and postage costs in an ever-increasing inflationary spiral, direct mail is an expensive promotion and sales tool, particularly when it is improperly or badly used. On the other hand, well-planned, creatively done direct mail can produce outstanding results. It can be as sophisticated in application, penetration of markets, coverage of potential audience, and selling ability as any other medium.

The list (or lists) to which your direct mail goes can be at once the most important and the weakest part of the program. The best layout, copy, paper, and graphics in the world won't sell church design expertise to a prospect for a sewage treatment plant—nor is the head of a state highway department apt to be impressed with your firm's design awards for hotels and shopping centers. In putting together a mailing list, try to stack the odds in your favor as much as possible by maximizing hot prospects and minimizing cold ones. List refinement or narrowing is just as important as list building.

For example, if you are located in Atlanta and your real expertise lies in designing clean rooms for industry, you have several targets for a direct mail program:

1. All U.S. corporations
2. The top 1000 U.S. corporations
3. The top 500 U.S. corporations
4. Corporations in list number 3 who must manufacture or assemble products in controlled environments
5. Corporations in list number 4 located east of the Mississippi River
6. Corporations in list number 5 located south of the Mason-Dixon line
7. Corporations in list number 6 within a 200-mile radius of Atlanta

Each successive list is narrower and theoretically better than the one preceding it.

Since you are selling a specialized service, the list you build yourself, based on your own knowledge of the market and potential clients, should be the most effective list for your purposes. In addition to your house list, trade directories may be helpful to your list-building efforts—such directories as *Standard & Poor's Register of Corporations, Directors and Executives, Dun & Bradstreet Reference Book of Corporate Management,* and *Polk's World Bank Directory.* If you can't find the right directory you might consult the *Guide to American Business Directories* (Public Affairs Press, Washington, D.C.).

For certain kinds of services and for most products there are list brokers to help you find the right list for your purposes. But for design services, ethical codes aside, mass mailings to unknown audiences probably will not be very productive. A few firms do direct periodic broadside mailings to corporate buyers of design services—and it might work for your firm, if you have heavy experience in office buildings and manufacturing and warehouse facilities.

If you decide to rent a mailing list for a direct mail campaign, remember that the original list is private property and you can use the list only as many times as the contract calls for (usually once). Naturally, any response gives you a name to add to your house list.

Say a list broker turns up a list of 30,000 city engineers, or 40,000 school district superintendents. If you design streets and water distribution systems, or elementary schools, these *might* be great lists. But the direct mail pro will test any list of more than 2000 or 3000 names. A test mailing will be made to some percentage (10 percent, for example) of the names; so many selected from each state. Another type of list test is the *n*th name mailing—every 10th or 20th name in the list, up to a total of 2000 or 3000, is mailed to.

It's important to specify how your random sample is to be selected; otherwise the broker can furnish only the newest additions to the list—a form of sandbagging. Based on the returns from the test mailing you decide whether it is worth your time and money to mail to the entire list.

Avoid using lists with inaccurate or out-of-date individual names, titles, company names, and addresses by periodic list cleaning. One method of cleaning lists is by a postcard mailing every six months or so, asking for corrections. According to the U.S. Census Bureau, the average American makes twelve moves in his or her lifetime, and 18.6 percent of the population changes residences during any given year. If you have "Address Correction Requested" printed on the outgoing envelope, you'll get back the undelivered mail or a Form 3547 with the new address or the reason for nondelivery. The cost is 25 cents per returned piece.

Once you have a good house list built up, consider it an important business asset. Keep it clean by regular weeding—and keep it growing by feeding in good new names.

The relationship between the use of color in direct mail and the amount and quality of responses has been proved to the satisfaction of most direct mail professionals. Unfortunately, as in most of the variables involved with this type of marketing, there is fairly wide disagreement about which colors pull best—and why. One company found that a yellow envelope drew 40 percent better than a white envelope. Another firm, according to its direct mail consultant, doubled the response by switching from one-color to four-color printing.

Even though there is much that the experts, including psychologists, still don't know about the effects of color, there *are* a few points of reasonably general agreement:

• Black on yellow, green on white, and orange on blue give strong legibility. The least legible combinations are red on yellow, green on red, and red on green.

• The most exciting color is red; the red-yellow-orange family spells action. Violet and blue are the quiet, reserved, and subduing colors. Green is the most tranquil and neutral; yellow is the most cheerful and sticks in the mind as does no other color.

• Dark tones suggest stability, weight, and closeness. Lighter colors tend to make objects look lighter in weight and more distant.

• The favorite color of most women is red, while most men prefer blue. (Another expert advises: "Navy blue for him; blue-green for her.")

• Red is the best impulse color, quickly attracting the eye and motivating the individual to action.

• In the spring of the year tints and pastel colors have the widest appeal; in autumn public taste shifts to the richer shades of red, green, brown, or purple—presumably in imitation of nature.

Direct mail can serve, in its simplest sense, as a straight, passive advertising medium, but most mailers want to engender some kind of action (response) as a check on the mailing's effectiveness, if nothing else. You've probably received mailings from publishers with a response card that required you to insert one of two punch-out tokens in a coin slot; either a "yes" or a "no." You might have wondered why a company goes to all of the expense of the mailing, just to get a negative response from some recipients. The answer is simple—involvement. Psychologists advise that any time a reader is involved in pushing, pulling, licking, stamping, tearing off, punching, or any other kind of overt participation in the reply procedure, the better the response.

In the example of asking for a "yes" or "no" answer by inserting the proper token in a coin slot, many recipients put the "no" token in the slot and return the reply card in the belief that this action will cause the sender to lose interest in them as a prospect. The opposite effect results, since the mailer has gotten some type of response. Even the negative reply causes your name to be worth more on a prospective name rental list, for example, than someone who did not return the card at all.

In marketing professional services, the response mechanism is somewhat more limited than if you were selling encyclopedias, records, or Christmas gift baskets. Perhaps you are doing some market research; the desired response would be the return of a questionnaire aimed at giving you a better idea of your market profile. People like to be asked for their opinion or suggestions, but keep the questionnaire simple.

If the primary purpose of your mailing is to maintain client and prospect contact, you might offer to send a new study on solar energy collection by your engineering division, or you might offer a report on computer developments in project planning. Any premium offer should be of fairly widespread interest and relate to the primary interests of those on your mailing list.

We included Figure 5-4 to show that even the most experienced direct mail pros slip up occasionally on a mechanical detail. In a mailing to its millions of card holders, the American Express Company used the wrong postage indicia on the business reply card (BRC). In theory, the postal service could have refused to accept any of the order cards for delivery.

## EXHIBITS

Exhibiting, to be an effective public relations tool, must be considered an active, not a passive, marketing medium. Here are a few tips from the pros on getting the most for your exhibit dollars:

• If the exhibit itself wasn't designed as a professional marketing tool, nothing will help.

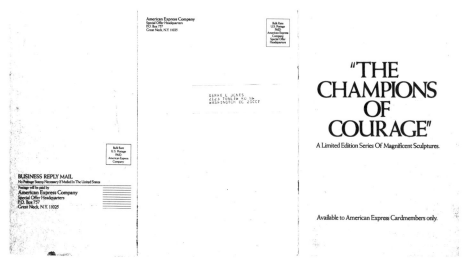

Figure 5-4. Even giant mailers can goof. This combination booklet cover-mailer business reply card, sent out by the American Express Company in 1977 to its millions of credit card holders, has a third-class bulk mail indicia on the business reply card section (left panel) instead of the required first-class permit number. Of this mailing the Postal Service said, "Business reply mail may not be sent to the original distributor [American Express] at the bulk third-class rates. Consequently, the bulk third-class permit imprint should not be shown on such mailing pieces . . . we will advise the mailer accordingly."

- If all you really want to do is just "talk to people," design the exhibit booth as a parlor and serve cookies and tea. It will be a lot easier on your staff's feet.
- Don't get caught up in the numbers game. It's always better to talk to 30 real prospects than to have 300 "lookers" who'll just waste your time.

Design competitions and awards can be considered a form of exhibit—at least for the winners. Since the sponsoring of competitions has become such a popular marketing gimmick for so many building material and equipment suppliers and their trade groups, it is difficult to compile a current list of such award programs. If you want to utilize more fully competitions as a public relations tool, write to your professional organization for an up-to-date list of sponsors, rules, and addresses.

## REFERENCE SOURCES

There is almost an embarrassment of riches in media contact information sources. One of the most complete listings will be found in the various *Standard Rate & Data* indexes, available in most libraries. Some other publications in the field we have used and found to be helpful:

*Ayer Directory of Publications,* Ayer Press, 210 W. Washington Square,

Philadelphia, PA 19106. Issued annually. Contains information about 23,000 newspapers, magazines, and trade and special interest publications.

*Bacon's Newspaper Directory,* Bacon's Publishing Company, Inc., 14 E. Jackson Blvd., Chicago, IL 60604. An annual listing of all daily, weekly, and semi-weekly newspapers in the United States. Twice-yearly revisions.

*Bacon's Publicity Checker,* Bacon's Publishing Company, Inc., 14 E. Jackson Blvd., Chicago, IL 60604. Published annually in October, with three revision supplements. Lists over 4000 business, trade, farm, and consumer publications under 99 market classifications, plus business and financial writers with over 700 major daily newspapers, news services, and syndicates.

*Federal Editors Directory,* Federal Editors Association, 7204 Clarendon Rd., Washington, DC 20014. Lists more than 300 active editors and writers in government bureaus and departments.

*The Gebbie House Magazine Directory,* National Research Bureau, Inc., 424 N. Third St., Burlington, IA 52601. Information about 4000 major house magazines; published annually.

*Gebbie Press All-in-One Directory,* Gebbie Press, P.O. Box 1000, New Paltz, NY 12561. Lists all daily and weekly newspapers, AM and FM radio stations, television stations, trade press, business papers, general magazines, and farm publications. Published annually.

*Hudson's Washington Directory,* Hudson Associates, 44 W. Market St., Rhinebeck, NY 12572. Issued annually; revisions quarterly. Information on more than 2500 members of the Washington press corps.

*National Directory of Weekly Newspapers,* National Newspaper Association, 491 National Press Building, Washington, DC 20045. Issued annually in spring, with information on almost 8000 weekly, semiweekly, and triweekly newspapers in the United States.

*Professional Guide to Public Relations Services,* 3d ed., by Richard Weiner. Prentice-Hall, Inc., Englewood Cliffs, NJ 07632. Covers more than 650 services, including clipping bureaus, media directories, and newspaper feature release services.

*Television Factbook,* Television Digest, Inc., 1836 Jefferson Place, N.W., Washington, DC 20036. Comes out yearly, with almost everything you ever wanted to know about television, including names of key station personnel.

*The Working Press of the Nation,* National Research Bureau, Inc., 424 N. Third St., Burlington, IA 52601. A five-volume set of directories covering newspapers, magazines, radio and television, feature writers and syndicates, and house magazines.

Prices for most of the directories change frequently (always upward), but most of those listed above are in the $30 to $60 range. *The Working Press of the Nation* is in the over $200 range. We suggest that you review them in a nearby library before investing in any of the directories.

Newsletters and magazines dealing at least occasionally with public relations subjects include:

*Columbia Journalism Review,* 700 Journalism Building, Columbia University, New York, NY 10027.

*Editor & Publisher*, 850 Third Ave., New York, NY 10022.

*The Gallagher Report*, 230 Park Ave., New York, NY 10017.

*Impact*, Venture Publications, 333 N. Michigan Ave., Suite 2025, Chicago, IL 60601.

*Media News Keys*, Television Index, Inc., 150 Fifth Ave., New York, NY 10011.

*Jack O'Dwyer's Newsletter*, 271 Madison Ave., New York, NY 10016.

*PR Aids Party Line*, PR Aids, Inc., 221 Park Ave. South, New York, NY 10003.

*pr reporter*, PR Publishing Co., Inc., P.O. Box 66, Exeter, NH 03833.

*Practical Public Relations*, P.O. Box 3861, Rochester, NY 14610.

*Public Relations Journal*, Public Relations Society of America, Inc., 845 Third Ave., New York, NY 10022.

*Public Relations News*, 127 E. 80th St., New York, NY 10021.

*Public Relations Quarterly*, Hudson Associates, 44 W. Market St., Rhinebeck, NY 12572.

*Public Relations Review*, College of Journalism, University of Maryland, College Park, MD 20742.

## References

[1]"Direct Mail Guide for Design Professionals," *Professional Marketing Report*, Washington, November 1976, p. 1.

[2]Anthony N. Mavis, "How to Organize and Manage a Public Relations Program." Reprinted from *Consulting Engineer*, August 1976, p. 57. Copyright © 1976 by Technical Publishing Co., a Division of Dun-Donnelley Publishing Corp.—all rights reserved.

[3]"Marketing for Design Professionals," *Professional Marketing Report*, Washington, April 1977, p. 1.

In 1927 there were 677 broadcasting stations in the United States and 1,949 daily newspapers. Today there are 8,434 broadcasting stations and 1,774 daily newspapers. . . . Americans spend, in an average week, 555 million hours watching television news broadcasts. Of these hours, 394 million are spent on locally produced news and 161 million hours on network news broadcasts.[1]

# CHAPTER 6
# Tools and Techniques: Advanced

AS MIGHT BE expected, television has generated more than its share of statistics and superlatives. A 1977 survey found that more than 64 percent of the American public depends on TV as its primary news source, with 51 percent saying it is the most believable medium. Nightly news programs from the three networks draw an average of 55 million viewers. "The average evening news show on the three commercial networks can manage to shoehorn 17 items into the 23 minutes that are left over after commercials in a 30-minute broadcast."[2] That works out to an average of 1 minute 21 seconds, or 203 words, for each news item, based on an average broadcast speech delivery of 150 words per minute.

According to the Radio Advertising Bureau, the average American spends more than 8 hours a day with various media—3 hours 48 minutes with television, 3 hours 22 minutes with radio, 37 minutes with newspapers, and 20 minutes with magazines. Or, for every minute in front of a televison set, the average American spends 9 seconds with a newspaper and 5 seconds looking at a magazine. If the total media time investment seems high (one-third of a person's life), compare the breakdown for each medium with your own viewing, listening, and reading habits. You'll probably decide it's not far off the mark.

We deal with print media in later chapters, but for the record and for comparison with electronic media, here are the numbers, in round figures, of various print media in the United States:

1,800 daily newspapers
1,000 major consumer magazines
10,000 weekly newspapers
8,000 special interest publications

And a few more TV statistics:

- At least 100 million Americans watch television for 6 hours every day.
- Approximately 112 million television receivers were in use in the United States in 1977.
- Some 98 percent of all American dwellings have TV sets; 30.1 million homes have two or more sets.
- A typical American will spend 10 years of his or her life watching television.
- There are more homes with radio or TV than with indoor toilets.

Some of the more caustic critics of the medium might not be inclined to pass over the last item without comment. As a matter of fact, a new twist to the TV ratings game was provided a few years ago when several municipal water departments noticed a definite correlation between sudden water pressure drops and the occurrence of commercials in local TV shows. Gauges in the Lafayette, Lousiana, water department, for example, measured a 26-pound pressure drop at the end of one particularly gripping movie. Some 80,000 gallons of water were used as 20,000 people flushed toilets simultaneously.

As with many of the statistics afloat in the sea of communications, these would be difficult to verify completely, but there is every reason to believe that any error is on the side of conservatism.

## EARLY HISTORY OF BROADCASTING

In 1898 Guglielmo Marconi made the first known newscast, a report on the progress of the Kingstown Regatta. Marconi thus became the first sportscaster as well.

Serious broadcast historians mark November 2, 1920, as the date radio newscasting began. On that night stations KDKA (Philadelphia) and 9XM (Detroit) broadcast returns from the Harding-Cox presidential race. The radio audience, estimated at about 1000, was the first to learn that Warren G. Harding was the apparent winner with a landslide 60 percent of the vote.

Four years later, an audience estimated at 17 million listened to gavel-to-gavel coverage of the first political convention to be carried on radio—the 1924 Democratic Convention in the old Madison Square Garden.

Television is much older than many realize. Experimental stations, using crude, mostly handmade equipment, were operating in the 1920s. At the

1928 Democratic convention in Houston a TV camera shared space with the candidates on the crowded platform. Al Smith presumably became the first televised presidential candidate—however small the viewing audience.

Ironically, both world wars served to delay the consumer phases of broadcasting, while improving the technical quality of the medium and training technicians. World War I had this effect on radio; World War II came along just as television was about to go commercial.

The first true nationwide TV broadcast did not occur until September 4, 1951, when AT&T finally completed a coast-to-coast hookup of its coaxial cable in time to carry an address by President Truman from the Japanese Peace Treaty Conference in San Francisco. Regular nationwide news service on television began a couple of weeks later.

## USING TV FOR PR

If you are among the many who have had no experience whatsoever with the on-the-air and production aspects of television, one of the best introductory booklets you can get is *If You Want Air Time,* published by the National Association of Broadcasters (NAB) for the user of lay persons. Check with a local radio or television station to see about getting a copy.

The 18-page NAB publication begins with definitions of publicity, promotion, and public relations; runs through the early steps for getting air time, including several good lists of DOs and DON'Ts; and concludes with sample announcements for radio and TV. While the booklet is aimed primarily at organizations eligible for public service time, almost everything in it will be helpful to anyone trying to break into the electronic media.

## TV NEWSCLIPS

Since television is such a popular news source, with greater mass credibility than even newspapers, how can design professionals put TV to work in their marketing and public relations programs?

There are two basic methods open to any individual, firm, or organization. One is to be your own talent, through participation in interviews and panel discussions; the other is to furnish television newsclips to stations. We'll take up the latter method first.

An article in *TV Guide* for October 5, 1974, posed this seemingly easy-to-answer question:

> If you were a businessman with a product to sell, or a special interest group with a message to promote to a TV audience, which would you choose: (a) to spend $25,000 for a one-minute commercial that viewers might turn off or ignore, or (b) to pay $2,500 for 60 seconds of exposure with built-in believability on that most popular of local broadcasts—the evening news?[3]

While practical experience with such handouts or sponsored "news items" will demonstrate that the answer to *TV Guide*'s question is not "either-or," newsclips do offer a way to get air time that cannot be bought in any market.

Newsclips can be on 16-mm sound film, on videotape, or in the form of a slide-and-script release. They are usually a minute or less in running time and the rule of thumb is one audio plug and one video plug (one mention of the sponsor in the narration and one shot of the sponsor's name on the screen) per newsclip. Most of the production and distribution of newsclips is handled by specialists such as Modern Talking Picture Service, Worldwide Films, Spotlight News & Associates, Gordon Newsfilms, and North American Precis Syndicate (NAPS).

Representative costs for newsclips, including production and national distribution, range from $2500 to $6000. Many factors such as talent costs, original artwork requirements, location shooting, and the number of stations to be covered affect the final cost of sponsored newsfilms. NAPS offers slide-and-script releases consisting of four to eight 35-mm color slides and accompanying script averaging around 30 words per slide (Figure 6-1). Cost of a four-slide plus script release to 300 stations is approximately $1300 when the client supplies the color photos or other artwork.

## Possible Newsclip Subjects

If you are interested in TV newsclip exposure, what are some of the potential subjects for design professionals? A few possibilities:

- Major design awards
- Groundbreakings
- Top outs
- Release of first renderings or model studies of major structures
- Unusual or record-breaking aspects of projects—highest, deepest, longest, largest, smallest
- Civic awards
- Anniversaries
- Unusual applications of design or materials—especially in energy conservation
- How-to subjects

Simpler and much cheaper versions of newsclips are still photos, 35-mm slides, or locally-shot film or videotape footage of relevant news and feature subjects. The vast majority of design firms would seldom, if ever, be faced with the need for more than regional distribution of TV news material. Costs for this more localized coverage would range from around $10 to perhaps $300.

## TV APPEARANCES

The more adventuresome practitioners may opt for the alternative to sending out newsclip material—personal appearances on the TV screen.

If you have an opportunity to be interviewed on television, here are some

▶ *The history approach pulls extremely well and is useful in making one key point. Is the key point below the one made in box three, with the Amoco name just "worked into" the next box? No. Instead, at a time when some people wondered whether Amoco was withholding supplies to cause the gasoline shortage, the key point demonstrated to newscasters and viewers by this release is that Amoco—far from causing the problem—wanted to solve it.*

**IN COLOR**

**TV TAKES**

NORTH AMERICAN PRECIS SYNDICATE, INC.
220 West 42nd Street ● New York, N.Y. 10036 ● LO 3-0400

ENERGY THROUGH THE AGES

1.  For thousands of years, people used petroleum for everything but fuel. They made mortar with it. They sealed boat hulls with it. The Indians and the early frontiersmen even drank it as medicine!

2.  The modern petroleum industry began in 1859...when Edwin Drake drilled an oil well in Titusville, Pennsylvania. Kerosene, not gasoline, was the major product at first. Kerosene lamps soon replaced whale oil lamps in 19th century households.

3.  Today we need programs to improve energy supplies...things like building the Alaskan pipeline and increasing offshore exploration.

4.  To save energy, keep your car in good shape. A poorly tuned engine can cut gas mileage by 10 percent. High speeds and jackrabbit starts also waste gas...so slow down! Amoco experts say there would be no shortage if each American used one less gallon of gas each week.

**Figure 6-1. An example of a NAPS slide-and-script television release prepared for Amoco. NAPS explains the key point made in this release: "At a time when some people wondered whether Amoco was withholding supplies to cause the gasoline shortage, the key point demonstrated to newscasters and viewers by this release is that Amoco—far from causing the problem—wanted to solve it."**

pointers gathered from various sources and personal experience that may be helpful.

• Personal appearance is important. Wear light-colored shirts or blouses rather than white ones. Ties and scarves with conservative patterns and colors are best. Avoid most jewelry; it can reflect and distract. Keep your head up to avoid sinister shadows around your eyes and chin.

• Get as familiar as possible with the technical workings of television.

• Know the format of an interview show well in advance. Watch a few of the shows if possible.

• Find out something about the host or moderator and ask about other guests, if any.

• TV time is always in short supply—there may be only 30 seconds to make an important point. Learn to say what you want to say in the briefest possible form.

• Anticipate questions that may legitimately be asked of you—and mentally form sample responses. If you don't know the answer, say so.

• Look at the interviewer when you're talking. Avoid looking directly into the camera unless you are on by yourself. If more than one camera is used for your show, remember that the one with the red light lit on the front is the live camera. The floor director or a camera operator will usually direct you by hand signals when the booth director switches to another camera.

- Don't fidget. Avoid all such nervous habits as tapping feet, drumming fingers, knuckle cracking (especially bad), throat clearing, blinking, and playing with hair, tie, or a pencil.
- Don't slouch or lean.
- Keep your hands off all microphones.
- Avoid sudden body movements. Standing (or sitting) quickly will take your face out of camera range.
- Don't sit between two questioners, especially if they may be hostile. Sit on either side of them and avoid being whipsawed into unintelligibility.
- Take a second or two to frame an answer if you need it. Avoid verbalizing while thinking or making transitions.
- Don't be confused by all of the lights and other equipment in the studio. Concentrate on the host or hostess and your subject.
- Avoid the use of scripts on television. Use brief notes, cue cards, or mechanical prompters such as the Teleprompter.
- Answer only one question at a time. If questioners cut you off, or more than one questioner speaks at a time, state openly that you would like an opportunity to finish your answer—and answer one question before moving on to another. Don't repeat questions, particularly if they are hostile.

A familiarity with all of the above pointers will not make you an immediate threat to veteran TV performers, but you will be more knowledgeable about the medium and come across better than most first-time interviewees.

## RADIO

The demise of radio, widely predicted in 1948 when the possibilities of television began to be evident, has obviously never happened. Some 30 years later, radio is stronger than ever as a news and entertainment medium.

The primary thing to remember in dealing with radio is that a listener must depend on one sense—hearing. A widely quoted Columbia University survey shows the roles played by the five senses in the learning process:

| Sight | 83 | percent |
|---|---|---|
| Hearing | 11 | percent |
| Smell | 3.5 | percent |
| Taste | 1.5 | percent |
| Touch | 1 | percent |

Among other things, these figures tell us that a purely verbal presentation, as on the radio or over a telephone, relies on a fairly ineffectual human learning sense. Hearing is about one-eighth as effective as sight in conveying lasting messages to the brain.

In their book, *Are You Listening?*, Ralph Nichols and Leonard Stevens explained some of the reasons for the rather startling decay ratio in the retention of aural information.

> Basically, the problem is caused by the fact that we think much faster than we talk. The average rate of speech for most Americans is around 125 words per minute (wpm). This rate is slow going for the human brain, which is made up of more than 13 billion cells and operates in such a complicated but efficient manner that it makes the modern digital computers seem slow-witted. People who study the brain are not in complete agreement on how it functions when we think, but most psychologists believe that the basic medium of thought is language. Certainly words play a large part in our thinking processes, and the words race through our brains at speeds much higher than 125 words per minute. This means that when we listen we ask our brain to receive words at an extremely slow pace compared to its possibilities.
>
> It might seem logical to slow down our thinking when we listen so as to coincide with the 125-word-per-minute speech rate, but slowing down thought processes seems to be a very difficult thing to do. When we listen, therefore, we continue thinking at high speed while the spoken words arrive at low speed. In the act of listening, the differential between thinking and speaking rates means that our brain works with hundreds of words in addition to those we hear, assembling thoughts other than those spoken to us. To phrase it another way, we can listen and still have some spare time for thinking.[4]

## PR Possibilities

In radio, as in television, there are several possible outlets for a public relations message. News shows are an obvious point of placement and probably offer the greatest potential to design professionals. Interviews, discussions, and features are other program formats to explore with news and program directors.

Interviews are often classified as "informative" or "personality." Informative interviews focus on what individuals know, rather than who they are. Personality interviews tend to exploit a name, accomplishments, special interests and skills, and the like. You don't have to be a celebrity to participate in this kind of program, but it helps.

Features can be broken down into news, human interest, and information features, all of which are often used as transitions between "hard" news items. A 5-minute radio newscast can include up to a dozen items—each containing about 50 words. These items are paragraphed or broken with transition features.

## Microphone Technique

For a definitive rundown on achieving maximum broadcast effectiveness—a not-so-mysterious art, as you'll see—we turn to a training booklet prepared for information officers by the Air Force Extension Course Institute.

Radio delivery and the fundamentals of public speaking have a lot in common. This does not mean that a good public speaker will make a good radio performer; it means that certain fundamentals of speech and voice training belong to both media. The big differences between public speaking and radio announcing are style and projection. A platform orator has to project his voice to every corner of an auditorium in order to reach his entire audience. In contrast, the radio performer directs himself to a single individual or a small group of people. The announcer may be a foot from the microphone while the listener is probably a few feet from the radio. You can consider these combined distances as the true distance between performer and listener. The miles between the microphone and the radio do not matter here. Radio is intimate; there is no need to throw or project the voice to the rear of a hall. Whenever a radio speaker addresses his listener, he should always remember how close he is to him. Even if all the announcer sees in front of him is a microphone, he needs to maintain the intimate, casual style of conversation.

Despite the fact that we talk every day, conversation is not an art that is as easy or as simple as it seems. A conversational style is a skill acquired through training, practice, and experience. One way for you to develop this style is to read aloud as often as possible while someone listens. Ask your listener if your reading style differs from your normal speaking style. If the styles differ, practice to make them sound alike. A tape recorder is a big help when you practice alone.

Nevertheless, the necessity for a conversational style is no excuse for sloppy speaking. You must use correct pronunciation, crisp enunciation, and the most agreeable voice tones that you can muster. To manage each of these requirements, you must hear yourself speak, identify your radio speech faults, and then try to eliminate them. Most people do not know how they sound when they talk until they have heard recordings of themselves.

The mediocre performer often forces his voice until he sounds completely unlike himself. Never be pretentious or gushing, and never assume the airs of someone other than yourself. The good radio performer pronounces correctly and enunciates crisply because he wishes to be understood, not because he wants to sound cultured.[5]

## SEMINARS AND WORKSHOPS

Seminars and workshops can work two ways for design professionals: as periodic personal educational experiences or as public relations opportunities for their firms. Our interest in this book is in the latter role.

The self-serving seminar or workshop has been around in various guises for many years. Basically, one looks for a subject with some potential for increasing business, lines up a panel of experts (mostly internal), and invites prospective clients to attend the workshop. To make the session truly productive, there obviously are many more points of concern besides the basics.

Selection of the subject should be a careful, logical process. Search for project types on the early interest plateau or at the beginning of the upward curve. Don't waste time with project types on the top plateau or on the downside of the market decay curve. Were you to design a seminar around vocational technical schools—or even energy conservation—today, it would be an extreme case of too little, too late.

With a good topic in hand, spend some time in structuring the presentation. Know where you (and the participants) are going. Select a faculty with equal care. Naturally, qualified internal staff should be used whenever appropriate, but don't overlook the aspects of third-party endorsement and added credibility to be derived from carefully selected outside government and academic experts.

Assemble the list of invitees with a lot of thought. Even if the participants will be paying part of the expenses through registration fees, the seminar is going to cost a fair amount of money; make it a cost-effective operation. And resolve to go first-class throughout—in invitations, meeting facilities, meals, handouts, and the like.

## Setups

There are a number of physical setups you can employ for the meeting room. One goal may be to promote interaction among attendees; the meeting setup can severely limit or facilitate this consideration. The most-used setups include:

**Theater (auditorium).** Appropriate for all-lecture sessions, maximizing the number to be accommodated in the room. This arrangement discourages audience participation and is essentially a signal to attendees that their role is to be a passive one—listening, absorbing, understanding, and believing. Developing any sense of group identity or a group dynamic is extremely difficult to achieve in a theater setup.

My personal reaction to the passive theater setup is almost completely negative. The audience is treated to a succession of talking heads parading across the front of the room—a series of 50-minute lectures (which often appear to be uncoordinated), in which the information is figuratively poured into the laid-back skulls of a passive group of listeners. Few, if any, questions are raised (sometimes they are expressly forbidden), no discussion worthy of the name results, and the whole exercise usually can be characterized as deadly and uncommunicative.

**Conference.** The name is more conducive to audience participation, but this setup has certain drawbacks of its own. Implied is a table around which conferees will be seated. Actually, the physical form can be a round, boat-shaped, or rectangular table, or a hollow square, or a U-shaped arrangement.

Size limitations for this setup fall within the range of fifteen to thirty people. A round table allows everyone to look at each other, but when more than fifteen to eighteen people are seated around it, eye communication and group identity suffer. Any table shape other than round has the psychological disadvantage of tacitly directing attention and discussion to those seated at the narrower dimensions of the table.

The U-shaped arrangement is preferred by some workshop organizers, but many meeting rooms do not allow for the most efficient utilization of this setup. Seating people on both sides of the legs of the U means that those on the inside will be uncomfortable if note-taking is expected.

**TABLE 6-1. How to Determine Per-Person Consumption**

| Number of guests | Number of drinks | | | |
|---|---|---|---|---|
| | ½ hr | 1 hr | 1½ hr | 2 hr |
| 25–55 | 2 | 3¾ | 4¼ | 4¾ |
| 60–104 | 2 | 3¾ | 4 | 4¾ |
| 105–225 | 1¾ | 3 | 4 | 4½ |
| 230–300 | 1½ | 2½ | 3 | 3½ |
| 315–up | 1½ | 2½ | 3 | 3½ |

**Classroom.** Sometimes called a "schoolroom" setup, this is perhaps the most adaptable arrangement for workshops of up to forty people. My personal preference is for a herringbone table arrangement, where the inside aisle ends of the tables are slightly slanted away from the front of the room. This avoids the precise military look of tables being squared up in columns, and seems to bring those at the outside ends in closer to the action.

It is important not to crowd people in a classroom setup. Standard hotel table sizes come in 6- and 8-foot lengths and 18- and 30-inch widths. Seat two people at a 6-foot table or three at the 8-foot model. Never settle for less than the 30-inch width. If the facility claims it does not have the 30-inch tables, have them set two 18-inch tables together.

## Facility Checklist

— Special needs of speakers
  — Projectors. Type _____.
  — Portable mike(s).
    — Check out all mikes.
  — Blackboard(s).
  — Flip chart(s) and easel(s).
— If a panel is to be used, how many microphones _____?
  — Check out mikes.
— Spotlights.
— Table for check-in.
— Table for handouts and other literature.
— Badges (in alphabetical order).
— Blackboard or bulletin board in reception area for telephone and other messages.
— Lectern at proper height.
  — Light, if required.
— Supplies. Ice water, glasses, ashtrays, and note pads on every table.
— Hats and coats. A rack or checkroom near the meeting room.
— List of attendees for distribution.

Other checkpoints will be found in Chapter 8, "Audiovisuals."

Figure 6-2. A few of the many books written by or about design professionals. They include books by John Portman, Louis G. Redstone, Peter S. Hopf, Ernest Burden, William Dudley Hunt, Jr. (about Welton Becket), and Edward Durell Stone.

## Planning

If a pre- or post-workshop cocktail party is planned, the consumption figures in Tables 6-1 and 6-2 may be helpful in your planning.

A final point on workshop planning has to do with questions and the discussion period. Most seminar speakers announce that questions are expected and welcome. To avoid an embarrassing silence, plant a few starter questions in the audience. Ask the speaker to furnish some. And the moderator or chairman should jot down a few during the presentation.

Some speakers prefer to respond to written questions. If this is the case, distribute question cards to attendees before the talk. As moderator, feel free to interrupt long-winded and irrelevant questions—and mini-speeches disguised as questions. The speaker and the rest of the audience have some rights too.

## BOOKS

The transition from self-serving seminars and workshops to books might seem somewhat abrupt, but the kind of books we're talking about are written for at least one of the same reasons as for producing a workshop—a public relations tool to establish expertise and credibility. Figure 6-2 shows a few of the many books written by or about design professionals such as Edward

**TABLE 6-2. How to Determine Drinks per Bottle**

| Bottle size, qt | Drink size, oz | Number of drinks |
|---|---|---|
| 4/5 | 1 | 25 |
| 4/5 | 1¼ | 20 |
| 4/5 | 1½ | 17 |
| 1 | 1 | 31 |
| 1 | 1¼ | 25 |
| 1 | 1½ | 21 |

Durell Stone, Hugh Stubbins, John Portman, Warren Platner, and Welton Becket.

Of the approximately 40,000 new book titles published annually in the United States, up to half will not sell enough copies to break even. According to *Newsweek* magazine, a first work of fiction may, with luck, sell perhaps 3000 copies in a hardback edition.

As a specific point of reference, the McGraw-Hill computer came up with a prepublication break-even point of 3612 sales for my last book, *How to Prepare Professional Design Brochures*. In other words, the 3613th sale would make a profit for the publisher. This was based on a $9.90 return per book of the original $16.50 retail price (the average dealer discount is around 40 percent). Simple multiplication—3612 × $9.90—shows that McGraw-Hill's costs for editing, printing, distribution, royalties, promotion, and other front-end expenses were almost $36,000. Paper, incidentally, represents almost one-third of the cost of producing a modern book.

Writing a book might seem like a large order for busy design professionals—or for anyone else who must hold down a full-time job in addition to writing. But once the determination is made, first-time, part-time writers are usually amazed to see how much can be accomplished in a regular writing schedule of an hour or two a day, plus 8 or so hours on weekends. Just 20 pages a week adds up to the average finished 500-page manuscript in about 6 months.

If you are among those who believe they have absolutely no qualifications or bent for writing, there are several alternatives—coauthorship, as-told-to, or use of a ghostwriter.

*Impact*, the communications newsletter, outlined the process of writing and submitting a book manuscript (ms):

1. Type ms on one side only, double-spaced, on good quality (14 lb. or better) bond white paper. Leave broad margins, top, bottom, and sides, and leave one-third of first page of each chapter blank. Make three copies. One for yourself; two for the publisher.

2. Number pre-text or "front matter" (title page, table of contents, preface or foreword, acknowledgements, introduction) in lower case Roman numerals in upper right-hand corner.

3. Begin numbering text consecutively with Arabic numerals in upper right-hand corner from beginning to end, not chapter by chapter. Place chapter numbers in upper center of page in upper case Roman numerals. Type your last name and slug for title in upper left margin of *every* page.

4. List "back matter" (footnotes, appendices, bibliography, glossary, index) with page numbers on your contents page. Type footnotes for each chapter on separate pages and number them consecutively by chapter.

5. Avoid hyphenating on right-hand margins, especially foreign words or technical terms. Use two hyphens for a dash; one for hyphenating words.

6. Be neat. No editor appreciates a messy ms, and the publisher could charge your royalty account with a retyping of the manuscript.

7. Write "end," that most wonderful word in the writing world, three spaces below the last line of the last chapter.

Many publishers request that writers query before submitting manuscripts. A query should include the book's title, length, and subject matter, as well as a detailed outline and synopsis, and one or more sample chapters. A stamped, self-addressed envelope should always be enclosed.[6]

One source says there are almost 6000 book publishers in the United States, plus thousands of "vanity" publishers. Bob Baker explains the difference:

Most trade publishers who sell through bookstores and newsstands are unrelenting about their basic criteria for considering unpublished writers: A book must be extremely well-written on a topic with a ready and massive audience; or the writer must be so famous millions of potential readers would buy on name alone.

Also, your chances of getting a hearing from a trade book publisher are better if your book is non-fiction. Novels by unknown writers . . . have almost no chance. So little, in fact, that a group of serious writers is reported to have formed a Fiction Collective at Brooklyn College to publish their own novels, with distribution by an established publisher.

Then there are the "vanity press" publishers, many of whom entice the unsuspecting through come-on ads offering to publish works by new authors. Often they do little more than the printing job, dumping the copies of the book and the bill for the printing into the author's lap.

The big three in this field built solely on the rock of the ego are Pageant, Exposition, and Vantage—all in New York.

If you can afford about $25 a page to publish your own book, the more reputable members of the vanity press will design, print, bind, and jacket the book. They will also handle promotion, publicity, distribution, and sales of subsidiary rights (motion pictures, book clubs, mail order houses, foreign reprints, etc.). You must reconcile yourself to the fact, however, that your actual income from the book will usually be very limited. For one reason, vanity press imprints are seldom reviewed by newspaper and magazine book reviewers. For another, sales promotion and advertising campaigns are minimal.[7]

Most books by architects and engineers, logically enough, deal with the practice and application of building design. But Los Angeles architect A. M. Kemper, AIA, wrote a book a few years ago that explored new areas in design. Kemper's book, *Love Couches—A Design Criteria*, is described in promotional literature as "the culmination of a research program conducted by [the author] to investigate the hitherto unexplored problems of basic criteria and parameters for the design of facilities to accommodate various acts of lovemaking." A further idea of the book's contents may be gained from the fact that sales are restricted to those over 21 years of age.

### References

[1]William S. Paley, "Broadcast Journalism: At the Crossroads of Freedom," speech given at Syracuse University, New York, May 31, 1974.

[2]Sander Vanocur, "Thinking News," *The Washington Post*, Jan. 7, 1976.

[3]Edwin Kiester, Jr., "That 'News' Item May Be a Commercial." Reprinted with

permission of *TV Guide* magazine. Copyright © 1974 by Triangle Publications, Inc., Radnor, Pa., p. 10.

[4]Ralph Nichols and Leonard Stevens, *Are You Listening?*, McGraw-Hill Book Company, New York, 1957, pp. 78–79.

[5]"Public Information," *Information Officer,* vol. 4, Extension Course Institute, Air University, Gunter Air Force Station, Alabama, 1974, p. 31.

[6]Robert Leon Baker, "That Book in Your Future," *Impact,* no. 175, Venture Publications, Chicago, 1975, pp. 3–4.

[7]Ibid., p. 1.

The good press agent understands that the virtues of his cause are not news, unless they are such strange virtues that they jut right out of the routine of life. This is because it is not worthwhile to say that nothing has happened when nobody expected anything to happen. So if the publicity man wishes free publicity he has, speaking quite accurately, to start something. He arranges a stunt: obstructs the traffic, teases the police, somehow manages to entangle his cause with an event that is already news.[1]

# CHAPTER 7
# Special Events

**W**HAT EDITORS CALL "news pegs" will be covered in more detail in Chapter 10, but since they are intimately related to special events coverage—or at least that of successful special events—a brief explanation is in order at this point.

A news peg, logically enough, is what the reporter or public relations practitioner "hangs" the story on. It is the *raison d'être* for carrying the story at all, and may be as important and serious as a terrorist attack on an airport—or as innocuous and flimsy as a state governor proclaiming a "Drink More Milk Week."

News pegs come in two basic models—real and created. Real news pegs will not concern us here, other than to mention that what may appear to the lay person to be a true and valid news peg often has been manufactured by someone on somebody's behalf—probably by a public relations counsel for a client.

Created news pegs are unabashedly manufactured. They are often manifested in the form of an event, and include press conferences, staged events (groundbreakings, top outs, dedications), appearances by newsworthy individuals, and the like. There is nothing ethically or morally wrong with a created news peg that (1) actually is worth building a story around (has inherent news value), and (2) serves the interests of the client on whose behalf it is created and staged. Go back and reread the Walter Lippmann quote at the beginning of this chapter. While Lippmann used the term "press agent" rather than public relations counselor, it *may* have been an unintentional slip. (In another context, Lippmann once commented, "Some people think of a publicity man as a press agent with a tie, and believe that when he puts on a coat he becomes a public relations counselor.")

At any rate, consider the last two sentences in the chapter-opening quote: "So if the publicity man wishes free publicity he has . . . to start something. He arranges a stunt: obstructs the traffic, teases the police, somehow manages to entangle his client or his cause with an event that is already news."

"obstructs the traffic"—a routine ploy, used by advance people for practically every candidate for state and national office. Motorcades and parades are scheduled by the knowing for only two times during the day; at noon, when sidewalks and streets are crowded with people on the way to and from lunch and shopping, and in the middle of the evening rush hour, when sidewalks and streets are again crowded with those on the way home, or to dinner, or the theater.

"teases the police"—a principle of news creation demonstrated ad infinitum by social and campus activists in the sixties, and by political activists, terrorists, and others today. Jim Moran, one of the most imaginative and durable of all publicists, developed the science of traffic obstruction and police-teasing into an art form.

" . . . somehow manages to entangle his client or his cause with an event that is already news." This phrase is the key to success for many publicity and promotion stunts, and it has almost infinite variations and applications.

## GIMMICK PUBLICITY

Alan Dessoff, then press secretary to Senator Charles Mathias of Maryland, once described the creation of a Capitol Hill media event. Senator Mathias had introduced a resolution to make "The Stars and Stripes Forever" the country's official march. To call attention to his legislation Mathias's staff decided to create a media event, in the form of the U.S. Marine band playing Sousa marches on the steps of the Senate.

The television networks were represented, along with all four Washington, D.C., television stations. An assortment of other correspondents, still camera people, and a few unoccupied tourists also showed up. Standing near the piccolo section, Mathias explained his resolution during a band break. The army of camera operators and correspondents, according to Dessoff, were busy "capturing on film and tape the Mathias words and Sousa music for the city, the country, maybe the entire free world."

The Mathias gimmick was not only pseudo-news, it wasn't even new news. After the event was well into its planning someone discovered that Ohio Congressman Delbert Latta had introduced a similar bill in the House earlier in the session by simply dropping it in the hopper—no Marine band, no television cameras, no publicity.

Dessoff cites another example of a Capitol Hill media event—the day someone brought some trained lobsters to the Capitol to demonstrate something. TV news programs that evening covered the lobsters' performance as if it had been a presidential news conference. Many remember the lobsters; no one recalls the reason for their visit.

Dessoff concludes with the admission that media events are not new and often are not news, either. "Still, everyone needs them. Senators and Congressmen need them to get themselves in front of the pack. When you are one of 535 and your pet bill is one of thousands and you are not running for President, how do you get anyone to pay attention? Anything unusual will do, and hang the subject matter."

## GROUNDBREAKING

In an earlier book I discussed the five story possibilities basic to practically every construction project.[2] They included groundbreakings, top outs, and dedication ceremonies, and several examples of each were given.[3] Since many readers seemed to find the material of interest, we will take up each of the three construction site activities in some detail.

Groundbreakings, top outs, and dedications all share one feature in common. They are essentially nonevents—created, staged affairs to obtain a little more publicity for what is hoped to be an above-the-ordinary, if not a semisignificant, structure. After seemingly every possible gimmick has been used at least once in the breaking of the first ground for a building, coming up with an original approach is a challenge to anyone in public relations.

The originator of a groundbreaking ceremony for the purpose of publicity generation is unknown. The event apparently began with a single, cheap, unadorned shovel; then someone thought of painting the shovel gold; several shovels were used (see Figure 7-1) on the theory that more is better; then a bulldozer was substituted for the shovels and invited guests given hard hats as mementoes of the occasion—and so it went.

A few examples of the inventive PR mind at work attempting to take groundbreakings out of the ordinary:

• In downtown Los Angeles fake rocks were blown up by motion picture special effects people to signify the "groundblasting" for a new office complex.

• At the elaborate groundbreaking ceremonies for the 18-story Rehabilitation Institute of Chicago, the highlight of the occasion was described as "when Michael Williamson, a former rehabilitation patient who had lost both lower legs in an accident, was elevated on a fork lift to the crane to activate the machinery that dug the first hole." Among those witnessing this act were the Governor of Illinois, Senator Charles H. Percy, and the Administrator of the Department of Health, Education, and Welfare.

• A full-scale floor plan for the new special education center at Tusculum College was laid out with stakes and white nylon cord on the actual construction site. Volunteer guides took the invited guests through the unbuilt

Figure 7-1. This photograph, taken during the 1969 groundbreaking ceremonies for the A. H. Robins Company corporate distribution center in Richmond, Virginia, possibly proves that more is more when it comes to shovels. Each of the shovels carries its wielder's name on the handle and information about the occasion on the gold-painted blades. (Photo courtesy A. H. Robins Company.)

building. One stop on the tour was to observe a class of retarded children and their teacher in a rope-and-stakes classroom. The tour ended with a look at a three-dimensional scale model of the new center.

• An Indiana-based financial services company sometimes substitutes a sign-raising for a groundbreaking. Before construction begins, a sign identifying the new building is bolted into place on the site with "ceremonially decorated wrenches" by company officials and local VIPs.

• The building for which ground is being broken sometimes has an influence on the ceremony. At the 1959 groundbreaking for New York's Lincoln Center, the silver-bladed shovel was operated by the President of the United States, with background music by the New York Philharmonic Orchestra.

• When groundbreakings are spectacular enough they may even be noticed by the *Wall Street Journal.* On April 4, 1974 the *Journal* reported on groundbreakings for new headquarters for two companies. A skydiver floated down to one site and presented a gold-plated child's shovel to officials of Revco D.S., Inc., one of whom promptly used it to turn over a bit of earth. At the other ceremony the head of Allied Supermarkets swung a 9-foot-long aluminum-bladed meat cleaver to mark the construction start of his company's new headquarters. Presumably the grocery executive cleaved the earth, although the *Journal* did not say.

• One of the more imaginative groundbreaking events occurred in Las Vegas a few years ago to mark the construction start of a 16-story tower addition to the Caesars Palace hotel-casino complex. Seven pounds of earth from Rome's ancient Circus Maximus were flown in to be mixed with the desert soil. The Roman dirt was accompanied by the mayor of Rome and his wife. A spade covered with 333 silver dollars (one for each of the suites in the new tower) was used to blend the Roman and Las Vegas soil. The scoop of a nearby earthmover was filled with magnums of champagne on ice for the guests. All of this, as one bystander observed, was "real class"!

• The University of Florida used a 2000-year-old spade to break ground for the Florida State Museum.

## Remote Groundbreakings

The Chicago public relations firm of Daniel J. Edelman claims credit for staging "the world's first fully automated, remote groundbreaking cere-mony," for an industrial facility in Columbus, Ohio, in 1968. A few para-graphs from the press release will tell most readers perhaps more than they really want to know about the technology of such an event.

FOR IMMEDIATE RELEASE
*Via CCTV, Remote Activation*
DESOTO GROUNDBREAKING BREAKS NEW GROUND

COLUMBUS, OHIO—In a unique fashion, the corporate pennant was raised and the traditional shovel full of dirt was turned today for DeSoto, Inc.'s new 241,000 sq. ft. paint manufacturing and warehousing facility here—but no one was there.

Three miles away in the downtown Columbus Athletic Club, the groundbreaking was automatically cycled via a multiple-switch, transformer, leased telephone line circuit and relay switch system that activated a special servo-mechanism at the construction site—with 74 hands "turning the shovel."

First, DeSoto Executives, Dignitaries and guests closed 73 special knifeblade switches, then at the invitation of DeSoto President B. A. Malm, Columbus Mayor M. E. Sensenbrenner pushed the button that sounded a Klaxon and sent the activating impulse to the site.

As the shovel lifted the dirt and the DeSoto pennant moved up the flagpole, the action was transmitted via closed circuit TV to the Athletic Club over a special Ohio Bell Telephone Co. micro-wave system, installed in bleak, wet and windy weather by technicians still bone-weary from constant shifting of micro-wave equipment needed by the major TV networks to cover fast-moving election developments.

The backdrop for the unusual groundbreaking scene was an inverted "V" of flags, with the center 12-foot pole carrying the U.S. flag at its peak, the Ohio and Columbus Flags lower and on either side on cross-bars, and the DeSoto pennant rising on the mast to a point just under the Ohio and the Columbus Flags.

The main flagpole was flanked by 8-foot staffs flying the Canadian Flag and the flags of the other eleven states in which DeSoto has major facilities, with multi-plant state flagpoles bearing a streamer for each plant.

S. U. Greenberg, DeSoto's Chairman of the Board, said that while DeSoto believes the automated remote groundbreaking constitutes a "first," the decision to stage the novel ceremony basically was made because it seemed to be appropriate for this highly mechanized and automated paint manufacturing and warehousing facility.

"Groundbreaking is more a symbolic than a physical act, marking an important step in the growth of a corporation. But while the tradition is worth observing, we felt there was no more reason to turn dirt by hand than to manufacture paint that way," Greenberg said.

The special groundbreaking and flag-raising unit and the activating equipment was engineered by Hans Schulz, president of Delta Manufacturing Co., Chicago, which has constructed displays used throughout the world. The display firm is noted for its animated displays, including an eight-foot model of the earth circled by a spacecraft and space-walking astronauts developed by Delta to commemorate that space feat.

The closed circuit television system complete with cameras, switching equipment, monitors and video tape recorders, was installed and operated by Taylor'd Sound, Inc., Columbus, with the Columbus and Southern Electric Company providing power at the site.

The above is quoted verbatim from the first two pages of the four-page Edelman press release, with sentence structure and punctuation unchanged from the original. We'll explore the subject of writing press releases and other public relations items in Chapter 9, but a few comments are in order here about this release.

The first four paragraphs of the release say essentially all there is to say about the event. Note that most paragraphs consist of a single sentence. The fourth paragraph is a windy 67-word sentence. The "bone-weary technicians" installing microwave equipment in "bleak, wet and windy weather" conjure up a kind of downbeat note to the ceremony.

Note also that the release writer annexed Canada to the United States in the sixth paragraph through a little sloppy writing. The lengthy coverage of flags, flagpoles, and pennants midway through the material seems overdone and not particularly pertinent. The same observation applies to the description of Delta's earth model built to commemorate America's spacewalk.

The complete release runs on for ten more paragraphs. It is not an outstanding example of the release writer's art.

## Checklist

Let's assume that your groundbreaking ceremonies will be held on the site—no closed circuit television and no robot dirt diggers—just regular people with standard gold-plated shovels. Planning for such an event can get rather complicated, especially the first time around. The Public Relations Society of America provides a checklist for public relations activities connected with groundbreakings, which has been expanded somewhat for this chapter (Table 7-1). The groundbreaking checklist is a good general guide for almost any special event.

As a final note on groundbreakings, one public relations director, noting that chrome- or gold-plated shovels can cost up to several hundred dollars, recommends minimizing risk of damage to the implement by preshoveling the bed of earth, then raking and sifting the loose dirt to remove rocks, nails, and other scratchy objects.

### TABLE 7-1. Groundbreaking Checklist

|  | 10 weeks prior | 8 weeks prior |
|---|---|---|
| Press Relations |  | Begin press kit: <br> 1. General release <br> 2. Biographies & pictures <br> 3. Facility renderings <br> 4. Company information <br> 5. Product literature |
| Invitations |  | Draft invitations with RSVP. |
| Staff and guests |  |  |
| Food, entertainment | Hire entertainment if desired. | Reserve room; hire caterer. |
| Plant | Order sign for plant site. |  |
| Speeches |  |  |
| Transportation |  |  |
| Letters |  |  |
| Biographies | Write Chambers of Commerce, cities for names of key people. |  |
| Miscellaneous | Write for telephone book from town or city involved. Check all legal, safety, and insurance regulations. | Order company display for event. Arrange with local police for assistance in routing and parking cars. |
| **4 weeks prior** | **3 weeks prior** | **2 weeks prior** |
| Draft advance release. | Prepare special media list. | Send preliminary company information kit to editors. Arrange with utility for power at site. |

(Continued)

## TABLE 7-1. Groundbreaking Checklist  (Cont'd)

| 4 weeks prior | 3 weeks prior | 2 weeks prior |
|---|---|---|
| Mail to company officials, local people, state officials, customers, suppliers. | | Mail invitations to press. |
| Make reservations for PR staff. | Type guest badges. Make guest reservations if necessary. | |
| Set menu. | | |
| Order directional and parking signs. | Select escorts for VIPs. | Order necessary safety gear. Order sound equipment. |
| Prepare first draft of speeches. | | |
| Order buses, cars, etc. | Arrange transportation for PR staff. | |
| Draft letters of welcome to new employees. | Draft thank-you letters. | |
| Request biographies of city, state officials, featured guests. | Write biogs. for company people. Write city, area profiles for company people. | |
| Hire photographer. Plan remembrance items. | Arrange for secretarial help at site. Get company logo. | Order remembrance items. Recontact local police on arrangements. Order print of company movie. |

| 1 week prior | Day of event | 1 week following |
|---|---|---|
| Complete press kits, including speeches and site maps. Advance release out. Arrange for media to cover arrival of company party at airport. | Meet with press; distribute kits. Check for special photo requirements. Set up press area. | Follow-up letters to press. |
| Draft final guest list. | | |
| Make final transportation arrangements for guests. | Press kits for guests. Set up tables for badges. | |
| Confirm final arrangements for food. Give final count. | Check eating area, sound system, recording equipment, place cards, table souvenirs, program. | |
| Plan housekeeping site cleanup. | Check grounds, plant sign, platform, podium, etc. | |
| Finalize speeches. | Have extra copies on hand. | |
| Confirm arrangements for motorcade to bring party from airport to hotel. Check on police escort. | | |

(Continued)

**TABLE 7-1. Groundbreaking Checklist (Cont'd)**

| 1 week prior | Day of event | 1 week following |
|---|---|---|
| | Mail letter of welcome to new neighbors, city officials, etc. | Mail thank-you's the week following. |
| Distribute biogs. to company people. | | |
| Order flowers. Arrange for extra phones. Set up guest register. Arrange for message board. Have local airline schedules on hand. | Check company display and logo. Check on movie to be shown. Check on company photographer. Get safety glasses and hard hats. Secure shovels. | |

## TOPPING OUT

Sometimes erroneously called "topping off," this practice is rooted in the history of construction. In the beginning, topping out was more a private than a public ceremony. Since it basically is a celebration of reaching a certain stage in the still uncompleted building's construction, topping out was more significant to the designers, owners, and those actually engaged in the construction, than to the general public. Over the years, however, topping out has been made into a day of hoopla, speeches, corny and funny gimmicks, and an occasion for politicians, bankers, and the media to don hard hats and join the real construction people at the job site.

Germans generally are credited with starting the custom of placing an evergreen tree on the highest part of a building to signal completion of the framework. Known as "raising the roof tree," the ceremony was an excuse for a party for the builder, foreman, and the entire construction crew—at the owner's expense.

A certain amount of confusion has crept into the literature (for example, press releases) about which is the proper top-out piece of steel. References will be found to topping out at at least three different stages in the construction of the steel skeleton: the *last* piece of steel in a building frame, the *highest* steel bar in a structure, and the *first* piece of steel at the building's highest elevation. Actually, it makes no real difference and any of the three stages may be considered correct. Purists are referred to *On High Steel*, written by ironworker Mike Cherry (Quadrangle Books, New York, 1974), where on pages 201–203 he describes the topping out of a New York City skyscraper. "The topping out column is the *first* piece on the highest elevation, not the last."

Because most of the more elaborate ceremonies involve multistory structures, it can't make any real difference to those in the audience: (1) they wouldn't know the difference and (2) the location of the steel beam is too high for them to see it anyway. Weather and site conditions, the availability of company and political VIPs, and several other variables may have much more effect on establishing a date for the top out than whether it's the first, highest, or last piece of steel at the top.

The following release, for top-out ceremonies of a few years ago on a building for the Chicago Mercantile Exchange, is representative of the modern-day approach to the event.

FOR RELEASE AFTER 2 P.M.

TUESDAY MAY 4 1971

CHICAGO—"We're not superstitious, but why take chances?"

This was the question posed and answered by Everette B. Harris, president of the Chicago Mercantile Exchange, as he described how the CME plans to avert bad luck in its new building now under construction at 444 W. Jackson Blvd.

"We used just about every symbol ever employed at topping out ceremonies over the past 3,000 years when we moved the last piece of steel into place on our new building today," Harris said.

"And just to be doubly safe," he added, "we included a few new items."

Attached to the final beam as it was hoisted skyward a young fir tree, the Scandanavian [sic] symbol for fruitfulness, good luck and a long life. It ties in with the European custom of attaching a sapling to the ridgepole or highest member of a building, a practice believed to go back to an ancient belief in the kindly influence of the spirit inhabiting the tree.

The tree, which also represents the CME futures contracts in lumber, was decorated with eggs, potatoes, and yellow grain sorghum (milo), representing food for the steeds of the god Woden to persuade him to keep lightning away from the building. Coincidentally, the Exchange trades in these three commodities.

Departing somewhat from tradition, the tree also was decorated with other CME commodities substituting for chicken blood which the Chinese previously had substituted for the human beings sacrificed by the ancient Aztecs and Romans to placate the spirits on such occasions.

The array included a packet of ground beef (live cattle and boneless beef contracts), a package of bacon (live hog and pork belly contracts), a small ham and a small turkey (ham and turkey contracts).

Alongside the tree will be an American flag representing, Harris said, "our appreciation of and contributions to the American system of free enterprise."

Finally, a pair of handcuffs was attached to the tree in a ritual dating back to Xerxes, the Persian general who ordered the waters of the Hellespont to be lashed and the shackles thrown into it to punish the waters for causing one of his pontoon bridges to collapse during his invasion of Greece about 480 B.C.

"Since our building adjoins the Chicago river," Harris said, "we thought this might be a wise precaution."

"We don't know whether these symbols will bring good luck to our members and their customers," he added, "but we feel that they can't hurt anything. In any event, we wish everyone concerned the best of good fortune, health and happiness on the occasion of reaching this most significant milestone in our 51-year-history. Of course, we hope futures traders follow well thought-out plans instead of relying on superstitions."

This release, as was the one on the DeSoto groundbreaking of a few pages back, was reproduced verbatim from the original, just as it was sent out by the Chicago Mercantile Exchange's press department. While certainly more lively in tone and content than the DeSoto release, it is not a good example of PR attention to detail. A few examples: the misspelling of the exchange president's name at the end of the third paragraph, the omission of a verb in the first sentence of the fifth paragraph ("was" obviously should have followed "skyward"), misspelling Scandinavian in the same paragraph, and misspelling "substituted" in the seventh paragraph. Since any editor must take what is sent as the best example of a firm's writing capabilities, it is patently counterproductive to issue an error-filled release.

The basic top-out observance currently in vogue involves attaching an American flag to a symbolic steel beam. The beam often is signed by owners, contractor and supplier representatives, and workers before being hoisted upward (Figure 7-2). At the top out for the Occidental Center in Los Angeles, VIPs were given magnetic horseshoes (for good luck) with their names on ribbons attached to the horseshoes. The horseshoes were placed on the top-out beam and spotwelded to it after the steel was bolted into place.

**Figure 7-2. A 28-foot-long, half-ton, flag-bedecked ceremonial top-out beam is hoisted to the top of the 39-story One Oliver Plaza in Pittsburgh, marking completion of the steel framework.** (Photo courtesy of Bethlehem Steel Corporation.)

**Figure 7-3. Before the steel beam in Figure 7-2 began its 400-foot climb to the top of One Oliver Plaza, executives of the developer, the steel supplier, and the contractor signed the top-out symbol. Hundreds of Pittsburgh residents had previously signed the beam during the week it was on display at the site. The American flag is a traditional part of top-out ceremonies in the United States.** (Photo courtesy of Bethlehem Steel Corporation.)

In late 1975 the Bicentennial spirit caught up with top-out ceremonies for a five-story office center in Philadelphia. For the occasion two employees of the general contractor, dressed as Revolutionary War soldiers, hoisted a thirteen-star flag from the nearby Betsy Ross house to signify completion of the steel frame of the city's newest office building.

Occasionally, the top-out beam will be painted white and invited guests, workers—even passersby—asked to sign it prior to its installation (Figure 7-

3). There's a story about one such beam that was covered with X-rated graffiti by disgruntled workers and those from neighboring office buildings who had grown weary of the construction din. Luckily, someone from the public relations staff thought to check out the jottings and signatures early on the morning of the top out. Two cans of white spray paint restored the steel to its pristine condition just before the invited guests arrived.

The Bethlehem Steel Corporation's public relations department compiled this list of items for inclusion in a top-out press kit:

- News release
- Fact sheet
- Schedule for topping out ceremonies
- Releases on the architect and major consultants
- History of topping out
- Photos
- Sketches
- Feature article on fabrication
- Feature article on erection
- Prayer
- Invitation to the event

Media coverage of the topping out of a major building can usually be counted on, since it's a fairly visual event. A little imagination and creativity on the part of the public relations staff will increase the odds of getting at least minimal coverage for the ceremony.

## DEDICATIONS AND OPEN HOUSES

Building dedications, as a general rule, are more dignified occasions than either groundbreakings or top outs. But not always when symbolic ribbon cuttings are scheduled, as these examples illustrate:

- The opening of a west coast commodities exchange was signaled by the sight (and sound) of one of the exchange's executives cleaving a coconut with a machete (coconut oil futures would be traded on the exchange).
- From a UPI report of a few years ago: "Instead of cutting the ribbon at the dedication of the new police firing range in Brigham City, Utah, it was decided to have two officers snap the ribbon with gunfire. The two marks-men aimed their automatic pistols and fired—500 times. When the smoke cleared, the ribbon was tattered, but unsnapped. A third officer finally finished it off with a shotgun."
- The 3M Company had better luck with a plant opening in Brownwood, Texas, when the company president and then Governor John Connally successfully used old dueling pistols to break a ribbon.
- A new golf course near San Diego was opened with the driving of an over-sized golf ball through the ribbon.
- For the opening of a new race track a model rode a specially trained

horse into the grandstand, where the horse chewed an oats-baited ribbon in two. Unfortunately for several dignitaries standing nearby, the horse's education did not include toilet training.

• In what has come to be known as "the great sponge plunge" in PR circles, a hotel chain elected to have a diver jump from a high perch onto a large air cushion circled with a ribbon. The impact of the diver's landing cut the ribbon.

• At least one financial services company uses a string of dollar bills in place of the traditional ribbon when opening a new branch office. The bills, somewhat the worse for wear, are donated to a local charity following the ceremony.

• Since Eugene, Oregon, is the self-proclaimed timber capital of the United States, it was only logical that a local community college would opt for a 40-foot log in place of a ribbon for its opening. The governor used a chain saw to do the honors.

• While it did not involve a building dedication per se, some may recall the 1972 UPI photograph showing Cleveland Mayor Ralph Perk with the top of his head in flames. The mayor's hair was ignited by sparks from an acetylene torch he was using to cut a metal ribbon to open a convention of the American Society of Metals. A wire service update on the incident 4 years later said the mayor had had extensive hair transplant operations—and was sticking to scissors since the unfortunate and painful accident.

• The Wickes Corporation opened a furniture warehouse outlet by having a key lowered from a balloon to a former Miss America, who used the key to unlock the store's front door.

• A slightly classier approach was taken for the opening of the Metropolitan Boston Arts Center. From contemporary news reports: "The boom of a brass cannon and the blare of trumpets heralded the Center's opening. A flotilla of motor launches ferried special guests from the Boston Museum of Science to the theater site on the bank of the Charles River. Guests were greeted by torch bearers and trumpeters dressed as Yeomen of the Guard."

Dedications do not, of course, have to be honky-tonk, theater-of-the-absurd events.

> The ceremony should reflect the client and the public he wishes to reach. Everyone is looking for something different, and while a happening such as a rock festival, a horse show or some other way-out function might be fine, being different just for the sake of being different does not generally accomplish the objectives of the program. If the client is dignified, and most are, let dignity reign.
>
> A building dedication can be one of the most useful means of bringing a completed project, as well as client and architect, to the public's attention. For the client, nothing is as illustrative of the organization's progress, stability, strength and concern for its employees and for its community as a well-conceived new building. The same is true for the architect. A well-executed project glowingly illustrates his firm's abilities to meet the needs of the client and the community.

A dedication is an excellent opportunity to invite the neighbors to meet the organization's officials. It may also signal the point in time when the mass media will present the building—and thereby the client and the architect—to a wide audience.[4]

## CORNERSTONES

Those of us who have reached a certain plateau in the aging process can still remember the elaborate ceremonies attendant to the laying of a cornerstone. Libraries, Masonic halls, schools, churches, city halls, and other government and public institutions were not to be considered really finished without the insertion of a hollowed-out granite block, presided over by the mayor and other dignitaries. Since most modern urban structures have an average life expectancy of 30 years or less, it is understandable that the historically inclined no longer get excited about the idea of preserving artifacts for their successors only 3 decades down the line. The odds are that contemporary historians will outlive most of the buildings they see completed.

In New York City not one of the many skyscrapers built during the office building boom of the sixties can boast of a cornerstone, to my knowledge. This is not to say that the tradition has passed away completely. Designers with a feel for history and tradition have come up with a few variations on the hollow granite block.

An insurance company in Syracuse, New York, has its cornerstone enshrined on a pedestal off the lobby in an enclosed patio. At Kennedy International Airport in New York, Eastern Airlines has a cornerstone of sorts in its passenger terminal. In a container are three reels of taped predictions by some sixty government and industry leaders of what aviation will be like in 2009—50 years after the building was dedicated. The Transamerica pyramid in San Francisco has a time capsule, as does the Hancock center in Chicago. The Hancock capsule, called a "skystone" (there'll always be a public relations counsel) is a replica of a space vehicle on display on the ninety-first floor observation deck.

Architect Philip Johnson, among others, casts a modernist's jaundiced eye on the whole business of cornerstones. "If your name isn't worth preserving, a cornerstone won't do it," Johnson observes. His attitude seems a practical one—at least for the style of design for which he is known. Where in the world would Johnson put a granite cornerstone in an all steel and glass building?

## OTHER SITE ACTIVITIES

Job signs and various forms of sidewalk superintendents clubs are traditional publicity activities at the job site. The job signs of the Oliver T. Carr Company, a Washington, D.C., developer, are usually interesting, original, and educational. These two were posted on the construction site of the company's building at 1800 M Street, in Washington:

> For those of you who know it takes a long time. . . .
>
> The design drawings were commissioned on September 15, 1972, and after studying several alternatives, we moved ahead with final construction drawings in the Spring of 1973. The site was cleared and the parking lots were closed down in June and July, and ground was broken on July 23, 1973. At this time, the completion date for 1800 "M" Street is March, 1975.
>
> During the twenty months it will take to construct this building, 28,251 cubic yards of concrete and 12,000 tons of structural steel will go into its frame. On approximately March 1, 1974, the first elements of the facade will go into place, which will be grey precast and over 71,000 square feet of solar bronze glass with brick pavers at street level.
>
> The result will be a ten story, fire proof office building, 110 feet tall and containing over 528,000 gross square feet of space. Building services will be divided into two sections, north and south, each with a separate lobby and six high-speed elevators. The typical floor will contain 52,428 square feet of rentable space, which will be custom designed to suit individual needs.
>
> THE OLIVER T. CARR COMPANY
>
> *    *    *    *    *    *
>
> TO: All Sidewalk Superintendents
>
> After the recession of the Acadian Mountains and the beginning of the formation of the Appalachian Range, this area of the East Coast became sedimentation "source land" during Paleozoic time. The materials removed from this site are a record of this part of our geologic history.
>
> The bedrock here has been identified as granite-gneiss, rock which was recrystalized approximately 1000–1100 million years ago. The gray colored micaceous sand and clay accumulated as sediment during paleozoic and ordovician time, and it may contain microfauna in the form of mollusks or other marine life.
>
> The site area is 62,127 square feet, and excavation will go down approximately 31 feet. This brings the total amount of earth to be excavated to 71,331 cubic yards weighing over 190,000,000 pounds or 95,000 tons.
>
> THE OLIVER T. CARR COMPANY

Figure 7-4. Hard Hat Club membership card issued by the Mark Hopkins Hotel in San Francisco. Recipients were certified to be "members in good standing as evidenced by exceptional fortitude, understanding and kind patience during the refurbishing of the Top of the Mark 1973 A.D."

A switch on sidewalk superintendents clubs was the Hard Hat Club set up by the Mark Hopkins Hotel in San Francisco during the 1973 renovation of the bar and observation area known as the Top of the Mark. The membership card is shown in Figure 7-4.

In summary, special events may be termed acts of news engineering—created publicity situations aimed at translating staged events into media coverage. One practitioner suggests the essential ingredients of special events publicity include time, place, people, activities, drama, and showmanship. And never forget that a major special event may have many subsidiary, or spinoff, events—each one a potential challenge to the skills and abilities of PR counselors and their clients.

## References

[1]Walter Lippmann, *Public Opinion,* Macmillan Publishing Company, Inc., New York, Copyright 1922 by Walter Lippmann, p. 262.
[2]Gerre Jones, *How to Market Professional Design Services,* McGraw-Hill Book Company, New York, 1973, p. 307.
[3]Ibid., pp. 310–318.
[4]Martin A. Brower, "How to Dedicate a Building." Reprinted with the permission of the *A.I.A. Journal,* copyright 1972; The American Institute of Architects.

There are important craft aspects of visual aids (which influence selection of the correct types) as well as elements of over-all and detailed design generally applicable. When these are observed, the visual portion amplifies the presentation; when ignored, visuals produce interference and obstacles to comprehension. Like all powerful tools, visual aids do constructive work only when guided by trained intelligence. Otherwise they are dangerous. Their use does not automatically improve a presentation any more than a power saw automatically improves carpentry.[1]

# CHAPTER 8
# Audiovisuals

**V**ISUAL AIDS HAVE been with us since the first cave dweller scratched an outline of a prehistoric animal into the wall of an underground shelter. Henry Boettinger observes:

> Language itself employs the visual aids of metaphor, simile, and anecdote when actual ones cannot be used, as in novels and essays. Motion pictures and television programs are nothing but ensembles of visual aids glued together by some coherent idea. (At least the good ones are.) Examples could be multiplied, but they would all make the same point: the eye can help the ear to understand.[2]

Few are the public relations professionals who have never been called upon to produce an audiovisual presentation. (Definition: If you can see it and hear it, and it involves the use of hardware, it's audiovisual.) The presentation to a prospective client has been called the payoff in the marketing sweepstakes. For a design professional, the first plateau in business development is reached when the firm makes the client's shortlist and is invited to be interviewed. But the real prize, of course, is selection for the job. Since any position lower than first is meaningless in most businesses, the sales arm of marketing becomes paramount in an interview.

As might be expected, a major source of information about audiovisual presentations is the Eastman Kodak Company. A sampling of the publications available from Kodak's Motion Picture and Audiovisual Markets Division would include *Slides with a Purpose*, VI-15, *Audiovisual Planning Equipment*, S-11, *Legibility—Artwork to Screen*, S-24, and *Simple Copying Techniques with a Kodak Ektagraphic Visualmaker*, S-40.

Some other recommended Kodak publications on the subject include:

| | |
|---|---:|
| *Audiovisual Projection*, S-3 | $ .30 |
| *Producing Slides and Filmstrips*, S-8 | 1.25 |
| *Motion Picture and Audiovisual Publications:* Selected References, S-10 | .35 |
| *Artwork Size Standards for Projected Visuals*, S-12 | .15 |
| *Planning and Producing Visual Aids*, S-13 | .25 |
| *Kodak Projection Calculator and Seating Guide*, S-16 | 2.00 |
| *Effective Lecture Slides*, S-22 | .15 |
| *Kodak Audiovisual Literature Packet*, U-915 | 2.50 |

The last item contains about thirty specially selected technical pamphlets and information sheets, and includes the *Kodak Audiovisual Products Catalog*. The price for the packet works out to about one-half the regular charge for the same items if ordered separately. The prices shown in the right column are for single copies. The publications may be ordered from

Eastman Kodak Company
Department 454
Rochester, New York 14650


## PLANNING

In the initial planning for any presentation, the first question should be: "What are my objectives with *this* audience?" In the great majority of cases the primary objective is to create a change in the listener-viewer. Mostly, the change desired is in attitude—toward your product, service, or organization. The objective may be as simple as imparting factual information. Perhaps you want to teach the members of the audience to perform a certain function. But for design professionals, most presentations will be some combination of imparting information and motivating the audience to take action—to retain *your* firm for the project.

A decision must be made early in the planning process as to whether the presentation will be purely oral, purely visual, or some combination of the two. Advantages of the strictly oral presentation—maintenance of eye contact with the audience throughout; observing the interview team for face and body language, nonverbal communication, and other nuances; and keeping full control of the presentation—are all overshadowed by one big drawback. In all-oral presentations the speaker must rely on one of the least effective learning senses of the human body—hearing. Of all that we learn, only about 11 percent is acquired through the sense of hearing. Contrast that with the fact that we learn about 83 percent of what we know through seeing. (A General Electric education study found the eye 22 times as powerful as the ear in transmitting messages to the brain.) If the presentation is heavy with statistical data, for instance, an oral presentation is a poor, if not useless, approach.

Retention of information, as opposed to learning, has its own set of statistics. On the average, about 20 percent of a spoken message is retained, some 30 percent of purely visual intake is retained, and a combination of aural and visual messages raises the retention factor to between 50 and 75 percent. A somewhat more discouraging statistic is the long-term retention factor, estimated to be around 10 percent. In other words, out of ten points initially retained, the receiver eventually will forget all but one—or perhaps worse, recall only the unimportant one-tenth of the whole presentation.

Effective communicators are audience-oriented. They give careful consideration as to why they are presenting information to a particular audience—and what they want the audience to do after the presentation is over. One consultant suggests the presenter define the objective by finishing the sentence, "After seeing this slide presentation, I want my audience to . . ." However this aspect is approached and answered there should be only one *primary* objective for each presentation, and every element of the presentation, visual *and* oral, should support that objective.

Audiovisual experts suggest several ways in which good visuals can improve communication:

• A visual can be a great asset in holding an audience's attention. Statistical information can be made interesting and easily understood, for example, through visuals, rather than boring and difficult to follow. (But never forget that today's audiences are accustomed to well-prepared visual presentations through years of watching television programs and commercials. Any presentation that does not meet or exceed this arbitrary standard will probably miss the mark.)

• Visuals help to clarify major points and concepts. Differences of vocabulary, experience, and general background among members of the audience can be overcome. At the same time, areas of agreement can be reinforced.

• Visuals help to establish the same starting point for the presenter and the audience. It might be difficult to describe the esthetic effect of a well-sited structure to an audience who has never seen it. With a visual everyone has at least seen and talked about the same thing. (Consider the problems of giving a words-only description of Pisa's leaning belltower or the Piazza San Marco.)

• Visuals can overcome limitations of time and space, providing experiences otherwise impossible or impractical. Time's passage can be speeded—or slowed—or stopped completely. One can visit London, the Taj Mahal, or even the moon, through the time and space potential of visuals.

There are two cardinal rules for effective presentations: Keep it moving and keep it simple. Once the objective is defined, all content—visual and verbal—must support it throughout the presentation. Another way of putting it: The success of any presentation is dependent upon one thing—the timely occurrence of events effecting the desired impressions.

## AUDIENCE ANALYSIS

By now we presumably know what it is (objective) we want to get across to the audience. It is time to ask (and answer) a few questions about the listener-viewer group—the members of which you want to change in some manner. How can you motivate them to listen, understand, and react to your message? Some of the factors to consider:

**Size of the group.** If it's a large audience with wide variations in personality, background, and interest, the presenter ordinarily will opt for broader examples and less intimate and specific discussion techniques than would be used with smaller, more cohesive groups.

**Occupation and education.** What are the levels of intellectual ability, training, and income of the audience? The same ideas sometimes must be presented in vastly different ways to different groups.

**Age and sex.** These factors have much to do with the subject matter, as well as with any examples used. Quite different illustrations may be required for a mixed audience of mostly the under-30 age group, from those examples that would be appropriate for a largely middle-aged audience of women.

**Audience level of knowledge about the subject.** The presenter should know as much as possible about the group's existing knowledge so as to avoid spending time in giving needless elementary information. It is equally important not to make too sophisticated a presentation to an unprepared audience. Never talk over the heads of an audience—and try not to talk down, either. Boettinger counsels: "Start where THEY are, not where YOU are."

**Audience attitude toward subject and speaker.** An apathetic or hostile audience can throw off even the most experienced speaker—particularly if the speaker is unprepared for a less than friendly audience.

**Existing beliefs and prejudices held by the audience.** Depending upon the subject and the presenter, an attempt may be made to change or use identifiable beliefs, biases, and prejudices, however accurate or unfounded they may be. As a general rule, try to support beliefs and avoid prejudices, toward the end of creating an atmosphere of acceptance for yourself and your ideas.

**Potential information intake of the audience.** Never try to cover more than an audience can digest, relate to, and remember. Short presentations almost always are to be preferred over long ones. Remember the earlier admonition to keep it moving and keep it simple. Rather than throwing a complicated graph or a diagram or a long list of items on the screen in its entirety, and then trying to lead the audience through the visual maze step by step, use a gradual buildup of elements. This technique sometimes is called "progressive disclosure" of information. Start at the beginning, both visually and verbally, with the simplest possible diagram. As you move on to a new step, use another slide to add the next element. In addition to making the overall subject easier to understand, progressive disclosure tends to step up the tempo (always important) on the screen while the speaker discusses a long list of items. Carefully lead the audience down a simplified path to the whole by showing the information under discussion along with previous information on the screen. Otherwise you run the danger that at least some of the viewers, bewildered by a mass of lines and color, are still trying to figure out what happened in step three, while you are explaining step eight.

Incidentally, the gradual buildup of elements, or progressive disclosure through a series of studies, is a much better process than the technique sometimes employed with overhead projectors, where the operator uses an opaque sheet to cover all but the first item in a list of points, slowly sliding the cover down the page to reveal each new item in turn.

**Why is this audience here?** Were they ordered to attend, or do they really want to hear the presentation? Voluntary audiences usually are more receptive than captive ones. Know in advance which type you have.

Audience analysis might sound like a lot more trouble than it really is. In the majority of cases you will have most of the information from various sources early on. And, of course, not every item needs to be fully developed for every presentation. Always try to take advantage of the edge that audience analysis gives you. The prepared presenter is a better communicator.

## ORGANIZING THE PRESENTATION

Far, far too many design professionals (and others) show up for a presentation with a handful of slides pulled together at the last possible moment, and usually with little or no thought given to the proper sequence, their relationship to the client's project, or their general effectiveness. A slide show of such a haphazard collection of visuals almost has to be a disaster—and a waste of all parties' time. Whether or not such a state of unpreparedness involves aspects of a self-fulfilling prophecy for failure has been the subject of numerous masters' theses and doctoral dissertations.

Kodak's booklet, *Audiovisual Planning Equipment*, gives a thorough introduction to the use of planning or story boards for organizing a slide presentation. Plans for constructing low-cost planning boards and slide sequence illuminators are included.

Individual slides commonly are planned on plain white 3 × 5 inch or 4 × 6 inch index cards. (See Figure 8-1.) The rectangle in the upper left corner is for a rough sketch of the proposed visual. If the desired shot is not in your slide files, try to visit the site to avoid visualizing shots that later prove impossible to make because of intruding objects or buildings, space limitations, and other restrictions.

The job number or title of the presentation goes in the upper right corner. The illustration number also is entered—first in pencil, later in ink after the sequence has been finalized. If slide pairs are to be used they may be shown

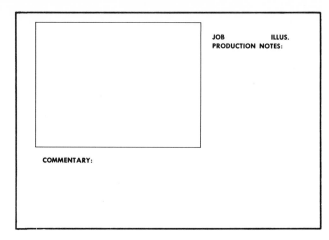

**JOB** **ILLUS.**
**PRODUCTION NOTES:**

**COMMENTARY:**

Figure 8-1. Planning card
on a 4 × 6 inch index card.
The ruled rectangle
should be 3¾ by 2½
inches to approximate the
dimensions of a 35-mm
transparency.

as 1*a* and 1*b,* 2*a* and 2*b,* and so on, with *a* and *b* referring to the two slide
trays.

Production notes are for the photographer or artist, and include such
information as background colors, camera angle, subject identification, and
lettering styles desired. The space for commentary may contain anything
from a single word to several sentences. It is, in a way, the first draft of the
final narration. Be sure to put no more than one idea or point on each card.
By using the planning board, the cards are all on view and easily moved. The
slide presentation is then edited by shifting, deleting, and adding cards. The
final arrangement should represent the continuity of ideas in the finished
presentation.

Ernest Burden, in his book *Architectural Delineation,* suggests using a large
board ruled off into 2 × 2 inch frames for programming a slide show. A 30 ×
40 inch board could represent almost 200 slides and can be set up for a single,
double, or other multiple projector arrangement. He reminds us that the
most difficult parts of a slide show will fit into an easily seen, logical pattern
by the use of some type of planning board. In most cases the planner must
apply a systematic plan, appropriate to the content and to the audience. This
might be a chronological arrangement, a problem/solution approach, or a
cause-to-effect plan.

Burden also suggests that the opening and final sequences be planned first,
since they are both the most important and the most difficult parts of most
slide shows.

Kodak suggests this final slide-by-slide check of the planning board
arrangement before beginning production.

1. Does this slide help me achieve my presentation objective?
2. Is there good continuity between this slide, the previous one, and the
following one?
3. Does this slide add to the audience's knowledge of the subject?
4. Does this slide focus attention on one main idea? Is the idea clear?

5. Have I removed all unnecessary elements without destroying the one main thought in this slide?

6. Have I presented the information in this slide in the most effective manner?

7. Are the titles legible and short enough to be read in the time they will be shown?

8. Does the commentary add anything to this slide? Does it distract?

## PRODUCTION PLANNING

In a single slide, show only the information you intend to discuss. Make sure the slide is relevant to the script and vice versa. Don't make the audience wonder why extraneous detail is on the screen. By the same token, don't explain the obvious when the slide says it all.

For most ideas a single slide should be enough, although occasionally a sequence of slides will be required to fully explain a fairly complex subject. Unless it's a summary, avoid putting two or more ideas into one visual. In a discussion of the ten steps of marketing planning, for example, all ten steps might be shown on the first slide. Each of the next ten slides would then cover one of the steps—preferably by one- to two-word summarizations of the step. (Showing all ten marketing steps on one slide is not a contradiction of the potential intake factor under ''Audience Analysis'' of a few paragraphs back—as long as each of the ten steps is covered individually on separate, following slides.)

Avoid too many visuals. Each should relate and contribute to the oral presentation. Excessive visuals tend to confuse an audience.

Intermix long, medium, and close-up shots to add variety and to provide a better vehicle for the message. Remember the standard motion picture technique of a long shot to establish, medium shots for more detail, and close-ups for emphasis, impact, and reaction. Use visuals taken from different angles as well as from varying distances.

Slide sequences were mentioned earlier. Sequences are particularly effective in a progressive disclosure series, wherein a word, picture, or diagram is gradually revealed (and explained) to the audience. This prevents the audience reading ahead of the narration and can assist in building from a simple to a more complex idea. Progress shots of a building under construction is one form of progressive disclosure.

Side-by-side comparisons, to show differences or relationships, also are effective. A hot air balloon and an Apollo-series moon rocket shown side by side on a split screen could illustrate technological development in air travel. The preparation of multiple images on a single slide is thoroughly explained and illustrated in *Architectural Delineation*, pages 288–289, and in *How to Market Professional Design Services*, pages 141–144. The same two images could also be shown on two separate slides projected side by side on one or more screens.

The latter technique is effective in a presentation responding to a Request for Proposal (RFP), or when the prospective client has a reasonably defined and written program. The pertinent section of the RFP or program, underlined or indicated by an arrow, is projected on the left side of the screen. On the right side are shown simultaneously views of plans, models, buildings under construction or completed—anything from your slide library that relates to the client's project and helps to explain your expertise and capabilties for handling the job.

## MEDIUM VS. MESSAGE

There is an inherent danger in getting overly fancy in a slide presentation. The reference here is to the multiscreen and so-called multimedia shows, wherein nine or twelve or eighty projectors are used to imitate such widescreen motion picture processes as CinemaScope and Cinerama.

I have yet to see a demonstration of a multiprojector, multiscreen presentation, using more than two projectors, that has not ended up as a demonstration of all that can go wrong when too much sensitive and complicated projection and audio equipment is hooked up to a computer.

The National Visitors Center in Washington, D.C., features a sunken screen with eighty projectors throwing images on it in rear projection. Perhaps the activating computer has been debugged by now, but during the Bicentennial year there were not many trouble-free performances. Often, only three or four projectors were out of sync, but that was enough to ruin the effect of a spectacular sunset view of the Jefferson Memorial, as parts of the preceding, unrelated scene showed up in the center of the Tidal Basin.

If you feel that you must explore the world of multiple screens–multiple projectors, first read the Kodak pamphlet, *Wide-Screen & Multiple-Screen Presentations* (S-28).

## AUDIOVISUAL SHORTHAND WITH CHARTS AND GRAPHS

Use charts and diagrams wherever appropriate. A wealth of information can be transmitted and made understandable with a few well-designed charts. In an audiovisual presentation pictorial comparisons usually are more easily grasped than bars and lines.

The *Graphic Arts Encyclopedia* defines a graph as the "diagrammatic representation of changes in a variable quantity in comparison with those of other variables. The term is used in preference to 'chart' in scientific and technical work."[3] "Chart," on the other hand, is defined as a "graphical representation showing values and quantities by means of bars, curves, columns, and symbols."[4]

The *Encyclopedia* breaks chart nomenclature down into five types: bar, column, curve, pie, and surface. Those definitions:

> **Bar Chart:** Graphic representation comparing numerical values by means of rectangles of equal width. The bars extend horizontally on the chart and usually represent quantity. . . . Time, distance, or some other value is shown on the

other dimension of the chart. Shaded patterns may be used to construct a chart with parallel double bars, divided bars, and symbols. A bar chart may also have a vertical baseline that divides the bars. Distances to the left of the baseline would show negative results, while those to the right should show favorable results.[5]

**Column Chart** (also called Vertical Column Chart): Graphic representation having juxtaposed vertical columns that usually denote a quantity, with the horizontal dimension representing time or some other value. An additional value can be represented by using double or divided columns or symbols such as a pig, cow, and sheep, interpreted to indicate pork, beef, and mutton.[6]

**Curve Chart:** Graphical representation that uses curves to reflect values such as time, distance, or any other condition desired. For example, the base of a chart may show a time value in years, months, weeks, or days, and the vertical dimension may reflect quantities. The curve chart is probably the most popular type of chart.[7]

**Pie Chart:** Circular chart divided into wedges resembling the cuts of a pie. Each wedge represents a percentage of the whole ''pie.'' This type of chart is easy to understand, but its use is limited because only one quantity can be compared with the whole.[8]

**Surface Chart:** Graphical representation with plotted points moving across it from left to right in a logical sequence. The pattern thus reflected is extended to the base of the chart by shading or crosshatching. The shaded area is the predominant feature of the chart. The vertical scale may indicate quantities, while the base may reflect periods of time, expressed in hours, days, weeks, months, or years.[9]

The relationship between a curve chart and a surface chart should be apparent. Remember, the wrong chart is apt to obscure the point you want to make, while an appropriate chart will not only inform viewers, it will emphasize the point. All the above graph and chart variations are illustrated on pages 141–144 of *How to Prepare Professional Design Brochures.*

Good visuals are easily read. When making visuals, limit the number of words or ideas on each. Allow enough space for letters to be large and clear. Leave plenty of blank space (air), especially between lines of copy. And choose a typeface that is familiar and easy to read. If one word on a visual will do the job, resist the urge to use two, three, or four words.

## TITLING TECHNIQUES

Titles are used in audiovisual presentations to introduce the program, make transitions between main points or subjects, to ask questions, to answer questions, to provide graphic explanation and exclamation points to the narrative, and to conclude the presentation.

Ready-made titles exist all around us—newspaper headlines, proposal covers, street signs, the office entrance door, plans, and so forth. There is no need to produce art for a title slide if it already exists.

*Always* use an opening title in a slide presentation of projects representing past and current work of an association or joint venture. Many clients are unsure about how well the various elements of a joint venture may perform together—particularly if there is little or no past history of collaboration among the joint venture members. The psychological impact to be made on a potential client by a simple title slide introducing "The Joint Venture of Jones, Doe & Roe; Able, Baker & Charley, and Smith and Brown, for the Murtah Museum, Murtah, South Carolina," has never ceased to amaze this writer. The effect comes cheap, considering the cost of one 35-mm slide. If a formal proposal has been put together for the project by the joint venture, a shot of the proposal cover often is sufficient.

## COLOR CONSIDERATIONS

Kodak's publication, *Simple Copying Techniques with a Kodak Ektagraphic Visual-maker,* contains much useful information about making your own slides. In making up title slides, consider carefully the background colors. Black photographs best as a general rule, but can get monotonous in quantity. Deep reds, blues, greens, and browns are also recommended. Avoid white backgrounds because of inherent exposure problems and use pastels carefully and infrequently.

Strictly on the basis of legibility, psychological tests rank color combinations in the following order, from most readable to least legible:

1. Black (printing) on yellow (background)
2. Green on white
3. Blue on white
4. White on blue
5. Black on white
6. Yellow on black
7. White on red
8. White on orange
9. White on black
10. Red on yellow
11. Green on red
12. Red on green

Texture as well as color may be imparted by choice of paper or fabric for the background. Backgrounds should never overpower the lettering or artwork on them. Photographs, drawings, postcards, maps, and other artwork can also serve as backgrounds for titles of three-dimensional plastic or ceramic letters; slightly side-lit they make effective introductory or transitional slides.

## LEGIBILITY IN LETTERING

Lettering may also be of the dry transfer variety, from stencils, or even in standard typewriter type. Letters for titles should be a minimum of $\frac{1}{25}$ the height of the area to be photographed and included in the projection area of the slide. If a 10 × 12 inch board is used, letters should then be at least ⅜ inches high; a ½-inch minimum height would be better. For lower case letters the measurements refer to the body of the letter only, and exclude ascenders and descenders. An ascender is the upright line on such letters as "b," "d," and "h." Descenders are the tails on "q," "p," and "y."

Remember, we've been talking about *minimum* heights. Larger letter sizes are more legible, increase emphasis, and usually will result in a title that speeds up rather than slows the presentation. Leave at least the height of a capital letter between lines.

When using printer's type, check the typeface for legibility. "Light" faces usually mean thin lines, which tend to be become indistinct or even disappear in projection. Type is measured in point sizes, but don't be fooled into thinking that all type of the same point size has the same legibility; it doesn't. Script and other ornate type styles are difficult to read. The best typefaces for projection are sans serif types. Applying the lettering vertically or on other unusual angles on the slide is not recommended for optimum legibility and rapid comprehension.

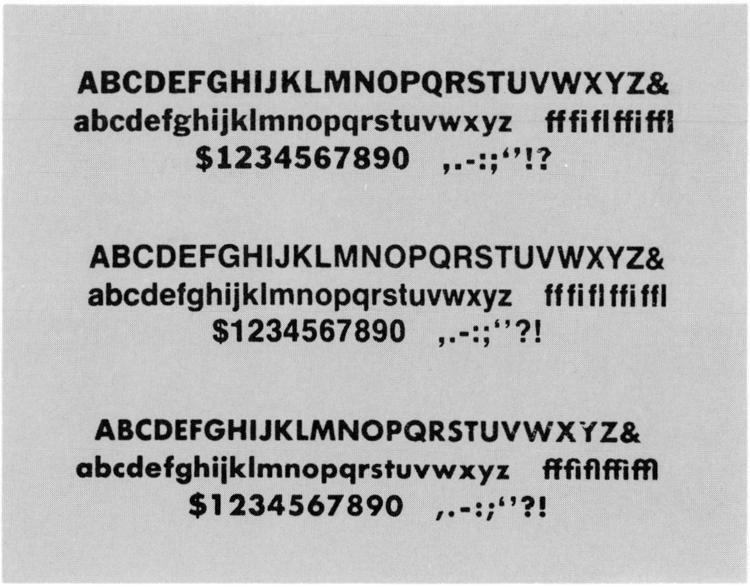

ABCDEFGHIJKLMNOPQRSTUVWXYZ&
abcdefghijklmnopqrstuvwxyz  ff fi fl ffi ffl
$1234567890  ,.-:;"!?

ABCDEFGHIJKLMNOPQRSTUVWXYZ&
abcdefghijklmnopqrstuvwxyz  ff fi fl ffi ffl
$1234567890  ,.-:;"?!

ABCDEFGHIJKLMNOPQRSTUVWXYZ&
abcdefghijklmnopqrstuvwxyz  ff fi fl ffi ffl
$1234567890  ,.-:;"?!

Figure 8-2. Showings of three sans serif typefaces. Top, Franklin Gothic, center, Vega Medium, and bottom, Futura Bold. Any of these faces can be read easily in projection.

If duplicates of certain title slides are apt to be required—to repeat or return to a point during the presentation, for example—it is best to shoot the original layout enough times to give the necessary number of slides. No commercially made duplicate of an original slide is ever quite an exact duplicate in color, and if the lettering on the original is large and close to the margins many commercial dupes will cut off parts of the letters. As you get into third and fourth generation duplicates there is usually little left of the original's snap and color.

## THE NARRATION

Never lose sight of the fact that the best set of slides will not compensate for an inept narration. One audiovisual consultant points out: "Behind every good presentation is much experimentation, some selective analysis, and a lot of imagination. When shows are brought before the public they must be polished to meet the occasion and the story line must be clear, concise, and convincing. There should be an introduction, a statement of ideas, a development of these ideas, and a conclusion." Or, as in the formula for writing a novel, there must be a beginning, a middle, and an end.

A script has been called the mortar that holds slides together. Before starting to make notes for the narration, run through the slides in order. On the first run-through, just look. You probably will discover that a few seem out of sequence or unnecessary. The second time through ad lib a commentary into a tape recorder. Use the tape to help in writing the first draft of the script. Finally, read the script back against the slides to smooth and edit it. Always strive for clarity and continuity.

Rather than memorize the material, know it well and try to give it as a conversation with the audience. If presenters tie themselves to a set piece they will have difficulty in reacting to unexpected audience comments and questions—and may not be able to adequately restate or rephrase a thought when someone in the audience misunderstands or misses a point. Always rehearse with the visuals.

Time the presentation to fit the number of minutes allotted. Try to get under by 2 or 3 minutes to allow for emergencies. A rule of thumb for the written narration is to allow about 120 words per minute of presentation. Thus, for a 10-minute show some 1200 words are needed; a 30-minute talk requires about 3600 words. One double-spaced sheet of typing paper averages about 250 words, so fifteen typed pages should suffice for a 30-minute presentation.

### TABLE 8-1. Projection Distances, Feet*

| Screen image width, ft (in) | Lens focal length, inches | | | | | | | | |
|---|---|---|---|---|---|---|---|---|---|
| | 1.4 | 2 | 3 | 4 | 5 | 7 | 9 | 11 | 4 to 6 (Zoom) |
| 3⅓(40) | 4 | 5 | 8 | 10 | 13 | 18 | 23 | 29 | 10 to 16 |
| 4⅙(50) | 4.5 | 6 | 10 | 13 | 16 | 23 | 29 | 35 | 13 to 19 |
| 5 | 6 | 8 | 11 | 15 | 19 | 27 | 34 | 42 | 15 to 23 |
| 6 | 7 | 9 | 14 | 18 | 23 | ·32 | 41 | 50 | 18 to 27 |
| 8 | 9 | 12 | 18 | 24 | 30 | 42 | 54 | 66 | 24 to 36 |
| 10 | 11 | 15 | 23 | 30 | 38 | 53 | 68 | 83 | 30 to 45 |
| 12 | 13 | 18 | 27 | 36 | 45 | 63 | 81 | 99 | 36 to 54 |

*Projection distances are measured from the front of the projector to the screen.

## THE PRESENTATION

The wise presenter always checks out the room to be used before the presentation. From this point on, checklists can be helpful. The Office of Information of the Secretary of the Air Force has developed a good presentation checklist.

### Slide Presentation Check List

The content of this check list represents years of professional planning experience. Although many of the tips will seem self-evident, use of this check list will make any slide presentation much more effective. As with any preflight, it will help prevent accidents away from home base.

*35 mm slide projector.* Should be the best available and equipped with at least a 500-watt projection bulb. It should also have a lens of the proper focal length to match the screen distance or room size. A projector with a zoom lens is even better. This will eliminate the possibility of having to put your projector in the middle of the audience. Clean the lens and test run the projector before you set forth.

*Projection screen.* Use a projection chart to help you determine what size screen and what size lens you will need for the room in which you are working. [See Table 8-1.]

*Fly-away kit.* A kit of spares and other items you should take along—just in case:

- Extra projection lamp of right type and wattage
- Extra fuses for the projector
- Extra 15- and 25-watt house fuses
- Lens cleaning tissues
- Small insulated screwdriver
- A heavy cloth or cloth gloves to use if you have to replace a projection bulb in the middle of a program—to prevent burned fingers
- At least two 25-foot lengths of extension cord
- Plug adapter for two-pin to three-pin grounded outlet
- A roll of masking tape to tape extension cords into wall outlets and to tape cords to the floor to minimize chances of someone tripping over them
- A roll of electrician's tape

*Slides.* Be sure you have them all and that they are in the right sequence in your slide tray. Also make certain slides are inserted in the tray in the proper position. Avoid handling slides unnecessarily. A black slide should be inserted before the first slide and after the last slide to avoid the distraction of a white screen. Check all of this before each presentation! Rehearse, rehearse, rehearse! Professional actors would never go on cold. And remember, you personify your organization to your audience.

*Slide and narrative synchronization.* Your narrative copy may contain important slide change cues. Test this cueing with the projector you will be using. If your machine changes slides faster or slower than the standard Carousel, advance or retard cue marks accordingly to insure proper synchronization. If you are using a projector operator, make sure he has a copy of the same cued narrative.

*Questions from the audience.*  You can expect questions after completing most slide presentations. Welcome the opportunity to elaborate and clear up misconceptions. This also is a good time to tie in your local situation.

*Tough questions.*  Your audience may be peopled by experts. This means you should bone up on your subject from many vantage points.

*Your answers.*  Answer as completely, factually, and truthfully as you can. It is no crime to say, "I don't know, but I can get the answer for you." Should you make this promise, take the questioner's name and address and make sure he receives the promised reply.

## Slide Presentation – Setting the Stage

*Arrive early.*  You then have time to set up properly and solve unforeseen problems.

*Speaker's light.*  Make sure a speaker's reading light is available and that it doesn't throw a distracting light on your screen.

*Room lights.*  Locate the switch and arrange to have it turned on and off as required.

One of the most comprehensive checklists for meetings of all types is the *Checklist to End Checklists,* which originally appeared in the magazine, *Meetings and Conventions* (Gellert Publishing Corporation). The public relations department of Quality Inns reprinted the checklist in booklet form and a few copies may still be available. Section 12 of the *Checklist to End Checklists* covers pre-meeting audiovisual checks, including acoustics, audio, projection booth or stand, lectern, room lights, doors, size of audience and length of meeting, screen size, seating, equipment, audiovisual materials, and persons involved in the presentation.

## SCREEN FORMATS AND VIEWING DISTANCES

The Eastman Kodak book *Designing for Projection* discusses maximum and minimum viewing distances and screen sizes and shapes. The maximum allowable distance between viewer and screen image is approximately eight times the height of the screen image. If the screen is 40 inches high, then no viewer should be seated more than 27 feet from the screen. Conversely, the minimum image height should not be less than one-eighth the distance from the screen to the viewer seated farthest from the screen.

Also, according to *Designing for Projection,* the closest viewer should be not less than twice the height of the screen, that is, with a 40-inch screen height, no viewer should be seated closer than 7 feet from the screen. The obverse of this rule of thumb is that the maximum image height should be no more than one-half the distance of the front row of viewers.

A projection distance table should be part of the carry-along kit. The constants are the screen image width to be filled and the focal length of the projection lens. The variable is the distance the projector must be placed from the screen to give the desired screen image width. Table 8-1 gives the projection distances for a variety of screen widths and focal lengths of lenses, based on a standard 35-mm slide (with actual aperture dimensions of 34.2 mm × 22.9 mm) projected horizontally in a Kodak Carousel projector.

On screen formats the Kodak publication has these recommendations: "The shape of your screen should be determined according to your needs. For movies it should be 3-to-2. A compromise for multiple formats is a square-shaped screen that is 1½ times the intended image height. This will permit the use of different formats without any image falling off the edge of the screen."[10]

## MISCELLANEOUS TIPS

People have been conditioned by television and motion pictures to visuals in a horizontal format, so it makes sense to plan slide shows in the same format. Vertical and horizontal slides intermixed can create audience distraction. An occasional superslide for emphasis or contrast is acceptable in most presentations.

Motion picture and television camera operators have coped with an all-horizontal format for years, so you should have no problem in composing slides within that limitation.

Narration and visuals must work together to communicate a message and to cause the audience to react in the manner desired. The combination of sight and sound should come across in a smooth and harmonious way. If each slide has been kept as simple as possible, and the message is gotten across in small, easily understood increments, then the presentation will be professional, understandable, and effective.

Here are ten additional tips from the Kodak publication *Effective Lecture Slides:*

1. Limit each slide to one idea.
2. Limit each slide to fifteen to twenty words; include no more information than you will discuss.
3. Leave space—at least the height of a capital letter—between lines.
4. Include titles to supplement, not duplicate, slide data.
5. Use duplicates if you need to refer to the same slide at several different points in your talk. It is impractical for the projectionist to reshow a previous slide.
6. Plan your slides for a good visual pace in your presentation. Don't leave a slide on the screen after discussing its subject.
7. Thumb-spot all slides in the lower left corner when the slide reads correctly on hand viewing.
8. On a trip, carry your slides with you—in the tray, if possible. Don't trust them to checked-through luggage.
9. Use slides to supplement and support your local presentation, not simply to repeat what you are saying.
10. Consider your audience size in terms of screen size and projector output. As an example, an audience of 400 needs a screen image 12 feet wide.[11]

## HOW PROS ORDER AV EQUIPMENT

Earl Bauer, a Dallas-based audiovisual equipment specialist, recommends giving tight specifications when renting audiovisual equipment for a presentation or a meeting. He suggests specifying manufacturer, model number, and projection lamp. Bauer uses an order for an Eastman Kodak carousel-type 2 × 2 slide projector as an example of how the unwary can end up with what was ordered—but not with what was wanted.

The original carousel-type projector, Kodak Model 550, made its first appearance in August 1961; obviously, many of the 550 models are now at least 18 years old—but some audiovisual equipment rental companies still have them—and may supply them if the model number is omitted from the order.

Kodak Model AF-2 is one of the current carousel models. The AF-2 has autofocus, accepts the 140-slide tray, is quiet, relatively light in weight, and uses a quartz iodide lamp for brighter, better color reproduction with less heat. Model 550 lacks all of these features.

When model and lamp are not specified, a supplier could furnish any one of more than a dozen different Kodak slide projectors. They range in cost from around $70 to almost $300 for the AF-2.

Bauer also gives a guide for specifying various kinds of audiovisual equipment. Some examples:

- *2 × 2 slide projector.* Kodak AF-2 with ELH lamp.
- *Screen.* Da-Lite (size) Picture King Matt White.
- *16-mm movie projector.* Kodak 126TR with DFD 1000-watt lamp.
- *Overhead projector.* Beseler VGC 614 with DYS lamp.
- *Projection stand.* Welt Safelock Model 56.

Having used all the above equipment in my own workshops and in-house seminars, I am in agreement with Earl Bauer's recommendations. If local shortages cause you to settle for an "or equal," make certain it is very close to equal. Be sure the equipment is delivered early enough to give it a thorough checkout, verify model and lamp numbers, and to arrange for substitutes if some of it doesn't work to your satisfaction.

Many hotels—especially those with plentiful meeting facilities—now keep a selection of audiovisual equipment on hand to service clients. Unfortunately, a lot of such in-house equipment is not maintained to the standards you should expect, so be particularly careful in checking out all hotel-owned machines.

## SOURCES OF COLOR SLIDES

A fair in-house inventory of stock and scenic slides often can be developed from among staff members. To supplement the staff contributions there are a number of commercial sources of color slides on various subjects. A Kodak pamphlet, *Some Sources of 2 × 2-Inch Color Slides* (S-2), lists almost fifty domestic suppliers.

Several firms offer stock slide art, as opposed to photographic scenes. One such company is Visual Horizons, 208 Westfall Road, Rochester, New York 14620. For around $5 Visual Horizons supplies its "Slide Idea Library" packet of four filmstrips, illustrating more than 300 stock art illustrations available. *Successful Meetings* magazine, 633 Third Avenue, New York, New York 10017, offers more than 200 key word stock slides, for adding visuals to all types of speech material. Any number of slides may be ordered; the entire library of 206 slides costs $375. A full color catalog is free on request.

## SLIDE CARE AND STORAGE

Little of the foregoing has much point unless adequate provision is made for the safe storage of slides and other visuals when they are not in use. Always remount defective glass-mounted slides as soon as they are discovered, to save both cut fingers and embarrassment the next time they are used. The same advice goes for cleaning dust and fingerprints from the surface of slides.

Exposure to light will eventually cause the dyes used in color transparencies to fade. The longer the exposure, the greater the color loss. Some audiovisual specialists recommend that original color slides *never* be used in a projector. Instead, use originals only for making sets of working slides—and store the originals carefully and well.

All of us have the occasional problem of getting slides into a tray so they will project right side up and read from left to right. The rule about having the emulsion side of the film facing the projection lens is not foolproof if there are some duplicates in the set. The safest method is to project all of the slides in a quick run-through just before the actual presentation. This is not always feasible.

But there is another system for getting the projected image right. Lay out the slides in sequence on a light table or a light box so that they look the way they should appear when projected—right side up and everything reading from left to right. Put a mark on the lower left corner of each mount. Without turning them over, rotate the slides to an upside-down position (your mark will now be on the upper right corner of the mount). Now, next to the mark add the sequence number—1, 2, 3, and so on. When you load the slides into a tray for a standard front projection, keep the numbers up and facing you. To ensure that the slides stay in sequence, stack them and make a couple of diagonal ink marks along the top edges. Any slide out of sequence can be picked up immediately.

One of the best slide storage systems we've worked with is the Abodia system. Made in Germany, the full line of slide cabinets is imported by Eldon Enterprizes, Inc., P.O. Box 3201, Charleston, West Virginia 24332. Abodia storage cabinets range in capacity from 1000 to 10,000 slides, and allow for easy storage, inspection, editing, and viewing of all slides. The storage units feature an illuminated back panel to facilitate sorting and editing.

The annual buying guide issue of *Audio-Visual Communications* lists several other suppliers of slide storage cabinets. This monthly publication, located at 750 Third Avenue, New York, New York 10017, is a prime source of all types of information about the audiovisual field.

## OTHER AUDIOVISUAL TOOLS

While the emphasis thus far has been on one audiovisual tool—35-mm slides—most of the points that have been made are equally valid for and common to other types of visuals. The 35-mm slide has been called the mainstay of corporate communications. In 1976, according to *The Wall Street Journal,* $583 million was spent in the production of 113 million slides.

New equipment for presentations comes on the market in a pretty constant stream, so we'll take a brief general look at some of the other tools, beginning with simpler ones and working our way through to the more complex types.

**Blackboard.** The advantages of a blackboard are its versatility, access, and relative cheapness. It is considered a good medium for evoking spontaneity and an aid to involving audiences. The disadvantages of a blackboard include the limited available surface, the difficulty of writing on it while maintaining eye contact, and the distraction of having to erase it periodically to make room for more information.

**Flip charts.** Here we use flip chart in the sense of a large easel-mounted pad of blank paper (developmental), as well as the version prepared before a presentation on which text and drawings similar to 35-mm slide material have been placed. The blank version of a flip chart is similar to a blackboard in utility, with the added advantage that completed sheets may be posted and saved. Prepared charts may be made fairly cheaply in-house or, when justified by the importance of the audience or the possibility of multiple use, put together by outside graphic professionals.

**Transparency projectors.** Sometimes called overhead projectors, the machine uses clear acetate sheets, usually mounted in cardboard frames. It offers a flexible presentation approach for audiences of all sizes. The projection sheets may be hand lettered or drawn on, or prepared professionally. The use of additional sheets, hinged to the frame of the basic slide, allows the projectionist to show progressive views of an illustration by overlaying the attached sheets on top of each other. This type of transparency is called a dynamic projectural.

**Motion pictures.** Because of their high initial cost, motion pictures are not for everyone—particularly 16-mm sound color productions. If a film can be planned for multiple showings to amortize its high first expense, it is difficult to improve upon the appeal, interest, and dynamism of a good sound color motion picture. Just remember that a commercially produced sound motion picture in color, speech lip-synched, and with music background and special effects, can cost from $1200 to $3500 or more per finished minute. For a 30-minute film (approximately 1100 feet) that is a range of $36,000 to $105,000 and up. The "and up" comes into play if a lot of remote location shots are required, through use of name actors and narrators, and a host of extras that seem endemic to film production. In addition to the cost disadvantage, once finished, a movie is expensive to change or update. Motion pictures are discussed in more detail in Chapter 11.

**Videotape.** This medium is excellent for training and rehearsing as well as for presentations. Equipment is reasonably inexpensive to rent and is rapidly becoming more feasible to purchase outright. The constant introduction of new equipment and technology for closed-circuit television (CCTV) makes it difficult to recommend specific manufacturers and systems. In early 1977 the cost of a good black-and-white ½-inch CCTV setup was around $3500. This included a camera ensemble (camera, zoom lens, and tripod), a videotape recorder, a playback only unit, a monitor for playback, microphones, a mike mixer, and a half-dozen reels of videotape.

By the end of 1977, with the introduction of several new models of "home" videotape recorders (VTRs), the cost of an equivalent black-and-white system had dropped to around $1600. For under $3500 one could go into a color CCTV operation. Rental charges for all CCTV equipment dropped proportionately.

Whatever technique and equipment you select for an audiovisual presentation, never allow the medium to upstage the message—or the hardware to overshadow the software. We pointed out a few pages back that complex, spectacular multimedia, multiple screen presentations are subject to equally complex and spectacular breakdowns. By all means, exert some creative effort to take your visuals out of the ordinary—but it rarely requires a larger-than-life representation of a Boeing 747 in a full power takeoff over their laps to get and hold an audience's attention. And what is there left for an encore?

## PRESENTATION DOS AND DON'TS

As a kind of summary to this chapter, particularly for those who regularly make presentations to clients, here is a list of things to do—and not to do:

### DO

• plan, structure, dry run, and analyze presentations before inflicting them on potential clients.

• write for a copy of *A Layman's Guide to Audio-Visual Jargon*. Single copies at no charge from The Multimedia Forum, Crown Center, P.O. Box 1435, Kansas City, Missouri 64141.

• research clients and their projects thoroughly before outlining your presentation.

• determine early who the decision makers are.

• select the presentation team carefully. No one should be on it without a good reason or if they cannot make a significant contribution to the presentation.

• relate everything possible in the presentation to the client's interests and the specific project.

- try to come up with at least one "competitive differential" or "unique selling proposition" for your firm.
- thoroughly prepare all audiovisuals and written media.
- check out the presentation room in advance of the interview whenever possible.
- find out the composition of the interview committee.
- learn who your competition is.
- dress appropriately.
- insure a good introduction to the client interview team by preparing it yourself in advance.
- avoid theatrics; strive for sincerity.
- assume a confident manner from the outset.
- be brief.
- be aware of time constraints. Make your important points within the time allotted.
- encourage discussion and participation by all present.
- anticipate questions.
- have a plan for answering questions.
- have one member of your team act as recorder during the presentation; to note important points and questions raised by the interviewers.
- use examples and case histories.
- prepare for contingencies and emergencies—in everything.
- stay flexible throughout the presentation.
- remember that clients have every reason to relate the way you handle an interview to how you would handle their project.

## DON'T

- check presentation materials and notes if flying to the interview. Keep them in your possession.
- show up late for any reason.
- let your presentation team outnumber the interview group.
- lose control of the presentation.
- *ever* debate or argue a point brought up by a member of the presenting team in front of the interview group.
- use overly-complicated audiovisual materials or setups.
- talk down to your audience.
- let the interview drag out or wind down to a close. Have a plan for an upbeat finish.
- forget to have some type of relevant leave-behind handout.
- assume anything.

### References

[1]Henry M. Boettinger, *Moving Mountains,* Collier Books, New York, Copyright 1969 by Henry Boettinger, pp. 160–161.

[2]Ibid., p. 160.

[3]George A. Stevenson, *Graphic Arts Encyclopedia,* McGraw-Hill Book Company, New York, 1968, p. 164.

[4]Ibid., p. 63.

[5]Ibid., p. 19.

[6]Ibid., pp. 75–76.

[7]Ibid., p. 105.

[8]Ibid., pp. 288–289.

[9]Ibid., p. 366.

[10]*Designing for Projection,* Eastman Kodak Company, Rochester, N.Y., 1970, p. 22.

[11]*Effective Lecture Slides,* Kodak Pamphlet No. 5-22, Eastman Kodak Company, Rochester, N.Y., 1971. Numbers 1, 2, 5, 7, 8, 9 are paraphrased.

The difference between the right word and the almost right word is the difference between lightning and the lightning bug.[1]

# CHAPTER 9
# Writing: An Endangered Art

IT IS HARDLY a secret that Johnnies by the thousands are being graduated from high schools and colleges not only unable to read—they can't write, either, and we seemingly have become a nation hell-bent on achieving near-universal illiteracy by the year 2000. As the blame-fixing reaches new crescendos, we're testing English teachers in some jurisdictions before allowing them to test their students. And the number of teachers unable to write a standard sentence or name the eight parts of speech has turned out to be scandalously high.

**Item.** Courtesy of a fast-expanding credit-by-examination process called the College-Level Examination Program (CLEP), thousands of college students receive a full year's credit in English composition by taking a test which requires them to write nothing more complicated than their name. The examination consists of machine-scored multiple-choice questions.

**Item.** An article by the editor of *English Today,* the official publication for members of the National Council of Teachers of English, derides the call from colleges for more fundamentals at the high school level. ''The English teaching profession—for the most part—has progressed well beyond thinking of writing instruction solely or principally in terms of basic skills instruction,'' wrote the editor, who is a professor at Michigan State University.

**Item.** Across Lake Michigan, the neighboring University of Wisconsin had to set up a special 6-week writing lab in the English department to tutor students unable to pass a simple English usage exam required for admittance to the journalism school. (The University's English department stopped requiring introductory English composition for first-year students several years ago.)

**Item.** The Council on College Composition and Communication, in an official policy statement, "Students' Rights to Their Own Language," states: "Simply because 'Johnny can't read' doesn't mean 'Johnny is immature' or 'Johnny can't think.' He may be bored. . . . If we can convince our students that spelling, punctuation and usage are less important than content, we have removed a major obstacle in their developing the ability to write. . . . We should not insist on accuracy in [spelling, grammar, punctuation and vocabulary] lest we inhibit the students' creativity and individuality."

**Item.** In 1975 the Yale English department voted to reinstate a composition course because so many Yale students could not handle English. They were unable to make a sentence or a paragraph, to organize a paper, or to follow through well enough to do college work.

Paradoxically, the situation has spawned a whole new writing industry, as defenders of the language write best-selling books and go on lucrative lecture tours. Anti-English-debaser Edwin Newman, with two successful books about words, is perhaps the best known of this new breed, but others are trying to climb aboard the pro-English bandwagon.

Newman and his fellow defenders have, in turn, spawned attackers. Not attackers, we hasten to add, of good English, but of the Johnnies-come-lately who are cashing in on our current obsession with good and bad English. British journalist Henry Fairlie, who claims to have been an early warrior against language debasement, shot off this dart in the pages of the *Washington Post:*

> With a few other old soldiers . . . we had just got the enemy in our sights—when there is a whoop behind us, and we look over our shoulders to see a bunch of raw recruits riding idiotically to back us up.
>
> Among the raw recruits I include Edwin Newman and the purchasers of his two books about words. He has got it all wrong. The debasement of our language is not the result of the offenses that he criticizes. Even where he is right, he is right for the wrong reasons, and I would not let a budding writer near his books. Like all raw recruits, he does not lose the battle: much worse, he destroys the battleground. He does not know the terrain.[2]

Ken Langbell of the *Las Vegas Sun* (Nov. 2, 1976) wrote a strange sort of column about the unimportance of being able to read or write—because "the written word is being replaced, rapidly, by the spoken word.

"There has never been a time in this century or, for that matter, several centuries, when it was less important to be able to read than it is now," declared Langbell. "And this is good. The spoken word is where it's at. The spoken word is the basic means of communication in the years ahead, just as it was for those thousands of years before 1456, when man began to use movable type."

Actually, as we pointed out in *How to Prepare Professional Design Brochures,* movable type was in use in China by the middle of the eleventh century. And Langbell's apparent reference to Gutenberg's movable type (1456) is some 16 years too late. There are several other flaws in his logic, but suffice it to say Langbell's strong suit is not history.


## WORD ARRANGING

While the old soldiers and the raw recruits stake out ever-widening battle lines over the right to represent the rest of us in their defense of good English and clear writing, let us civilians move along to a discussion of effective writing and some of the tools for accomplishing it.

Thousands of books have been written about grammar, punctuation, usage, and style. Some of the most helpful ones are listed in the bibliography at the end of this book. Since that is the case, only a brief review of some of the more important considerations and principles of writing will be covered here.

First, have a clear purpose in mind. This should not be much of a problem in public relations writing, assuming writers understand their clients and their businesses, since the basic purpose of public relations is to cause others to take some kind of action—overt, immediate, passive, or long-range.

All creative writing should affect readers in *some* way. Unless deliberately written as a soporific for congenital insomniacs, writing will do one or more of these four things:

Direct
Inform
Persuade
Entertain

Experienced writers occasionally work all four elements into the same piece; most novice writers should try for only one at a time.

There is no magic formula for good writing, but there is a structured process of sorts which most professional writers employ. In outline form it might look like this:

    I.  Planning (thinking).
   II.  Make a rough outline (notes, really).
  III.  Do preliminary research.
  IV.  Make a detailed outline.
   V.  Do formal, in-depth research. (Don't hurry this!)
  VI.  Digest and understand the material.
 VII.  Decide how it will be handled.
VIII.  Write the first draft.

    A.  State the central idea or purpose.
        1.  Set the scene.
    B.  Develop and explain the central idea.
    C.  Give examples of the central idea.
    D.  Complete the statement.
    E.  Recap or reaffirm what was said under A.
  IX.  Revise; do additional research as needed.
   X.  Write the second draft.
  XI.  Revise and edit—through perhaps two more drafts.
 XII.  Do the final editing—cut, slash, hone, polish.
XIII.  Write the final draft—for publication.

Note that no real writing was done until step number VIII.

Experienced writers do not need to keep such an outline before them as they write, of course. The steps eventually become a routine, a part of the writer's mental discipline. (Undisciplined people, incidentally, seldom become productive or effective writers.) Throughout the writing process, the writer must keep in mind the fact that the amount of time an average reader will invest in understanding a message is in direct proportion to the perceived importance of the message to that reader. Another sobering thought: the reader doesn't know as much about the subject as the writer does; he or she doesn't *want* to know as much about the subject as the writer; and of this a writer can be certain—the reader will not have the same inclination to read the writer's material as the writer does.

## WORDS, WORDS, WORDS

For most people in public relations, words are their stock-in-trade *and* their most valuable product. Immediate and long-range responsibilities of all types require them to spend much of their time dealing with written communications. Looking at it one way, writers have some 750,000 tools; including technical and scientific terms, that's the approximate number of words we have to draw on when speaking or writing in English.

Our basic vocabulary has been developed by the time we finish the tenth grade. While most of us are "aware" of around 20,000 words (of which some 2000 are slang), the average working vocabulary includes from 600 to 1000 words. So as a practical matter most speakers and writers are limited to less than 1 percent of the total. Even if we knew all of the 600,000 nontechnical words of English, we'd have to learn about 20 new words every day just to keep up with the changes.

According to telephone company officials, people seldom use a vocabulary of more than 100 words when talking on the telephone. About half of all our communication is based on 44 words. While this tells us to keep most writing fairly simple if we want it to be (1) read and (2) understood, simplicity is not necessarily bad. In less than 2 minutes at Gettysburg, Lincoln spoke 271 words; 201 were one-syllable words, 51 were two-syllable words, and only 19

(7 percent) were words of three or more syllables. (Based on the second Bancroft copy of the Gettysburg Address.)

Even though they have no place in most writing, discovering or coining extreme examples of multi-syllable words is a form of relaxation for some writers. A long-time favorite of mine is "ultra-antihypersyllabicsesquepeda-lianist"—a 39-letter word for a person who is violently opposed to the use of long words. In 1935 the Boston Puzzler's Club came up with what may be the champ in English—"nonaeroresisticaltraceleriticarticulataautomotivinter-noncombustionary"—a 68-letter word for streamlined train.

## HOW IMPORTANT CAN ONE WORD BE?

That the "almost right word" has a great mischief-making potential has been proved many times. This has been particularly so in diplomatic circles when translations enter the picture. There is the oft-told story about *moku-satsu*, a Japanese word that can mean "consider" or "ignore," and the possibility that an error in translation ushered in atomic warfare. Following the surrender of Germany and Italy in 1945, the Allies called on Japan to surrender. At a press conference Japan's premier responded that his country would *mokusatsu* the ultimatum. It is now believed his meaning was "consider," but English-language translators in the Japanese press agency, Domei, broadcast it as "take no notice of." U.S. B-29s, with cargoes of atomic bombs, were soon on the way to Hiroshima and Nagasaki, closing the deadliest of all communication gaps.

Long before the present problems with Panama, a mini-crisis arose over the English verb *negotiate* and the Spanish verb *negociar*. Our State Department, not especially known for the preciseness of language generally used by its representatives, used *negotiate* in the noncommital sense of "to discuss"—while Panamanians interpreted it as a specific commitment to negotiate a new treaty.

Some foreign words have no real counterpart in English, and vice versa. Literal translations in such cases at best can sound foolish; at worst they can result in international repercussions of the highest order. And for those Americans whose working vocabulary is limited, most English words could as easily be Hindi or Urdu. In *Effective Public Relations*, Cutlip and Center tell of adman David Ogilvy's use of the word "obsolete" in an ad, only to find out that 43 percent of the women in the United States had no idea what it meant.

We all recognize that words are symbols of meaning, but words do not always or necessarily have the same meaning for both writer and reader. Communication begins when a word is found to express the writer's meaning; it is completed when the reader understands. Because of this potential source of misunderstanding between writer and reader, writers should always try to imagine the situation of their readers and make it, along with the nature and purpose of the message, a basic consideration in written communication. It is not enough to say *almost* what you mean. You must say it exactly.

## WORDS TO SENTENCES

Since a word cannot convey definite meaning until it is combined with other words in a sentence, sentences are the smallest units for transmitting complete thoughts. Sentences may consist of a single word (with "you" implied), as in "Ask." or "Go!"—or, in extreme cases, they may run on to several hundred words.

There is no ideal or magic sentence length, but it may be helpful to know that a 7-year research study found that sentences in the *Reader's Digest* averaged 16 words in length. *Time* magazine sentences averaged 16 to 17 words. The same study found that no popular magazine averaged more than 22 words per sentence. An old rule of thumb tells us to strive for an average of around 20 words per sentence, which is in line with the study findings.

In general, an effective sentence

- makes a clear, positive statement.
- contains no unnecessary words.
- is made up of definite, specific, concrete words.
- uses the active rather than the passive voice.
- if a simple sentence, it contains one, and only one, *central* idea. If a compound, complex, or compound-complex sentence, it contains one central idea, plus other ideas related to it, or at least to each other, as shown by appropriate coordinating or subcoordinating conjunctions.

## SENTENCES TO PARAGRAPHS

Paragraphs should be communication units for setting forth one topic. Topics are subdivisions of the total message to be communicated, and the reader is assisted in understanding the message by good paragraphing. The visual break of one paragraph ending and a new one beginning is a signal to readers that one step in the developmental pattern is complete.

To avoid a feeling of abruptness when moving on to a new paragraph and topic, transitional sentences or phrases are used. A transitional sentence will carry forward enough of the preceding topic to enable readers to make the mental adjustment to the new idea with no difficulty. Often a single word or short phrase will enable the transition to be made smoothly. Some examples:

Besides
Again
Consequently
As a result
Although
For example
In other words

In addition to a transitional word, phrase, or sentence, most paragraphs contain a topical sentence—a capsule version or summation of all that is to follow. The rest of the paragraph expands on, explains, and emphasizes the topical sentence.

Paragraph lengths, like sentence lengths, are flexible. There is no recognized ideal length, but remember that long paragraphs usually make readers work harder, by requiring them to hold a number of ideas and relationships in their minds. Also, solid-print pages are forbidding in appearance. A certain amount of white space invites the reader in. Newspaper stories traditionally are composed of fairly short paragraphs—30 to 50 or so words—on the theory they are more readable in that format. Don't be bound by any such artificial rules, but do organize and structure your writing so that paragraphs hold together in the reader's mind.

## PR WRITING

Public relations writers have four very different bosses to satisfy—themselves, their clients, editors, and readers. It seems axiomatic that any press release or PR feature arriving on an editor's desk should be better researched, better written, and more interesting, and should promise more benefit to readers than most of the material editors get from any other source, including their own staff writers.

General assignment reporters constantly work under daily and hourly deadline pressures. Little great writing results from a pressure-cooker atmosphere. While deadlines are an inescapable factor in most public relations writing, they are usually much less rigid and demanding. The point is, given equal writing experience and capabilities, PR writers, with days instead of hours or minutes to research, outline, be concerned about the reader, go through three to five drafts, edit, and polish their material, should routinely turn out a superior product. And superior writing is the minimum allowable. Newspaper space or air time must be earned by public relations practitioners—usually at the expense of staff-written stories. The examples of press releases in Chapter 7 show that there is still much room for improvement in public relations writing. Additional examples of sloppy, unchecked, uncaring writing in the next chapter should convince any remaining doubters.

## WRITING ERRORS

Lengthy monographs and entire books have been written on this subject. Our purpose here is to provide a few examples of how near misses—use of the "almost right word"—along with out-and-out errors in grammar and syntax can slow down, confuse, and lose readers.

For openers, take "few" and "less." Less applies to quantity or amount; few to number. From a Nicholas von Hoffman column in the *Washington Post:* "The other side of the coin is that there are less and less people to do the dirty work."

The simple word "me" is a problem for many. During the 1976 presidential campaign former Governor Paul Laxalt said on television, "The President's selection of Bob Dole has the entire support of Governor Reagan and I."

Few words are more troublesome than "its" (the possessive) and "it's" (the contraction of it is). We could easily fill ten pages with examples of the misuse of these two words.

Headlines, which by definition must briefly, clearly, and accurately summarize stories using active words in the present tense, are a fruitful source of humorous errors. The pressures of deadlines and brevity can cause mistakes in spelling, modifiers, subject references, verbs, and abbreviations. The occasional typographical error, in 18- to 36-point type, only compounds the problem. A few examples from our personal collection:

DEAD FLYER WARNED NOT TO START STUNTS
YOUTH BORN IN U.S. IN POLISH UNIFORM
MICHIGAN MAN DIES: BAKED FOR QUEEN
UNCOVER SKELETON OF MAN DIGGING FOR NEW CITY
    FLAGPOLE
ALLEGED WOMAN TOSSED OUT OF CAR IN MOTION
PRESIDENT OF FRANCE ASSASSINATED: DIES
MAN ON WAY TO ITALY TO SEE FAMILY KILLED
TWO CONVICTS EVADE NOOSE; JURY HUNG
WIFE CHARGES BATTERY
TWO TEENAGE GIRLS ARRESTED ON POT
'MISS AMERICA' TO BE SELECTED FROM 48 CONTESTING QUEERS

## METAPHORICALLY SPEAKING

Incorrect or mixed metaphors contribute their share of confusion to speaking and writing. Add in malapropisms and the stew becomes murkier. Lawrence Harrison, a government employee, coined the word "malaphor" to cover a wide range of such fluffs. A few examples from his extensive collection:

He said that with his tongue in his mouth.
That guy's out to butter his own nest.
He's cutting off his nose in spite of his face.
We are diabolically opposed.
It's like pulling blood.
She went through it with a fine-tuned comb.
It fell between the tracks.
He said it off the top of his cuff.
They treated him as if he had Blue Bonnet plague.
It was a case of the tail biting the dog.
They were raking him over the ropes.
It all became a mute question.

Related to the above is the radio commercial which described a product as "the most unique new innovation ever!"

## STREAMLINED WRITING

Padding of any kind is to be avoided in writing, on the grounds it takes up valuable space and slows a reader's progress. A few examples:

| Padded | Streamlined |
|---|---|
| of a very complex nature | is very complex |
| in the year 1957 | in 1957 |
| bright orange in color | bright orange |
| eight in number | eight |
| oval in shape | oval |
| at the location of the site | at the location, or at the site |
| repeat it again | repeat it |
| costs the sum of $10 | costs $10 |
| for the period of a year | for a year |
| in the event of | if |
| for the reason that | because |
| with reference to | about |

Write it the shortest possible way. The unnecessary modifiers and superfluous phrases in the examples above do nothing to move a reader through the material. When Neil Armstrong became the first man to set foot on the moon on July 20, 1969, he *could* have said to the waiting world, "One pedal movement of limited scope for homo sapiens, one pedal movement of massive scope for all present and future inhabitants of planet earth." And what kind of show biz would that mouthful have been?

One form of streamlining writing, in the sense that it can convey a mood or feeling with minimum wordage, is the use of onomatopoetic words—words that have the same sounds as their referents. These are generally strong words, such as buzz, plop, sizzle, thump, croak, tinkle, whiz, crack, swish, burp, whir, bang, hiss, whoop, chortle, bash, and peep. But don't go overboard onomatopoetically; the effect may exhaust some readers.

## EXPERTS, RULES, AND GUIDELINES

Brandeis's great truth: "There is no such thing as good writing; only good rewriting."

George Orwell, from whom we'll hear more shortly, on the decline of language, in "Politics and the English Language" (1946): "The great enemy of clear language is insincerity. When there is a gap between one's real and one's declared aims, one turns as it were instinctively to long words and exhausted idioms, like a cuttlefish squirting out ink."

Anatole France had a reminder for those who seek undeserved consensus: "If 50 million people say a foolish thing, it is still a foolish thing." And T. S.

Eliot once characterized each foray into creative writing as ''a new raid on the inarticulate.''

Over the years many have set out rules and guidelines for good writing. As we pointed out a few pages back, there is no foolproof formula or set of rules to ensure that one's writing will always (or ever) be clear and effective. (Author MacKinlay Kantor points out: ''Good writing can't be taught by anyone—any time, any place. The author is his own and only schoolmaster.'') Nevertheless, the following listing, compiled from many sources, may serve to steer some in the right direction.

- Use short sentences. More than 20 words leads to obscurity.
- Never use a long word when a short one will do as well.
- Prefer the plain word to the fancy.
- Prefer the familiar word to the unfamiliar.
- Prefer nouns and verbs to adjectives and adverbs.
- Vary your sentence length.
- Start sentences with their subjects. Subjects at the end confuse and slow both writer and reader.
- Use the active voice.
- Avoid imitation. Write in your natural style.
- Avoid gobbledygook and jargon.
- When making an abstract point, rephrase or restate it afterwards with a concrete example.
- Watch all punctuation. The writer's own eye, ear, and common sense are often the best guides.
- Paragraphing is also punctuation. Separate thoughts and ideas by proper paragraph packaging.
- Bait the reader's interest with live subheads and eye-catching titles.
- Personal words and sentences are desirable in most writing.
- Don't write over reader's heads—or your own.
- Consider the reader's situation. Tie into his or her interests.
- Write to reach the reader, not to exhibit your personal skills or intelligence.
- Go easy on the superlatives.
- Anticipate questions. Answer them.
- Seek fresh forms of expression.
- Avoid using the same words, phrases, and sentence structure. Mix sentence and paragraph lengths for variety, interest, and emphasis.
- Accuracy is essential. Double-check names, facts, and figures.
- Revise and rewrite. Improvement is always possible.
- Be brutal in editing. Most writing can be shortened by 40 to 50 percent and vastly improved in the process.

George Orwell, in ''Politics and the English Language,'' laid down six rules of writing that are worthy of your consideration.

1. Never use a metaphor, simile, or other figure of speech which you are used to seeing in print.

2. Never use a long word where a short one will do.

3. If it is possible to cut a word out, cut it out.

4. Never use the passive where you can use the active.

5. Never use a foreign phrase, a scientific word, or a jargon word if you can think of an everyday English equivalent.

6. Break any of these rules sooner than saying anything outright barbarous.

On the not-so-serious side, here is a list of 13 tips for writers. The original author understandably prefers to remain annonymous.

1. Don't use no double negatives.

2. Make each pronoun agree with their antecedent.

3. Join clauses good, like a conjunction should.

4. About them sentence fragments.

5. When dangling, watch your participles.

6. Verbs has got to agree with their subjects.

7. Just between you and I, case is important too.

8. Don't write run-on sentences they are hard to read understand?

9. Don't use commas, which aren't necessary.

10. Try to not ever split infinitives.

11. Its important to use you're apostrophe's correctly.

12. Proofread your writing to see if you any words out.

13. Corect speling is esential.

And to conclude this section on guidelines, *Writer's Digest* once carried a list of "things for all writers to think about." Here are a few of my favorite "things":

• For 90 percent of all writers, writing is slow, tedious, agonizingly difficult work. The other 10 percent are no doubt lying.

• If you would learn good writing, read good writing.

• If nothing else works, try writing as soon as you wake up in the morning. You may discover that some of your best work is done when you're semiconscious, but don't let it bother you.

• Chances are the word you're looking for, the word you need to impart precisely the shade of meaning you intend, does not exist. At least not in English.

• It takes more than a little talent and a lot of hard work to succeed at writing. It takes know-how. There are two ways to acquire know-how: (a) the slow, dumb, expensive way, and (b) the fast, smart, economical way. (b) is better.

## OBFUSCATION, FLAPDOODLE, AND GOBBLEDYGOOK

Things have come, as they say, to a pretty pass when a bureaucrat makes headlines across the country by telling his staff lawyers to keep their writing uncluttered and understandable. Or when insurance companies issue press releases by the bushel to point out their policies are now written "in simple, everyday English."

Shortly after his appointment as chairman of the Civil Aeronautics Board, Alfred E. Kahn apparently decided there was some truth in the observation by a former Yale law school professor: "There are two things wrong with almost all legal writing. One is its style. The other is its content."

Kahn wrote a memo to all bureau and office heads, division and section chiefs, with carbon copies to other board members. His opening paragraph: "One of my peculiarities, which I beg you to indulge if I am to retain my sanity (possibly at the expense of yours!) is an abhorrence of the artificial and hyper-legal language that is sometimes known as bureaucratese or gobbledygook."

An arresting beginning, certainly. A little editing might have cut the 42-word lead sentence-paragraph into two easier to follow sentences. But you hesitate to nitpick someone on the attack against gobbledygook. The rest of Kahn's memo dealt with specific words and phrases particularly abhorrent to the new chairman. Not to be outdone, the chairman of the Interstate Commerce Commission appointed a gobbledygook committee, declaring to the commission's 2000 employees, "English is a remarkably clear, flexible and useful language."

Insurance companies, nudged in some cases by threats from state regulatory commissions, have been busy recently rewriting insurance policies. One firm, United Services Automobile Association (USAA), used several pages in a company magazine to explain how policy language has been simplified. The word count, in one type of policy, "has been reduced 40 percent—from 12,000 words to 7,000. Most of the legal jargon is gone . . . print size is about 25 percent larger than previously."

Before anyone gets the idea the millennium is here, let's take a brief look at some of the recent bureaucratic output. The State Department's explanation of its newly created post of coordinator of consumer affairs: "The consumer affairs coordinator will review existing mechanisms of consumer input, thruput and output, and seek ways of improving these linkages via the consumer communication channel." The implications for international diplomacy of a State Department consumer affairs coordinator boggles the mind. Or is all this, as one Washington veteran suggested, just an onput?

From the commandant of the Marine Corps: "It has been decisioned that some form of unit rotation may be a desirable objective. . . . Recent CMC decisions have alleviated the major inhibitors allowing a fresh approach and revaluation of alternative methods of unit replacement." I, along with many others, have decisioned that no Marine talks like that.

This is a notice posted in parks and recreation areas in and around Washington, D.C.:

## Trees, Shrubs, Plants
## Grass and Other Vegetation

(a) General Injury. No person shall prune, cut, carry away, pull up, dig, fell, bore, chop, saw, chip, pick, move, sever, climb, molest, take, break, deface, destroy, set fire to, burn, scorch, carve, paint, mark, or in any manner interfere with, tamper, mutilate, misuse, disturb or damage any tree, shrub, plant, grass, flower, or part thereof, nor shall any person permit any chemical, whether solid, fluid or gaseous to seep, drip, drain or be emptied, sprayed, dusted or injected upon, about or into any tree, shrub, plant, grass, flower or part thereof except when specifically authorized by competent authority; nor shall any person build fires or station or use any tar kettle, heater, road roller or other engine within an area covered by this part in such a manner that the vapor, fumes or heat therefrom may injure any tree or other vegetation.

The translation of that 140-word sentence monster (only 131 words shorter than the entire Gettysburg Address) is: Leave it *all* alone!

And what about the design profession's record on obfuscation? Architects have their own version of gobbledygook, as these two examples show:

"One of the basic notions of the . . . design methodology is to expand our visual language . . . and allow the natural development of an unconscious, nonmonumental esthetic. Such a design system, being inclusive, ad hoc, and opportunistic, tends much more to the vernacular than the academic." *(L.A. Architect)*

"An outstanding building. More refined, more complete than the FAA building which was its forerunner. Glass is treated as an all-enveloping vitreous skin. Siting is impressive. Not just an isolated building. Sense of the street is strong. The bridges do a great deal for it by connecting it to its surroundings. Sense of a complete organism." (Jury comment, Southern California AIA Annual Design Awards)

In dozens of marketing workshops for architects and engineers over the past half-dozen years, a common concern of participants is the lack of public understanding of the design professional's role. Is the reason for some of the confusion a little clearer?

Just in case there is any question about it, the *Guide for Air Force Writing* gives this definition of gobbledygook:

> The writer uses
> - Many words to say what could be said just as well in a few.
> - Unfamiliar words.
> - Words of three or four syllables when simpler words would give the same idea.
> - Military jargon and trite, overworked phrases.
> - Long and involved sentences.
> - Foreign expressions.
> - Jumbled, unrelated, illogical ideas.[3]

## WRITING FOR THE EAR: RADIO

While few readers may be called upon to write a radio newsscript, public relations writers should be familiar with the subject. The techniques for writing radio copy differ in several important respects from newspaper and magazine writing. Sentences are shorter (rarely longer than 25 words), but they must flow smoothly into each other without abrupt transitions. Ideally, radio writing duplicates normal speech patterns by avoiding stiff, formalized constructions.

Simplicity in expressing complicated concepts is one of the most difficult tasks faced by the radio news writer. Listeners have only one chance to grasp the meaning; they cannot reread or relisten to a foggy sentence. Therefore, in radio (and to a certain extent in television) one writes for the ear. To the five Ws and an H for a newspaper story (who, what, when, where, why, and how), radio adds four Cs—correctness, clarity, conciseness, and color.

The Associated Press, in its instructions to radio news writers, says, "It is a mistake to assume (and it has been assumed by some) that writing news for radio is a much easier task than writing for other media. Radio news writing demands greater compression which calls for greater skill."

It can be a difficult assignment to have to write a radio piece in words simple enough to be understood by an 8-year-old, clear enough to be heard by a 90-year-old who is half deaf, and still be interesting enough to appeal to a 40-year-old intellectual. Simplicity in ideas, thoughts, words, language, sentences, and punctuation must be attained by all possible means.

Begin by sticking with short, common words. This does not mean, naturally, that any word of more than three syllables is proscribed in radio writing. It should suggest the use of a short word, or three or four short words, instead of a long word or a word unfamiliar to many listeners.

Radio newscasters usually broadcast at the rate of around 150 words a minute—or at a slightly faster pace than a good speaker uses before a live audience. Spot announcements and news on radio are sometimes delivered at an even more rapid rate—up to 175 words a minute, depending on station policy and the announcer's style. The National Association of Broadcasters suggests 150 words a minute for a 1-minute spot announcement.

The briefer the story for broadcast, the better. Air time is at a premium, so if you can tell your story in 10 seconds, do it. Thirty seconds is about the maximum most stations will devote to a story.

## WRITING FOR THE EAR: SPEECHES

One veteran speaker characterizes a good speech as "a logically organized talk that contains ideas worth remembering which are presented in such a manner that they are in fact remembered. The key to getting ideas remembered is the judicious use of appropriate stories and sayings that illustrate and highlight the speaker's points."[4]

Much of what already has been said about writing for radio applies to preparing a speech for a live audience. As in radio, anything a speaker says must be grasped the first time around; there is little opportunity for listeners to ponder the meaning of words or phrases. Long and difficult passages should be avoided.

The advantage a public speaker has over the radio announcer is the ability to observe the reaction of listeners (nods, frowns, clapping, laughter, boos) and to make immediate judgments about what the audience thinks. The speaker thus has *some* opportunity to correct misunderstandings or confusion.

There are seven basic steps in preparing a speech. They are not unlike the thirteen-step formula for all writing.

1. Select and limit the subject.
2. Determine the purpose of the speech.
3. Analyze the audience and the occasion.
4. Prepare a tentative outline.
5. Collect data and expand the outline.
6. Plan visual aids, if any.
7. Word (flesh out) the speech and practice it.

Speeches, as any effective presentation, are organized into three conventional divisions: introduction, body, and conclusion (refer to the discussion of this point in Chapter 8). Speakers must introduce themselves and their message, develop ideas to achieve their purpose, and guide listeners in formulating logical conclusions. Strategically, the procedure is (1) attract attention, (2) arouse interest, (3) create personal desire, (4) motivate fulfillment of the desire, (5) suggest action, and (6) close on a strong note (inspirational).

Major speeches can require up to an hour of preparation by an experienced speech writer for each minute of delivered material. Inexperienced writers may have to use a preparation/delivery ratio of 3:1 or even 4:1.

When properly planned, executed, and merchandised, a speech can be a highly effective public relations tool. Because relatively few public relations practitioners are trained in oral communication and ghostwriting speeches, it is a PR tool often overlooked or mishandled. Since a speech should be viewed as a serious writing effort, requiring hours (sometimes days) of preparation, why not expand the potential audience far beyond the original 50 to perhaps 200 listeners? Reproducing the talk, or its highlights, in printed form with illustrations and attractive graphics can give you a good to excellent mailing piece for past, present, and prospective clients. Figure 9-1 shows the first page of a six-page reprint of a talk made by S. D. Bechtel, Jr., on the occasion of his initiation into the national engineering society, Tau Beta Pi. Bechtel's speech, on the energy situation, was reproduced on magazine stock in an 8 ½ × 11 inch format. Another common format for this purpose is the number 10 envelope–size booklet.

A list of speech writing DOs and DON'Ts might include:

## DO

• use concrete terms—definitions, examples, statistics, comparisons, case histories, anecdotes, and analysis—to create visual imagery.
• limit the subject in terms of your interests and qualifications, listeners' needs and demands, and the time allotted.

# An Engineer's Approach to The Energy Situation

If we do not accelerate the development of new energy sources, if we allow the gap between consumption and domestic production to widen, if we don't curb our reliance on imported energy, we are in for very serious problems.

S. D. BECHTEL, JR.

S. D. Bechtel, Jr., chairman of the Bechtel group of companies, was initiated into Tau Beta Pi, the national engineering honor society, at Purdue University, on April 17. His remarks on that occasion focused on a major national problem which is the concern of all thoughtful persons.

TO receive this honor from my Alma Mater means a great deal, particularly because of Tau Beta Pi's standards of professional excellence, character and integrity. Those standards are very important to me. I am honored to become a member of Tau Beta Pi.

I thought you might find it worthwhile for me to discuss two related subjects:

1) the energy situation in the United States, and
2) the engineer's role in helping our country meet its energy needs.

While the energy problem has received much attention over the last several years, and many of you are quite well informed on the subject, it probably would still be helpful to begin with a perspective of the situation, together with an appraisal of where we are, and where we need to go. Then we can consider the role of the engineer.

### A DECADE OF GROWING ENERGY CONSUMPTION

First, a few facts about the very great growth in the use of energy in this country during the last decade: During this period, total consumption of energy increased 51%. By comparison, population increased only 12%. The Gross National Product went up only 43%. So we not only used more energy in total, but more per capita and more per unit of economic activity. (A large part of this increase was in the consumption of electricity which rose 92% during the decade.)

### BUT NOT MUCH GROWTH IN PRODUCTION

During this same period, while consumption increased 51%, energy production grew only 33%. As a result, we have an energy gap. This gap between consumption and production has been filled by imports, which have risen substantially.

As we rely more and more on foreign sources of energy, the security of our country and the stability of our economy are in question. Further, our appetite for energy, and the consequent dependence on foreign sources, has enabled energy producers to increase prices far beyond what anyone ever anticipated.

It should be of little comfort to us in the United States that other developed nations have a bigger energy gap than we. For example, in 1973, the United States imported 18% of its energy requirements, but Europe imported 60% of its total consumption and Japan 80%. The problem these other countries have affects their economic and foreign policies, as well as their energy policies.

### THE ENERGY PROBLEM WASN'T A SURPRISE

We should remember that leaders in both government and the private sector have been concerned about a potential energy shortage for some time, well before the 1973 Arab embargo.

Figure 9-1. The first page of a six-page reprint of the talk, "An Engineer's Approach to the Energy Situation," by S. D. Bechtel, Jr., to members of Tau Beta Pi, national engineering honor society. Inside pages were copiously illustrated with photographs of energy-related Bechtel projects. Such reprints, sent to a firm's list of prospects and clients, is an excellent, reasonably low-cost way of expanding the audience for a speech.

• have something worth saying, the credentials for saying it, and a good reason for saying it to this audience, here, and now.

• be yourself; maintain your own style and identity.

• treat the audience with dignity.

• be relaxed, fresh, and alert.

• change the pace and vary the rhythm and force of delivery occasionally.

• pose a question occasionally to stimulate thought.

• try to get the audience involved.

• have a forceful summary and conclusion.

• rehearse the speech.

• try to avoid currently fashionable buzzwords—input, viable, prioritize, trade-off, and the like.

• use the pronoun "you"—a powerful motivator.

## DON'T

• use a full-length script. Cards are usually better.

• begin speaking the second you are introduced; give the audience a chance to size you up—and settle down.

• tell funny stories.

• use clichés.

• use visual aids unless they make a strong, positive contribution to the speech.

• try to write a multipurpose speech; no two audiences or occasions are alike.

• be afraid to express personal opinions.

We'll give the last word on speechmaking to the late Adlai Stevenson, and his 1960 introduction of Presidential candidate John F. Kennedy (who had beaten out Stevenson for the Democratic nomination a few weeks before): "Do you remember that in classical times when Cicero had finished speaking, the people said, 'How well he spoke'—but when Demosthenes had finished speaking, the people said, 'Let us march'?"

## EDITING

Now that you've finished that timeless text, or the priceless press release, what next? A thorough, merciless editing job is what's next. As Samuel Johnson once advised, "Read over your composition, and wherever you meet with a passage which you think is particularly fine, strike it out."

Everyone, as the saying goes, needs an editor. Most writers understandably find it difficult to be objective when editing their own material. For this reason, writing and editing are at their best levels when handled as separate processes—and by at least two different individuals. Air Force officer John Correll, an accomplished writer and editor (who does not edit his own written creations) gives these five editing caveats:

1. Don't rewrite.
2. Edit on the original manuscript (or keep a copy of the original ms for comparison).
3. Keep *your* ideas and sentiments out of it.
4. Rewrite *only* for transition.
5. Edit to
   first, shorten;
   second, sharpen;
   third, smooth.

An example from *Airman* magazine illustrates the point. First, the opening three paragraphs of the original manuscript:

> A German shepherd patrol dog who loves to ride in trucks and an Air Force security policeman who wants to become a veterinarian teamed up to stop a recent series of on-base robberies at Homestead AFB, Florida.
>
> A1C Mike H. Addis, from South Miami, has been a security police dog handler about a year-and-a-half. His patrol dog, Baron, joined the Air Force at the age of two and has four years in.
>
> Airman Addis described his arrest of the robbery suspect: "Baron and I were walking to our main post from the kennels. It was dark and a little cool, and we were enjoying the walk and the great Florida evening."

Now, the first three paragraphs of the published story:

> His bark *is* worse than his bite, but don't let that fool you. Two would-be robbers at Homestead AFB, Fla., correctly figured that his bite would be bad enough.
>
> And A1C Mike Addis, a security police dog handler at the base, discovered that Baron, a 6-year-old German shepherd patrol dog with a penchant for unrestrained barking while riding to work in a truck, is some kind of dog.
>
> It happened on a Saturday. "Baron and I were walking to our main post from the kennels," Addis said. "It was dark, a little cool, and we were enjoying the walk."

Publications expert Edith Seidel furnishes these examples of original and edited versions of the same material.

> (Original) Portland must rely on selling goods and services to populations other than its own in order to build sufficient commercial and industrial growth to provide the quality and quantity of employment opportunities necessary for maintaining and attracting population to the area. (41 words)

> (Edited) Portland must sell goods and services to an area greater than its own in order to create jobs that will sustain and attract people. (24 words)

> (Original) If Lake Smith were to have high-quality water (suitable for body contact) either controlled or uncontrolled, effective demand for commercial recreation at the park would be encouraged. (28 words)

> (Edited) The demand for recreation at the park would be increased if Lake Smith were safe for swimming. (17 words and the editing also eliminates any concern about what it is that's uncontrolled; water or body contact.)

(Original) The operation of the sewage treatment and disposal facility will vary with the type of facility and treatment process being used. The complexity of the operation is generally affected by the degree or level to which treatment is carried. The effort and complexity of the operation required is directly proportional to the amount of treatment or purification required. (59 words)

(Edited) The effect and complexity of facility operation will vary, being directly proportional to the amount of treatment or purification required. (20 words)

A tip for self-editing: read the copy aloud; listen to it. When you stumble you can be reasonably sure a silent reader will be blocked at the same spot. If it can be said, it can be read. Hard words lose readers.

## READABILITY FORMULAS

Not really a function of copy editing, an occasional application of one or more readability formulas may help evaluate your writing. It has been said that no worthwhile writing ever resulted from a slavish application of readability formulas—and we agree.

Readability formulas are not exactly new. *The Teacher's Word Book*, by E. L. Thorndike, came out in the early 1930s. The best-known and most-used indexes today include the Reading Ease Formula (Rudolf Flesch), the Fog Index (Robert Gunning), the SMOG Readability Formula (C. Harry McLaughlin), the Five-Letter Word Formula, the Dale-Chall, the Spache Readability Formula, and the Edward Fry Formula.

The easiest and fastest readability tool is the Five-Letter Word Formula.

1. Count the number of words on a page, omitting all proper names.
2. Determine how many words of five letters or less were used.
3. Divide the total obtained in (2) by the total in (1) for the score.

Around 75 percent is about right for most readers. As the percentage drops below 70, it's a sign that your writing is perhaps more difficult to read than it should be.

Gunning stresses the use of short words and short sentences, and his Fog Index is concerned with average sentence length and the number of words of three or more syllables in 100-word samples. The sum of these two is multiplied by 0.4 and the answer is the approximate number of years of education needed to understand the sample.

A ten-sentence sample, taken from a front-page *Washington Post* story (January 2, 1976) on operations of international commodity firms, was checked against the Fog Index and the Flesch Reading Ease and Human Interest Formulas. The first two paragraphs of the sample:

Five of the six largest grain conglomerates are closely held, private firms controlled by a few individuals or families. They don't publish any detailed financial information. The only one of the big six that does, Cook Industries, Inc., of Memphis, is required by law to do so because it has public stockholders, and Cook's outspoken boss, Edward W. Cook, in any case shows considerable contempt for the reclusive ways of his competitors.

Washington cognoscenti are even hard pressed to identify a grain company lobbiest here.

The ten sentences of the complete sample contained 264 words, for an average sentence length of 26.4 words. The selection had 56 words of three or more syllables, or an average of 21.2 such words per 100 words. The arithmetic:

$$\begin{array}{r} 26 \\ +21 \\ \hline 47 \end{array} \times 0.4 = 18.8\ (19)$$

The answer tells us that the equivalent of 3 years of graduate school, or a Ph.D., is required to understand the sample.

By Flesch's measurements, the reading ease of the *Post* sample is 38.5, or "difficult." The grade equivalent required, according to Flesch, is between 13 and 16 (first-year college student to college senior). From a human interest standpoint, based on a count of personal words and sentences, the piece rated 1.5 percent, or "dull." Part of the problem with the article is the writer's use of such vocabulary-loading, abstract words as

moguls
cryptic
reclusive
cognoscenti
oligopoly
pervasive
agribusiness

## CORRESPONDENCE

Every written business message should either initiate or maintain good will for the originating firm. Only the best writing will accomplish these goals, which are tied closely to public image and are therefore related to sales and marketing interests.

Effective sales letters should

- be direct. Don't hint or beat around the bush.
- be "you" and "your" oriented.
- be specific. How fast is "very fast"?—or how much better is "better performance"?
- be brief. People read the shorter letters first.
- be believable.
- be interesting.
- use active words.
- be clear.
- be cliché-free.
- avoid linguistic narcissism.

Letters to editors can be effective public relations tools. Many public relations campaigns include several published letters to the editor as part of the total program. Such letters represent the ultimate in going public with your correspondence, and should project literary competency of the highest degree and incorporate most of the points for effective sales letters as set out above.

## References

[1]Quotation attributed to Mark Twain, cited in AIA newsletter, Nov. 7, 1975.

[2]Henry Fairlie, "Our Misguided Defenders of the English Language," *The Washington Post,* May 29, 1977.

[3]Guide for Air Force Writing, U.S. Government Printing Office, Washington, 1973, p. 2.

[4]Jacob M. Braude, *The Complete Art of Public Speaking,* Bantam Books, New York, 1970, p. 1.

"You must orchestrate the press," said attorney Jerry Paul following his successful defense of Joan Little. "This country works that way. You have to deal with reality. . . ." Paul said Little's acquittal on charges she murdered a white jailer was "bought" and added, "given enough money, I can create illusion, anything," including valuable space in the press.[1]

# CHAPTER 10
# Press Releases

**A** COUPLE OF YEARS ago public relations executives were asked to rate their functions in order of importance. Four of the five top-rated functions involved written communications, and 99 percent of the respondents put "news releases and media relations" at the top of their list!

A press or news release, by defnition, should clearly have news import if there is to be any chance of the release fulfilling its mission. There are probably as many definitions of news as for public relations. One of my favorites: News is anything which excites, astounds, entertains, influences, or informs the reader, listener, or viewer.

News is also

- the report of a current event, idea, or conflict that interests consumers.
- anything timely that interests a number of people; and the best news is that which has the greatest interest for the greatest number.
- (from the reporter's standpoint) an account of events such that a first-rate reporter finds satisfaction in writing and publishing.

And the most important definition of all: News is what the editor decides it is, what he or she chooses to print, and not much else matters. What is worthy is not necessarily newsworthy. It should come as no surprise that the New York *Times* does not *really* carry "all the news that's fit to print."

In *How to Market Professional Design Services* we pointed out that "news is apt to be based on deeds rather than words; specifics rather than generalities; benefits rather than features; and it is practically always related to known public interests."

## PR OBJECTIVES AND PRESS RELEASES

In developing a publicity campaign as part of an overall public relations program, keep these pointers (based on an article in *Practical Public Relations*) in mind:

- Whatever objective you set up, be reasonably certain it is attainable.
- Be able to express a campaign's true objective in concrete, factual terms. If you cannot, it may be a sign that the campaign concept and structure are too abstract for it to ever get off the ground.
- Identify and relate the campaign's unique, worthy points to the self-interests of the target audience.
- Repetition of the publicity theme in all media usually is one key to a campaign's success; one of the challenges to a PR counselor is finding interesting ways to achieve thematic repetition without boring the audience.
- Issuing a press release doesn't guarantee its publication; publication is no assurance it will ever reach or be read by the target audience; and if it's read by the right people your objective is not attained unless it contributes in some demonstrable way to the setting or reinforcement of specific awareness or attitudes of the target group. *That* is the goal; all else is vanity—and it's *not* public relations.

## PRESS RELEASE FORMAT

There is something less than universal agreement on the "right" or "ideal" format for press releases. For example, most PR consultants put "FOR IMMEDIATE RELEASE" somewhere in the top right corner of the first page. "FOR IMMEDIATE USE" is my own preference, on the theory that it seems counterproductive to continually remind editors and reporters that this is a self-serving PR *release.*

Some releases require a time of release (advance stories on speeches, for example) and in those cases the line usually reads "FOR RELEASE AT 5 PM JANUARY 14" or "FOR PM RELEASE." Many more stories are made conditional on a time of release than deserve it. Like the boy who cried "wolf" once too often, some public relations writers find editors eventually ignoring a release hour—or, deciding the whole process is too demanding and complicated, the editor may simply release the item into the nearest newsroom wastebasket.

Some years ago I came across a list of twelve rules for effective press releases. The original compiler's name has been lost, which I regret, but here are his or her rules, which are still pertinent and useful:

1. Use standard letterhead size paper, 8½ by 11 inches—not legal length, half length, or other odd shapes.

2. Make your copy look like newspaper copy. Newsprint is the cheapest kind of paper and is preferable in editorial circles because it resembles the paper reporters use.

3. Use only one side of the paper. When using more than one sheet, clip them together; do not staple them.

4. Place the copy source in the upper left-hand corner. Give your name, the name of the organization, its address, and telephone number. Publicity is worthless unless an editor knows its source. Unless you declare yourself on your copy, its authenticity is open to question. Furthermore, the editor may be sufficiently impressed with your subject and treatment to follow it up for elaboration. Make it easy for him or her to reach you.

5. The release date and the periodical's name should go in the upper right-hand corner. It should say FOR IMMEDIATE USE—or FOR USE ON RECEIPT if you are sending the same story to many papers releasing at different times and want them all to release it at once. If the copy is not spot-news and the release date is unimportant, say FOR USE AT WILL. It is preferable when possible to specify the day and paper: FOR FRIDAY GAZETTE.

6. Write nonduplicated copy. When sending stories to competing newspapers, each release should be rewritten so that each paper has a distinctive story of its own. It flatters an editor to receive a special story.

7. Place no heading on the story. This only balls up the works because newspaper editors write their own heads anyway.

8. Allow ample margins. Starting a story well down the page allows plenty of room for the editor to write notes and heads. If you have a story somewhat too long for one page, and can trim it and force it into one page by cramping the top space, cramp it but do not entirely fill it up. Allow ample margins on both sides for editing. An inch on each side is sufficient.

9. Double space the copy. This makes copy easier to read and edit. Slug page two and all following pages with a two- or three-word identifying phrase (ABC Groundbreaking; Oak City Library). This helps editors and reporters keep the release all together.

10. Fold the release so that copy shows outside. News people are always in a hurry. When your envelope arrives the editor wants to see the release and identify the originator as soon as possible. Outward folding facilitates this.

11. Conform to style. The simplest interpretation of this rule is "be a former newspaper writer." You must know how to write a newspaper story. Express your lead, or first paragraph, in one compact sentence that covers the who-when-what-why-where angle. Make each paragraph self-contained so the story will heal after any editorial excision. Pack your facts like the parts of a puzzle. Be economical with words. Be specific. Use short, staccato, informative sentences. Be sure all names are spelled correctly, all initials and titles are right, all essentials are included, and everything mentioned is clear and

explained in the story. Do not editorialize. If your story justifies an expression of opinion, insert it in the form of a quotation from the source named in your lead.

12. Produce publicity with a purpose. Space is not the answer; most readers and all editors shun long columns of copy. An inch packed with punch is often worth more than a colorless, rambling full column. Abhorrent to editors are publicists who file stories three pages single-spaced when the item is worth no more than 2 inches. It pays to write your stories as compactly as possible and then try to cut them in half—unless they are of great importance (to the public, not to you). An axiom worth heeding: "Confine stories to one page." Really special material may run longer. Material lacking in historical importance should never exceed two pages. If you habituate yourself to pack, not pad, your stories, editors may get used to printing them "as is."

Concerning rule number 2, there is the story of a veteran publicist for circuses who, when making his annual rounds of newspapers on the performance schedule, would carefully gather and label a supply of copy paper at each stop. The next year he made certain that every editor got a release on his or her own copy paper; a commendable example of attention to detail.

Today so many releases are sent out in the name of serving the client that using paper clips rather than staples is probably impractical. But someone at the newspaper must remove the staples.

The rule about not putting headlines on news releases is subject to dispute. Many release writers include a brief head on the theory that it tells the editor at a glance what the story is about.

One detail omitted by the anonymous composer of the twelve rules for effective press releases—the word "more" should appear in parentheses at the bottom of each page when another page follows. Indicate the end of the story with "End," "-30-," or "XXX" centered below the last line of type.

It is considered bad form to split paragraphs at the bottom of a page—for a number of reasons connected with the mechanics of putting out a newspaper. Avoid carrying over part of a paragraph. A few other pointers on the elements of a professional news release:

• Dateline every release. Include a date at the beginning of the story, as CHICAGO (June 22)—. Some public relations writers have devised dating codes, which usually appear at the bottom of the last page. Unfortunately, in all too many cases this is the only place the date is shown. Few editors have time to play games with such codes.

• Some PR writers follow the old newspaper custom of labeling the second page ADD 1, the third page ADD 2, and so on. Since some of the new generation of reporters don't even know what that means, play it safe and put page 2 on page 2; page 3 on page 3.

• Deeper than normal paragraph indentations (eight to ten spaces) makes the release easier to read.

• *Never* ask an editor of anything to send you copies or clippings of stories based on your releases.

## DEALING WITH EDITORS

The importance of sending appropriate material to the right publication is underscored by the comments and complaints of Max Kerstein of the *Beverage Bulletin:*

> Ours is a newspaper which serves the licensed beverage industry in Southern California. Our daily mail is such that we can publish a 64-page daily newspaper on the strength of the publicity releases and photographs we receive from public relations firms.
>
> Of the material that crosses our desks, at least 95 percent ends up in the "round file" simply because it has little or no value to our audience, is not keyed to our industry, not directed to our marketing area, and contains practically no news value. It is little more than commercials for brands, or "puff pieces" to satisfy the egos of clients who would like to have their pictures published.
>
> I find that many public relations companies grind out volume rather than quality. Most do not take the time to study and review the industries they are servicing, the specific needs of their clients (in terms of achieving sales impetus through publicity), or the publications for which releases are intended. Publicity for the sake of publicity, regardless of how impressive the scrap book looks, means little if it does not achieve specific objectives.
>
> Another major problem we find is that a great number of public relations agencies and departments fail to keep their mailing list current. Although we moved almost six years ago, many companies still send releases to our old address, even though all have been notified several times.
>
> We find that most releases are too long. Many times short informational stories, even small filler-type stories, will achieve far greater results than the long stories which require considerable time to wade through and rewrite.[2]

Shotgunning releases by the thousands, in hope that a few responsive editors will be hit, has become more of a problem than ever in this era of high-speed presses, automatic folding and stuffing machines, and computer addressing. Any public relations operation that does not keep its mailing lists lean, clean, and current is a sloppy operation. Clients pay for such sloppiness.

For months I have received an average of three news releases a week (many with photographs enclosed) from a New York City public relations consultant on behalf of his client, a large New York architectural firm. Most of the releases have had the saving grace of brevity, but they all concern new projects in the client firm's office. I publish a marketing newsletter for the design profession and announcements of project awards have never been used in it—nor will they ever be. And I have yet to use a photograph in the newsletter. If just a tenth of the mailings for this client are wasted effort, as in my case, several thousand dollars are literally being thrown away annually.

A *few*—very few—PR firms have queried me to see if I have any interest in receiving releases about their clients. Media Distribution Services, Inc., of New York is one of this select group. The firm asked for a sample copy of my publication to evaluate its editorial interests and see if information about its clients would be used. Abbott, Langer & Associates, of Park Forest, Illinois, send out a business reply card inquiry (Figure 10-1) to editors.

☐ Please <u>remove</u> my name from all of your mailing lists.
☐ Please <u>place</u> my name on your mailing list(s) for future news releases regarding:

☐ "Available Pay Survey Reports: An Annotated Bibliography"
☐ "College Recruiting Report"
☐ "Compensation in Guidance & Counseling"
☐ "Compensation in Manufacturing"
☐ "Compensation of Industrial Engineers"
☐ "Compensation of MBA's"
☐ "Compensation of Sales/Marketing Execs"

☐ "Corporate Law Department Salaries"
☐ "Industrial Recreation Report"
☐ "Inter-City Wage & Salary Differentials"
☐ "Salaries & Benefits in Boat Manufacturing"
☐ "Salaries & Benefits in the Kitchen Cabinet Industry"
☐ "Salaries & Related Matters in the Service Department"

Name:_____  Title:_____

Name of Publication:_____

Street Address:_____

City:_____  State:_____  ZIP Code:_____

Figure 10-1. The business reply card distributed to editors by Abbott, Langer & Associates of Park Forest, Illinois. The editor may request news releases on various subjects—or ask to be taken off the firm's mailing list.

Once a productive mailing list is assembled, PR professionals do their homework. They obtain media recognition and use of their releases by their actions, by the quality (*not* quantity) and appropriateness of material submitted, and by becoming a reliable source of information. The real PR pro becomes an extension of the media. When public relations practitioners communicate as well or better than most reporters, editors have to use their releases because they know the competition will.

### THE SHRINKING MARKET

How many of these New York daily newspapers do you remember?

| | |
|---|---|
| American | Journal |
| Commercial Advertiser | Mail & Express |
| Evening Sun | News |
| Evening World | Press |
| Globe | Sun |
| Graphic | Telegram |
| Herald | Tribune |
| Herald-Tribune | World |

They are representative of the many that have folded in our largest city, as newspapers across the country became big business and ownership was concentrated in fewer hands. An example of the economic concentration of the media: 96 percent of the cities with daily newspapers have only one publisher. Some 100 million Americans were served by 2400 newspapers in 1910. Today 200 million are served by fewer than 1800 newspapers. More than 1000 of the survivors are published by just 174 companies.

Aside from the desirability of choice in newspapers (Walter Lippmann: "A free press exists only where newspaper readers have access to other newspapers which are competitors and rivals so that editorial comment and news reports can—regularly or promptly—be compared, verified and validated. A press monopoly is incompatible with the free press."), these figures tell public relations writers that more and more releases are going to a shrinking number of newspapers, with less and less editorial space available. Thus, the ability to write as well or better than staff reporters becomes a necessity, not a luxury, in the PR business.

And if all that isn't disheartening enough, the average reader of the New York *Times* spends about 20 minutes reading it. Average reading time devoted to other newspapers must be considerably less.

## PRESS ETHICS

Checkbook journalism, advertising to back up use of editorial matter, freebies for the print and broadcast media, reporters masquerading in pursuit of stories, and the growth of nakedly subjective "news" are some of the current internal ethical problems of the news media. Many of the present concerns of editors, publishers, and station managers are related to the activities and interests of those in the business of public relations.

Checkbook journalism, by and large, is not one of the mutual concerns. Some of the media, notably television, have fallen into the habit of substituting corporate funds for imagination, ingenuity, and perspicacity on the part of their news gathering staffs. Most of these efforts—at the least the publicized ones—have been less than a roaring journalistic success. The television networks denied they were buying news, and promised not to do it again.

In early 1976 print and broadcast media had a field day with a variation on checkbook journalism. *Esquire* magazine, the Xerox Corporation, and Harrison E. Salisbury (a former New York *Times* editor) entered into what appeared to be a cozy three-way arrangement holding out the prospect of benefits to perhaps everyone but the public. The facts, which were never in dispute:

1. Salisbury was to be paid $55,000 by Xerox to write a lengthy article, "Travels Through America." Of the total, $15,000 was to cover the former editor's expenses for gathering raw material for the article.

2. *Esquire* would get the article, at no cost, to run in its February 1976 issue.

3. Xerox additionally committed itself to buy $115,000 in advertising space in *Esquire* during the remainder of 1976.

4. Xerox could not dictate Salisbury's treatment of the subject, or exercise

any editorial judgment over content, but the company reserved the right to pull out of the deal, including the $115,000 ad package, if it didn't like the finished piece. The author still got his $55,000 writing fee, and *Esquire* got the article.

In the glare of the attendant publicity the deal finally fell apart, hastened perhaps by comments such as those by E. B. White (of *Elements of Style* fame) in the Ellsworth, Maine, *American:*

> . . . it doesn't take a giant intellect to detect in all of this the shadow of disaster. If magazines decide to farm out their writers to advertisers and accept the advertiser's payment to the writer and the magazine, then the periodicals in this country will be . . . indistinguishable from the controlled press in other parts of the world.[3]

Some professed to see little difference between the *Esquire* agreement and corporate sponsorship of radio and television programs. Others, more skeptical or less charitable, wondered about the future possibility of self-interest creeping into such sponsored journalism—especially if the sponsor and publication had less integrity than the principals in this case.

The Professional Standards Committee of the Associated Press Managing Editors Association looked into the can of worms called press ethics and conflict of interest a few years ago. Questionnaires were sent to more than 900 newspaper managing editors and to all members of the Public Relations Society of America, seeking comments on press freeloading. Almost a fifth of the PR people said they provided things of value to news people: 31 percent because the press expects it; 15 percent because the press solicits them; 35 percent because favorable coverage results; 15 percent because their competitors do it; and the remaining 4 percent to avoid unfavorable publicity.

The editors' responses generally paralleled those from public relations consultants. Two-thirds of the editors who answered will accept free trips; half accept expense-paid trips overseas; and three-fourths would not rule out accepting gifts. Acceptable limits for the gifts' value ranged from $2.50 to $25. Ten percent said they accept ads with the condition that a reporter will write a favorable piece about the advertiser. We make no judgments on the results of this survey—but do point out that the answers above are all from *editors* (who are the bosses of reporters) and suggest that freebies be dispensed carefully or not at all. Reporters and editors are not all that underpaid these days.

The ethical concerns of a reporter's obligation to identify herself or himself in pursuit of a story *could* be a PR concern if the masquerade is directed at one of your clients. Most media executives decry the practice—sometimes during undercover forays by their news people. The *Washington Star* approves of reporters adopting cover identities when that is the "only" way to obtain information the public is entitled to have. And who decides in such cases? The Star's editors, of course. Pulitzer prizes have been showered on writers of clandestinely gathered articles.

This particular journalistic anomoly would not justify public consideration or concern were it not for the hard-line stance taken by most news people against the occasional police officer who poses as a reporter while gathering information about criminal activities—or the Central Intelligence Agency employee operating under a journalistic cover. There seem to be different sauces for geese and ganders.

## PRESS CONFERENCES

Press releases go into press kits which are distributed during press conferences. That's tradition—and we don't fool with tradition. Except that at least half of all press conferences should never be held; the true figure for unnecessary gatherings of the PR and press clans may be closer to 75 percent.

Press conferences are one of the created events discussed in Chapter 7. The conference may be called in conjunction with a larger created event, such as a groundbreaking or a dedication, or it may be held in a company boardroom, a conference room, or a hotel ballroom. There are no hard and fast rules to tell you when or how to call and hold a press conference—other than you'd better have something important to say or show for the occasion that couldn't have been handled just as well by visits to the media represented.

## PRESS KITS

Bad-to-average press kits are to be found in every PR office and newsroom. To illustrate the subject in a positive way we'll deal with one press kit that was professionally written and assembled. More important, it resulted in excellent press coverage. We're indebted to Janet Rouse, who handled press publicity for the designer of the George C. Page Museum in Los Angeles, for our example. The cover of the press kit is shown in Figure 10-2.

Figure 10-3 is the cover of the *Los Angeles Times* magazine, *Home,* for March 6, 1977, featuring three color photographs of the Page Museum. The article inside, ''The Thrill of Discovery,'' got $3\frac{1}{2}$ pages (2 in color) for photos and a description of the project. The architects, Thornton & Fagan, AIA and Associates, are mentioned early in the story.

What goes into a successful press kit? The first sheet in the Page Museum folder is an index of the kit's contents:

1. Museum Dedication
2. Quotable Quotes
3. George C. Page Biography
4. Rancho La Brea History
5. Captain G. Allan Hancock
6. Architects: Thornton & Fagan
7. Exhibits
8. Acknowledgments

The museum, a branch of the Los Angeles Museum of Natural History, is located on the Wilshire Boulevard site of the famous La Brea Tar Pits. The

ARCHITECTS: THORNTON, FAGAN, A.I.A., AND ASSOCIATES • PHOTOGRAPHY: DAVID GATLEY • COPY BY: TIMOTHY BRANNING • PRESS/GUEST KIT GRAPHICS: © THORNTON, FAGAN, INC., 1977 ALL RIGHTS RESERVED.

**Figure 10-2. Press kit cover for the dedication of the George C. Page Museum in Los Angeles.**

## A Museum Is Born

Since 1913, the fossils from Rancho La Brea
have been an integral part of the Los Angeles
County Museum of Natural History, thanks largely
to the foresight and interests of George Allan
Hancock who originally owned the land.
A dream of Captain Hancock, as well as museum
directors for the past sixty-four years, has been the
development of a museum in which the mounted
fossil skeletons could be displayed at the site
of their discovery, and the story of Rancho La
Brea properly told.

George C. Page, museum patron, has long shared
that dream and is responsible for the funding of
a museum structure. Construction began in the
Spring of 1975 . . . . . . . . . . .

Figure 10-3. Color photographs of the Page Museum were featured on the cover of the *Los Angeles Times* magazine *Home* in connection with the opening of the museum.

dedication release is two pages in length. "Quotable Quotes" is a single page of comments—all are good and quotable. The Page biography, at eight pages, might be judged overly long. But Mr. Page does have an interesting personal and business background—and he *did* donate the $3.5 million required to design and build the museum.

On a 1-to-10 scale, the Page Museum press kit rates a 9.

## PRESS RELEASES – GOOD, BAD, AND INDIFFERENT

As proof that the quality of press releases is uneven at best, let's look at the opening paragraphs of some releases selected at random—much as they might arrive on an editor's desk. The excerpts are verbatim, warts and all.

### NURSE DOES RESIDENCY IN HOSPITAL ADMINISTRATION AT AN ARCHITECTURAL FIRM

Carolyn Kever has the distinction of being the only member of her class in hospital administration at UC Berkeley to be doing her six months of required residency at an architectural firm rather than a hospital.

A candidate for a masters degree in the School of Public Health, Carolyn received special permission for this first of its kind residency because of her desire to be a hospital consultant and because she is already familiar with hospital routine, having worked as a nurse for nine years.

These are the first two paragraphs of an eight-paragraph release from the San Francisco architectural firm of Stone, Marraccini and Patterson. Is the headline an interest-creating one (a "grabber")? Does it convey the uniqueness of Nurse Kever's residency? Would many nonCalifornia-based editors know that "UC" in the first paragraph means University of California? Is this version any stronger?

### QUICK NURSE, THE T-SQUARE— HOSPITAL RESIDENCY IN AN ARCHITECTURAL OFFICE

San Francisco (July 30)—Nurse Carolyn Kever is meeting the six-month residency requirement for a master's degree in hospital administration by working in a San Francisco architectural office.

Miss Kever won faculty permission from the University of California at Berkeley's School of Public Health for this first-of-a-kind residency because she wants to become a hospital consultant—and, as a nine-year veteran of nursing, she knows hospital routine.

Try your own hand at rewriting this and the following examples—to tighten, clarify, and make them more interesting. Here's the lead of a release from the public relations department of the AFL-CIO:

The AFL-CIO today urged the Senate Commerce Committee to recommend repassage of the no-fault auto insurance bill passed by the Senate during the last Congress, which died in the House, but with three important changes.

If you're confused about what died in the House, the bill or the last Congress, it's understandable. The position of the phrase, "but with three important changes," does nothing to help the awkward sentence construction. This rewrite is clearer in meaning, if not exactly inspired writing:

> The AFL-CIO today urged the Senate Commerce Committee to recommend passage of the no-fault insurance bill, with thee important changes. After being passed by the Senate in the last Congress, the bill died in the House.

We find no fault with the headline or lead paragraphs of this release from Litton Industries:

### GENERAL CREIGHTON W. ABRAMS
### HONORS FOUR ARMY ROTC CADETS

> Washington, D.C., Nov. 26—Four outstanding Reserve Officer Training Corps cadets received the 1973 Army ROTC Leadership Award from Army Chief of Staff General Creighton W. Abrams in ceremonies today at the Pentagon.
>
> Three of the winners were top honor graduates of their respective ROTC advanced summer camps; the fourth was top honor graduate of the ROTC class at the Army Ranger School, Fort Benning, Ga. .

In case you are curious, Litton's involvement is explained on page two; the president of Litton Data Systems division gave awards of $625 in savings bonds to each of the winners.

The PR people at the National Aeronautics and Space Administration usually turn out an excellent product, but this 1973 release shows that no one's perfect.

### JPL HOST TO INTERNATIONAL COLLOQUIUM ON MARS

> Four hundred space scientists from 10 countries will meet on the campus of the California Institute of Technology and at the Jet Propulsion Laboratory from Nov. 28 to Dec. 1 for an International Colloquium on Mars.

Counting the headline, "colloquium" is used seven times in the four-page release. For those whose native language is Latin, colloquium would pose no problem. It means meeting and is not in the average reader's vocabulary. Other useful synonyms include congress, council, conclave, assembly, convention, conference, session, synod, convocation, gathering, and union. (After you figured out what a colloquium is, were you relieved to find it was *about* rather than *on* Mars, as the headline implies?)

It's OK to say you're good in a release, but public back-patting can be overdone. How do you feel about this release?

### ELLERBE DRAWS ON 63 YEARS OF EXPERIENCE
### TO MOVE INTO FIELDS BEYOND ARCHITECTURE

> Ellerbe, the firm whose 63 years of experience in architecture, engineering and planning gave rise to Appletree Square, ranks as one of the country's leading practitioners in its field.
>
> Long a leader in the design of commercial, educational and medical facilities, the firm recently stepped to the forefront of a movement that extends beyond arcitecture. Ellerbe's part in this movement, for instance, gave birth to Landmark Development Corporation, the firm's real estate subsidiary.
>
> With the belief that the architect is the natural leader of the design-construction team, L. Kenneth Mahal, Ellerbe president, has within recent time guided the firm on this course.

While the architect is a key element in Ellerbe's international practice, he has since been increasingly supplemented by specialists in finance, master planning, land research and development, construction management, operations analysis, landscape and interior design, and other fields. The purpose is to provide the team necessary to cope with all the complexities of today's building and development programs, as well as to sustain a continuous growth in a more competitive market.

The remainder of the three-page release is in similar language. The final paragraph commits the sin of internal disagreement in numbers:

Mahal, who has headed the firm the past year and a half, is one of four principals. The others, all vice presidents who direct specific phases of the practice, are Robert F. Jacobsen, construction administration; Malcolm L. Neitz, electrical engineering; Donald G. Nelson, medical facilities; and William R. Shannon, Jr., branch operations.

Mahal obviously is one of *five* principals.

This next example of a lead is from a release sent out by the New York public relations firm of Richard Weiner, Inc., on behalf of an architectural client. The release was undated, but a transmittal letter is dated December 21, 1977.

The new Hyatt Regency New York constructed on the site of and utilizing the structure of the former Commodore Hotel located at the bustling Forty-second Street/Grand Central Station area, will give New York City its finest new convention hotel facility. The exterior design of the new Hotel consists of mirrored bronze-tinted glass with dark bronze mullions forming a skin over the existing masonry construction and reflecting the adjacent Grand Central Station, Chrysler and Bowery Savings Bank buildings. Below the third level, large areas of clear glass between cylindrical columns expose the activity of the Hotel public areas to views from the street. Acting as a dramatic symbol of the Hotel will be the Garden Room, a cantileavered glazed structure over the Forty-second Street sidewalk.

The lead paragraph is 129 words; the longest paragraph in the four-page release has 180 words. Throughout the release common nouns are capitalized haphazardly. Hotel is sometimes capped, sometimes not. Perhaps the most glaring error is the spelling of cantilevered as "cantileavered." (It appears twice in the story as cantileavered.)

In the third paragraph the writer notes " . . . the hotel will contain a variety of extensive space . . ." At another point: "A special aspect of [the mezzanine level] will be the inclusion of a taxi drop-off from the Park Avenue ramp over Grand Central Station." Aside from the awkward phraseology, anyone familiar with the old Hotel Commodore knows that there has *always* been a "taxi dropoff" at the Park Avenue ramp entrance.

## OTHER OUTLETS

So far in this chapter the emphasis has been on writing and placing articles in newspapers. Many of the same considerations, approaches, and techniques hold true for working with magazines. No one seems to know for certain, but some industry estimates place the number of commercial, regularly published magazines at more than 20,000. That figure does not include some 2400 trade (business and professional) journals published in the United States—with an aggregate circulation of perhaps 65 million.

McGraw-Hill is the largest publisher of trade magazines in the world, with publications ranging from *Medical World News* to *House and Home*. Some of the trades from various publishers whose names should be familiar to those in design and construction include *Progressive Architecture, Architectural Record, Building Design and Construction, Consulting Engineer,* and *Engineering News-Record.* Business magazines also include public relations periodicals such as those produced by Standard Oil of Indiana, DuPont, Dames & Moore, Kodak, and the airlines. Some of these began as strictly in-house magazines and developed into external publications.

Mention was made of Piedmont Airlines' in-flight magazine *PACE* in Chapter 4. Airline magazines have become a big business in the past 10 years, and publishing conglomerates such as the Webb Company (TWA's *Ambassador,* Northwest's *Passages*) and East/West Network (United's *Mainliner,* Delta's *Sky,* and several others) have largely taken over the lucrative in-flight magazine business. Attractive (to advertisers) upscale demographic analysis of the readers includes:

- 56 percent between the ages of 25 and 49
- 74 percent attended college
- 55 percent are professionals or managers
- 67 percent are male
- median annual income is $27,000 (1977)

With all of this going for the in-flights, they are a logical target for PR articles. Editors of these publications want thought-provoking, timely, topical articles aimed at business executives. Most of the material is from professional free-lance writers, which is one place to start.

## FREE-LANCE COSTS

Free-lance writers work on no long-term commitment to any editor or publication. Should you have an occasion to employ a freelancer to write a speech, the text for a brochure, or an article for a magazine, these examples of writing fee ranges from the October 1977 *Writer's Digest* may be helpful.

| | | |
|---|---|---|
| Annual report | to 3000 words | $750–3000 |
| Film script | 10–12 minutes | 500–1500 |
| Facilities brochure | 12–16 pages | 750–1250 |
| In-house magazine | per 12-page issue | 250–750 |
| Press release | 1–2 pages | 50–75 |
| Special news article | per 1000 words | 150–300 |
| Sales brochure | 12–16 pages | 500–1500 |
| Speech* | 10–15 minutes | 200–600 |

*At an average delivery of 130 words per minute, this would cover 1,300–1,950 words—a per-word cost range of 10 to 46 cents

The free-lance writer's words, from this price list, are worth anywhere from a dime to a dollar each, depending on the subject, use, schedule, and the writer's reputation and bargaining skills. Add from 5 to 10 percent a year to these figures to allow for inflation since 1977.

## SIGNED COLUMNS

A few design professionals have taken advantage of the publicity mileage offered by signed columns in newspapers and magazines. Signed columns on a wide variety of subjects are growing in popularity because readers want free expert advice. But a regular column by an architect, for example, does not have to be about house design or construction. James T. Potter, AIA, of

Figure 10-4. Architect James C. Potter has had a weekly column, featuring details and general views of Madison buildings, in the *Wisconsin State Journal* since 1969.

PAGE 4, SECTION 6          WISCONSIN STATE JOURNAL, SUNDAY, SEPTEMBER 19, 1976

## Have you seen this Madison?

A windmill used to be mounted in this tower atop King Hall on the University of Wisconsin-Madison campus, and was used for some of the first research on wind power. The building has an overall Tudor style and was constructed in the early 1890s. Ornate brick work is visible on the tower and curved, decorative fascia highlight the wall dormer on the tower. The building is named after Franklin Hiram King, a UW professor for 22 years and inventor of the round silo, barn ventilators and mechanical soil analysis.

— *Photo by James Potter, A.I.A.*

Potter Lawson and Pawlowsky, Inc., in Madison, Wisconsin, has gotten a lot of good exposure through his weekly *Wisconsin State Journal* feature, "Have You Seen This Madison?" Potter explains how it works:

> I photograph whatever interests me around the city; then a reporter writes the captions after I tell him what interests me about the picture.
>
> The feature grew out of a talk I give with the same title. During the talk I ask questions of the audience about my slides of downtown Madison. They always flunk! One day I showed the slides to the editors of the *Journal* and they flunked, too. That's how they decided to run the series.
>
> The feature has a surprisingly large following even in other parts of the state because the Sunday *Journal* covers Wisconsin. People often tell me they look for the picture each week, cover the caption, and try to guess what it is.

The weekly Potter photo feature has been running since August 31, 1969. Figure 10-4 shows one of his Madison mystery views.

One point to keep in mind about weekly or monthly signed columns—be reasonably sure you can maintain a high, professional level of worthwhile, interesting subject matter, once an editor buys your idea.

## RELEASES FROM NONPROFESSIONALS

Admittedly, much of the material in Chapter 9 and thus far in this chapter has been aimed at those who want to submit interest-provoking, professional-in-appearance news releases to the print and broadcast media. If you have neither the time nor the motivation to train yourself to be a professional news writer there is an alternative available to anyone with a newsworthy item and the ability to distill information into short, factual statements.

The alternative is a fact sheet; by means of which you submit only the important points of a story to an editor, who can turn it over to a reporter for conversion into a standard story.

If you go to the fact sheet route be sure to so label the submission. Always include your name and a telephone number where you can be reached in the likely event the reporter will want more details or verification of some point. Double space the fact sheet as you would a regular release.

There is no particular format for fact sheets, and they will vary somewhat by subject, but the following might be used as a guide for a building dedication fact sheet:

### BUILDING DEDICATION

*Project:* Office building
*Owner:*
    ABC Enterprises, Inc
    Sam Smith, President
    1400 East Main Avenue
    Putnam City, California 90000

*Project location:*
 200 North Anne St.
 Putnam City, California 90001
*Size of project:*
 20-story building, 100 × 200 ft
 400,000 gross sq ft
 250 underground parking spaces
*Architect:*
 Rhine, Hold & Jones
 300 West Main Avenue
 Putnam City, California 90000
*Consultants:*
 Spark, Watts & Fann (mechanical-electrical)
  100 Volta Place
  Hamletville, California 90002
 Standt-Strait Engineers (structural)
  200 Beverly Drive
  Putnam City, California 90000
 Goode, Earthey & Treeze (landscape architect)
  150 W. Endy St.
  Deenan, California 90003
*Contractor:*
 Over, Runn & Changling, Inc. (general)
 200 W. Endy St.
 Deenan, California 90003
*Construction started:*
 July 1977
*Construction completed:*
 January 1979
*Dedication time and date:*
 10:30 a.m., February 2, 1979
 (At the site)
*Program speakers:*
 Arthur M. Troops, California Lt. Governor
 Sam Smith, President, ABC Enterprises, Inc.
 Nadine O'Malley, President, Putnam City Chamber of Commerce
*Contact:*
 Diane Creason
 Rhine, Hold & Jones
 Telephone: 215-555-4120

This would suffice for transmitting basic information. A brief description of the building, its cost, some of the design rationale (in lay terms), and any special features (energy conservation measures, unusual materials used, unique design or engineering solutions, construction problems faced, and the like) are other points for possible inclusion in a fact sheet or to accompany it as an enclosure. Obviously, a release on anything about a project should always be cleared by and coordinated with the client. Include one or more photographs, with captions, with the fact sheet.

In deciding what and how much to include in a fact sheet keep in mind the four basic tests for newsworthiness: (1) timeliness, (2) interest, (3) value, and (4) proximity.

The same fact sheet approach works equally well with all types of magazines and with most broadcast media.

## References

[1]Charles Long, "Editor's Notes," *The Quill,* November 1975, p. 2.

[2]Max Kerstein, "Selectivity: Key to the 'Trades,' " *Public Relations Journal,* August 1975, p. 26.

[3]E. B. White, letter in the Ellsworth, Maine, *American,* Jan. 1, 1976, section 2, p. 1. Quotation from letter reprinted in an editorial in the Washington *Star,* Jan. 13, 1976.

Photography, as a fine art, can evoke in the viewer human feelings, sentiment, a sense of place and even passions. Moreover, by influencing the intellect as well as the emotions, photographs can move people to action.[1]

# CHAPTER 11
# Photography

DESIGN CAN BE broken down into seven components:

| | |
|---|---|
| Line | Texture |
| Direction | Value |
| Size | Color |
| Shape | |

Photography, in addition to the seven design components, must take these factors into account:

| | |
|---|---|
| Variety | Action |
| Unity | Dramatic impact |
| Human interest | Composition |

Composition, as we pointed out in *How to Prepare Professional Design Brochures,* has seven contributing principles of its own:

| | |
|---|---|
| Balance | Unity |
| Proportion | Clarity |
| Rhythm | Simplicity |
| Movement | |

## SIMPLICITY ABOVE ALL

If one had to pick the key to positive visual communication from among all of these factors, elements, and principles, it would be simplicity.

Hurley and McDougall, in *Visual Impact in Print*, suggest an oath for picture-handlers, which begins, "I will not mortise, tilt, mutilate, scallop, cookie-cut. . . ." Some examples of the offenses committed in the name of uniqueness include symbols superimposed on photos (clocks, exclamation marks, globes); shaping pictures in letter forms to spell out headlines; and forcing pictures into preexisting shapes (bowling balls, wheels, sacks, and musical notes)—all of which are a distortion of the photographer's vision to suit the picture-handler's vanity.[2]

## A BRIEF PHOTO GLOSSARY

While glossaries usually appear at the end of a chapter or a book, I believe this one will be more helpful as we get into our subject of photography.

**aperture**  The lens opening through which light passes. Expressed as a fraction of the lens focal length, or f-number, the size of the opening influences the depth of field.

**ASA index**  A standard for rating the sensitivity of film to light and for comparing film speeds. A film with an ASA number, or rating, of 250 is twice as fast (twice as sensitive to light) as a film with a rating of 125. ASA stands for American Standards Association.

**available light**  Also referred to as existing light, the natural nighttime or indoor low-intensity illumination.

**blocking**  Highlights in a negative so overexposed or overdeveloped that no detail is visible.

**bulb**  Referring to a "B" setting on some camera shutter speed dials, it allows the shutter to remain open as long as the shutter release is depressed.

**contrast**  In a black-and-white print, the gradation of tones from black to white.

**cropping**  Selecting part of the negative for printing.

**depth of field**  The zone in front of and behind the subject or object focused on, within which other objects appear equally sharp to the human eye.

**diaphragm**  An adjustable hole, or aperture, to control the amount of light passing through a lens to strike the film. The openings are expressed as f-stops. Small lens stops such as f/16 and f/22 offer great depth of field and overall sharpness. Larger f-stops (f/1.4 and f/2.8) reduce the depth of field and allow photographs to be made with less light.

**exposure**  The amount of light allowed to strike the sensitized surface of the film; a function of the f-stop opening and shutter speed.

**film speed**  Sensitivity of the film to light. Rated in ASA numbers.

**filter**    A colored transparent material placed over the lens to adjust color rendition or contrast.

**filter factor**    The number of times a normal exposure should be increased to compensate for the reduced light admitted by a filter.

**focal length**    Distance from lens to film when focused on infinity. The "normal" focal length of a lens depends on the film area covered, and will approximate the diagonal of the film size. Normal focal length of a 35-mm camera lens is 50 mm.

**focus**    Adjustment of the lens-to-film distance to create a sharp image of the subject.

**holography**    a lensless photographic technique for producing three-dimensional images of physical objects. Light beams (lasers) reconstruct the images from coded film strips or plates.

**interchangeable lens**    A lens that can be removed from the camera body and replaced by another lens of a different speed or focal length.

**latitude**    The degree to which a film may be over or underexposed without noticeable loss of image quality. Color film has very little latitude.

**overexposure**    The result of letting too much light reach the film, caused by too large a lens opening or too slow a shutter speed—or a combination of the two.

**parallax**    Difference between the image seen in the viewfinder and that recorded on film. Parallax is most noticeable at close distances.

**shutter**    A mechanical device that regulates the amount of light striking the film. Fast shutter speeds freeze action and tend to override camera movement during exposure.

**shutter speed**    The length of time the shutter remains open, usually from 1/1000 of a second to 1 or 2 seconds.

**stop down**    To reduce the size of the aperture.

**wide-angle lens**    Lens of short focal length which allows coverage of a greater field than a normal lens.

## HINTS FROM THE PROS

Even if you don't plan to shoot your own photographs for the planned brochure, newsletter, or annual report, these are all pointers you should know by rote.

1. Know your photographic equipment—how to use it and its limitations. If you have to stop and think about f-stops, apertures, and film speeds, you may miss a vital shot. Your equipment should be an extension of yourself, not an encumbering mechanical monster that overrides technique.

2. Strive to establish a point of view every time you aim the camera.

3. Don't think only in terms of a single photograph. The subject may be better covered by a photo series.

4. Mix long, medium, and close-up shots: long shots to show the entire subject, proportion it, and relate it to its environment; medium shots to

Figure 11-1. This is the original White House photograph which was cropped to give Figure 11-2. The straight line of the five heads is rather static and the separation of the figures is distracting, as is the fact that they are not all looking at the model.

show some detail; and close-ups to clarify important aspects of the subject.

5. Be alert to distracting backgrounds, crooked horizons, fuzzy foregrounds (unless planned that way), and leaning buildings.

6. For normal and wide-angle lenses don't shoot a handheld camera at a slower speed than the fraction of 1 over the focal length of the lens in use. To avoid camera shake, don't use a 50-mm lens at shutter speeds slower than 1/50 of a second.

7. Explore effects of sidelighting and backlighting the subject. Use a lens hood and an increase of one to two f-stops over the light meter indication.

8. Vary camera angles. All eye- or waist-level shots can be monotonous. Shoot down—from a chair, a table, a stepladder, the top of a staircase. Shoot up—from ground or knee level.

9. Compose shots in the smallest possible space. Don't take a group of ten people when two or three of them will tell the story. Avoid groups of more than four as much as possible.

10. Get action into the picture. Life is not static—show people doing things.

Figure 11-2. This tight two-shot of President John F. Kennedy and architect Edward Durell Stone, looking at a model of what was to become the John F. Kennedy Center for the Performing Arts, has considerably more interest and focus than Figure 11-1.

11. Put light subjects against dark backgrounds and vice versa.

12. Film is cheap. Photographers are expensive. Get as many pictures as possible from any assignment. Then pick the best negatives for printing. It is not unusual for a staff photographer for a magazine such as the *National Geographic* to shoot ten 36-exposure rolls of film of a subject, and have one frame from the group selected for the final picture layout.

13. Use a strobe light or flash only when you absolutely must. Natural light is just that—natural.

14. Crop carefully. The best print in the world can be ruined by poor cropping—and a so-so photo can often be improved by creative cropping. (See Figures 11-1 and 11-2.)

15. Know how to use selective focus. No human or natural law requires everything in a picture to be in sharp focus. Faster shutter speeds and wider apertures give the limited depth of field needed for selective focusing, especially in close-up work.

16. Be your own worst critic. Review your work and that of others for good and bad examples. Capitalize on mistakes by not repeating them.

## TECHNIQUE

Lack of composition, unplanned fuzzy focus, and camera movement are an unholy triad that plagues many photographers.

Avoid creating false horizons by looking for verticals and horizontals in the subject—and bring the edges of the viewer parallel with the natural lines of the subject.

Good composition depends on many things—and one of them is not necessarily an expensive camera with a dozen or more interchangeable lenses. Remember the Golden Ratio for locating the four strongest points of a composition. (See Figure 11-3.)

Depth of field is controlled by the focal length of the lens (in millimeters) and the aperture used (measured in f-stops). Smaller apertures indicated by higher f-stop numbers, give greater depth of field. Wide-angle lenses (15- to 35-mm lenses) give the greatest depth of field. A 28-mm medium wide-angle lens, set at f/16 and focused 6 feet in front of the camera, should give sharp detail from 3 feet to infinity. Opening up the same lens to f/11 will reduce the extreme end of the field from infinity to around 25 feet. Naturally, the speed of exposure will have to be increased to compensate for the additional light admitted by the larger f-stop. Telephoto lenses traditionally have shallow depths of field.

Be on the lookout for natural "frames" for your pictures. Frames do not have to appear on all four sides of a photo to be effective. Tree branches, windows, doorways, an open grand piano, a vase of flowers, a stack of books—all these and dozens of other objects can be used to frame and give additional interest to a shot.

When the shutter speed is 1/50 of a second or slower, steadying the camera on something is important. This is particularly so for a telephoto lens, where the slightest camera shake is magnified. Use a tripod, a special camera C-clamp, or a ready-made steadier—a wall, an automobile hood, a tree, or even the ground. A cable release is a useful accessory for telephoto shots. Another solution to the problem of camera movement is, whenever possible, to use a fast shutter speed—1/500 or 1/1000 of a second.

In shooting people the photographer becomes a kind of therapist-director. The subjects must be put at ease, in what is an uneasy situation at best for most people. When serious expressions are wanted, get a discussion going on a serious subject—of at least some general interest—taxes, defense, affairs of state. When smiles are desired tell a funny story—don't command "Smile!" unless you want a frozen slash across the faces.

Get the people you are photographing doing things together—talking, one showing a collection of something to the other, looking at illustrations in a book or magazine, doing something interesting with their hands, and the like. Don't be afraid to use props if they are related in any way to the picture subject. Explain what kind of picture you're trying to make. As the director, you must make the photo happen. And always be on the alert for new ways to show the mundane.

Be aware of the environment. What you see in the viewfinder is what

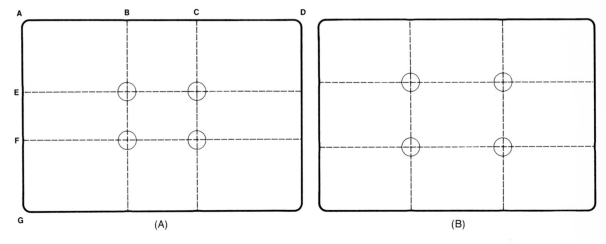

Figure 11-3. (A) Use of the Golden Ratio (0.38:0.62::0.62:1) to locate compositional strong points. Each of the four intersections within the viewing frame is an equally strong location for the main subject of the photograph. The viewing frame is in the 3:2 proportions of a 35-mm frame. If *AD* is 6 inches, then *AB* will be 2¼ inches (0.38 × 6). When *AG* is 4 inches, *AE* will be 1½ inches. Locate the grid points along the edges of the frame, then connect across. (B) Some professional photographers use a simpler "rule of thirds" grid, in which the picture area is divided into nine *equal* squares. As in the Golden Ratio grid, place the subject on one of the four intersections—looking or moving into the center of the picture. As a general rule, when subjects are placed to the left of center, with interest or movement to the right indicated, the picture will be more pleasing to most viewers. When subjects appear to be moving out of the picture, or coming into it from the right, it does not appear natural to viewers and creates a certain amount of tension.

you'll get, including telephone poles sprouting out of heads, unwanted shadows on faces, messy or cluttered foregrounds, busy backgrounds—even the photographer's shadow creeping into the bottom of the picture.

Be careful of all lines in a photo. To avoid the appearance of horizons cutting pictures in half, place the horizon line high or low in the shot. Lines running into a photo—tracks, fences, roads, shadows, stacks of hay, roof and building edges—can be used to draw attention to the subject. Lines from lower left to upper right generally give strength and direction to the composition—and add interest and unity to the overall effect.

Use people to give photographs an added dimension. Figures in the foreground increase the feeling of size and depth by giving scale to the scene. People can also add action to otherwise static pictures.

## THE CAMERA *CAN* LIE

Wide-angle and telephoto lenses can be used to propagandize and distort a scene. You want a picture of a school board or town meeting to illustrate a story. Instead of the expected packed meeting room it is less than half full. By

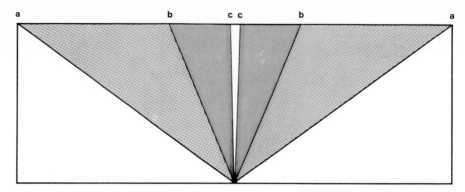

Figure 11-4. Relative coverage of a 15-mm extremely wide-angle lens ($a-a$); a normal 50-mm lens ($b-b$); and the 800-mm extremely long telephoto lens ($c-c$).

## Lens Coverage Chart

| Lens focal length, mm | Angle of coverage, degrees | Description |
| --- | --- | --- |
| 15 | 100 | Extremely wide-angle |
| 20 | 94 | Very wide-angle |
| 24 | 84 | Very wide-angle |
| 28 | 74 | Medium wide-angle |
| 35 | 62 | Wide-angle |
| 50 | 46 | Normal |
| 55 | 43 | Normal |
| 85 | 28 | Telephoto |
| 105 | 23 | Telephoto |
| 135 | 18 | Medium long telephoto |
| 180 | 13 | Medium long telephoto |
| 200 | 12 | Long telephoto |
| 300 | 9 | Long telephoto |
| 400 | 7 | Long telephoto |
| 600 | 5 | Very long telephoto |
| 800 | 3 | Extremely long telephoto |

his or her choice of lens the photographer can make the room look practically empty, half full, or jammed almost to overflowing.

By use of a wide-angle lens, emphasizing sections of empty seats, the photographer can spread the people who came thinly enough to justify the statement that "Only a few showed up for the meeting."

Switching to a telephoto lens, which might give only a 9- to 12-degree angle of coverage (see Figure 11-4 and table), and shooting from the right location, a photographer could make it appear that every seat was filled.

A normal lens (50- to 55-mm for a 35-mm camera) would result in a picture nearer the truth—a room half-filled.

## HANDSHAKE AND HANDOFF SHOTS

As in groundbreaking photographs, there are few new worlds left to conquer in the realm of shots showing new officers taking over, congratulatory situations, retirements, and presentations of things—gavels, plaques, checks, certificates, and the like.

Here are a few possibilities—some perhaps overworked; others still somewhat unusual.

### Handshakes

• Shoot a normal handshake from a high (at least head height) or low (ankle or floor height) level. Or even from directly overhead.

• While shaking hands, one puts arm on the right shoulder of other.

• New officer faces camera, retiring officer has back to camera. Shoot on about a 45-degree angle from the person with back to the camera.

• Both people have backs to the camera; heads turned in profile.

• Frame the handshakers with a doorway, furniture, window, building edge, tree limb, or piece of equipment. Remember, a photographic "frame" does not have to be four-sided to be effective.

• Stand the handshakers in front of a painting, statue, or a piece of appropriate equipment. Open the lens wide so the short depth of field will fuzz out the background prop.

• Have the pair touch wine glasses or beer mugs instead of shaking hands.

• Show them just before they touch each other's hands—the process before it's complete.

• Have one sit on a chair, table, or desk, while the other stands or leans over to shake hands.

• Instead of a handshake, have one hold the other's right arm high, as in a boxing ring victor's sign.

• Have the retiring officer use a prop sword to "knight" the incoming officer.

• Show the retiring officer handing a gavel to the incoming officer.

### Handoffs

• When the surface of a presentation plaque is reflective and large enough, show the recipient's face mirrored in the plaque (shoot over one shoulder).

• Use jumbo replicas of the object handed off—checks, plaques, gavels, and keys.

• Use stacks of money equivalent to the amount of a check. Show the donor pushing the money across a desk to the donee.

• As with handshakes, try for unusual angles—high, low, from the back.

• Pose a check handoff shot in front of a bank vault door.

• Show whatever is handed off in an insert or smaller accompanying photo, rather than being handed from one person to another.

## SELECTING AND WORKING WITH PHOTOGRAPHERS

Morton Tadder, the Baltimore-based commercial and architectural photographer, gave this advice to members of a marketing workshop I conducted a few years ago:

> In choosing a photographer, one of the ways by which you can distinguish quickly the type of photographic firm you're dealing with is simply to look at the tangible results of the photographic product. One of the prerequisites, especially for progress photography, is cleanliness in the area photographed. It is the responsibility of the photographer to come back to the client with pictures that are clear of empty cartons, coffee cups, and general debris. [See Figure 11-5.]
>
> In some instances a certain amount of litter is unavoidable, but with a little planning and effort it is relatively easy to have clean photographs. No matter what a client is paying, he has the right to expect this. Along the same line, photographs should be free of dust spots, clutter, or anything else that detracts from the overall design of the building or project. The finished print should be submitted on double-weight paper with half-inch margins to give editors the necessary space in which to mark cropping directions.
>
> A philosophy that accepts mediocrity rather than insisting on the optimum is responsible for the poor, non-productive photographs that generally dominate public relations and advertising in the architectural and engineering fields. At least 75 percent of the releases in business publications are a waste of space, time, and advertising dollars—and the client's marketing program is done a disservice as a result.
>
> Sharing responsibility with the prevalent philosophy of mediocrity in architectural and engineering public relations are the penny-pitching photo budgets authorized by some managements. Too many design professionals are using inept and lazy photographers who take pictures just good enough to get by.
>
> Thirty-eight out of a hundred people who are stopped by an illustration will read the entire text according to a recent survey. Obviously, the mediocre or static photograph that fails to stop the reader and get him into the text or advertisement nullifies all the work and expense that went into producing and placing the release. Economizing on photography, which at its best is only a fraction of the public relations budget, is utterly wasteful. Photography can make or break any release.
>
> The PR director has a right to expect just about what he and his agency or company are willing to pay for. If he pays for an outstanding photograph, then he should demand photographic perfection. A good photograph, regardless of the subject matter, should create excitement which draws attention to the product or service, the message, and the company—by being believable, by picturing an authentic situation with human interest, action, and real people; who may be posed but don't look it.
>
> The PR director can avoid poor photographs by refusing to accept pictures that are only adequate, and by knowing enough about photography and about his picture requirements to engage a good photographer, give him complete instructions, and, finally, to judge the results against the highest of standards.

After you've located a capable photographer, whose temperament seems to mesh reasonably well with yours, involve her or him in the project. A liberal

Figure 11-5. These two photos by Mort Tadder illustrate the wrong way (top) and the right way to shoot progress photos. A few minutes of preshooting cleanup make a world of difference.

application of equal parts of the Golden Rule, empathy, and treatment as a partner will pay off in getting the pictures and coverage you need.

If the pictures are to illustrate an article or a brochure, let the photographer read the text. And supply a shooting script as a guide to

• The setting. Exactly where are the pictures to be made—indoors or outdoors—what sort of background is desirable; what are the lighting conditions apt to be found indoors? If it's to be a series shot in a plant, arrange a tour of familiarization for the photographer.

• The people. Who are the individuals to be shown? Do they know they're apt to be photographed so their attire will be proper for the occasion? Schedule shots of executives and top managers to avoid unnecessary loss of time from jobs.

• The action. The photographer must have some idea of what you want the subjects to be doing in pictures. You should make certain that everyone involved has been notified of the schedule. Be sure all plant areas and machinery that may be shown are clean and orderly. (A good photographer will do this, as Mort Tadder pointed out, but it's apt to be an expensive cleanup.)

• Special effects. Unusual or technical composition details should be outlined in the shooting script.

Don't regard a shooting script as carved in stone. At least some of your original ideas will have to be modified or adapted to conditions at the scene. A few may have to be dropped entirely. But at least the photographer starts out with a fair idea of what is needed and expected.

In addition to the above points, the photographer will need to know

• The budget. Daily fees, allowable travel expenses, and the photographer's charges for extras, should be agreed upon early in the relationship. This includes legal matters such as who gets model releases signed, custody and ownership of negatives, and reproduction rights.

• Which shots are "musts."

• When contact sheets are needed, how many, and in what form.

• Who is responsible for getting names, titles, and other caption data.

Carol Lee, a Boston industrial photographer much in demand for business and trade paper and annual report photography, has this advice for her clients:

> Planning, scheduling, briefing—these are the essential ingredients for an effective and efficient working relationship between professional photographers and public relations practitioners. Without them, your photography will most likely be hit or miss. With them, you'll get better photographs, few headaches and probably spend far less money.[3]

## PHOTO SOURCES

Detailed information about nine sources of stock photographs can be found in *How to Prepare Professional Design Brochures* (page 139 and pages

203–206). Here are some others with identified specialties:

H. Armstrong Roberts
420 Lexington Avenue
New York, NY 10017
Advertising and editorial

Culver Pictures
660 First Avenue
New York, NY 10016

Charles Phelps Cushing
51 East 42d Street
New York, NY 10017
Geography, historical, industrial

Ewing Galloway
420 Lexington Avenue
New York, NY 10017
Commercial

Magnum Photos, Inc.
15 West 46th Street
New York, NY 10036

Photo Researchers, Inc.
19 East 51st Street
New York, NY 10022

Names and addresses of the principal stock picture companies can be obtained from

Picture Agency Council of America
520 Fifth Avenue
New York, New York 10022

There are many sources of photographs—some free, many at low cost—among federal agencies and departments in Washington. Besides the National Archives and Records Service, described in *How to Prepare Professional Design Brochures,* they include the Library of Congress, Department of Interior, Department of Defense, and the U.S. Geological Survey. Actually, every government agency maintains a public information office; feel free to query the director of public affairs in any office you believe may have photos of subjects you're interested in.

According to the information officer of the Library of Congress, the library's Photoduplicating Service will copy unrestricted items from the Prints and Photographic Division on request. Requests should refer to specific items in the collection or provide complete information about the subject. Depending on the material's availability, orders can take up to 6 weeks to fill. Cost of an 8 × 10 glossy print will range from $4 to $10.

The National Cartographic Information Center, U.S. Geological Survey, can provide aerial photographs of almost any area of the country. The pictures are taken at varying altitudes, from airplanes at a few thousand feet to orbiting satellites miles above the earth. Color photos are $7; black-and-white shots are $3. If you can furnish latitude and longitude specs for the area you want, fine. Otherwise, outline the area desired on a road map.

The Center can also furnish topographic maps for most sections of the country. Covering from 56 square miles up, 20 × 24 inches in size, the maps sell for $1.25. The U.S. Geological Survey's address is National Center, Reston, Virginia 22092.

If you ever have need for recent pictures of a building or general scene in a foreign country, keep in mind that there is a representative of the International Communications Agency (ICA, formerly the United States Information Service) in practically all U.S. embassies and in many consulate offices. (At last count we had over 125 embassies in capital cities, plus an additional 125 or so consular offices in other cities.)

You should be able to obtain the name of the ICA representative from the Foreign Service List, published by the Government Printing Office in Washington. Then write and ask for names of local photographers they have used and can recommend for your job. If your photo needs are fairly specific and communicated to the foreign city, the ICA representative may arrange for a photographer to fill the assignment and bill you directly.

I used this method several years ago to get new photographs of the U.S. Embassy in New Delhi. For $50 we received several dozen black-and-white 8 × 10s, plus four rolls of 35-mm color (unmounted). If I had commissioned an American photographer for the job, the bill would have come to several thousand dollars—for air transportation, local travel and living expenses, daily fees, and the like.

For names of domestic photographers there are two sources you should be familiar with:

Architectural Photographers Association
222 East 46th Street
New York, New York 10017

Professional Photographers of America
1090 Executive Way
Des Plaines, Illinois 60018

## PHOTO LAYOUT

We agree that this is a subject difficult to cover in a few paragraphs. Our intent is to cover a few of the main principles, hit the more obvious highlights, and recommend that interested readers engage in further self-education with some of the excellent books on the subject listed in the bibliography.

*Impact*, the excellent newsletter on all aspects of communications, carried a brief item on the use of art and photographs in issue number 158:

Simplicity should prevail. Reduce your elements to the bare essentials. Play down the use of meaningless and costly shapes—oblongs, triangles, ovals, silhouettes. And whatever you do stay clear of a variety of shapes on the same spread unless your intent is to create confusion. Some other thoughts:

1. For a dramatic change of pace, crop a picture close, then blow it up for a full-page display.

2. Use art when good pictures are not available or too costly to obtain, or to illustrate abstract subjects that need illustrations but don't lend themselves to photographic treatment.

3. Sometimes a severe vertical or horizontal crop can be an effective eye-stopper. Crop ruthlessly. It moves the reader in close.

4. On your spreads, the size of pictures, the cropping, and the arrangements of illustrations should be varied continually. Be extremely careful if you flop or butt pictures.

5. In the majority of cases when an editor relies on sur-printing over half-tones, the copy can't be read without considerable effort, and the halftone is defaced.

6. Bleeds, like white space, are useful for emphasis. But overused they can become tiresome and monotonous and self-defeating.

7. Cutlines [photo captions] look neater flush left *and* right with halftone edges. It makes cutline writing more difficult, but it's a mark of quality and editorial care.

8. Cutlines should be close to the pictures they describe. The cluster technique may appeal to artists, but it's confusing to readers. For cutline type, light sans serif or italic one size smaller than the body type seems to be preferred by many editors.

9. Line art need not stand alone. It can be reversed in color panels, or given tone shadings within some of the lines. Line art, too, can be overprinted on a photograph by doing one in black, the other in a second color. Or it can be reversed over a dark side of the photo to tie the photo and art closely together in mood.

10. Try for some variety in photo play (but don't overdo!). Some possibilities: silhouettes . . . partial silhouettes . . . geometric shapes . . . rounds and ovals . . . mood shapes (a chemist's flask for a lab story) . . . mortises . . . split illustrations . . . collages . . . montages . . . perspectives (the quest for a three-dimensional effect) . . . line extensions of a halftone . . . repetition in a sequence (the illusion of motion).[4]

We must comment that most of the effects suggested in number 10 should be considered DON'Ts rather than DOs—as Bob Baker himself suggested in the lead-in to the list. In the same issue of *Impact* editor Baker gave seven ways to play a single picture:

1. Split the photograph, horizontally or vertically. Use white space, heads or body copy between the split segments.

2. Use a second color with the picture (duotone).

3. Have the printer shoot for line only. Good for mood shots where identification is unimportant.

4. Use a coarse ben-day screen.

5. Print in a negative, rather than a positive position.

6. Fade-out, de-focus, or eliminate background (air brushing).

7. Send the photo to a studio that specializes in line (photomechanical) effects.[5]

Beyond these points, keep in mind that an effective layout figuratively takes readers by their hands and leads them into and through the pictures and text, while helping them to read or see the entire layout. An effective layout also makes use of the principles of graphic dominance, white space, and alignment—and is consistent internally.

Graphic dominance refers to the "grabber" or "stopper" photo—the picture that interests, stops, and pushes the reader into the page or spread (two facing pages). The grabber may tell a story in itself or pose questions, but it must somehow generate interest. It should be the largest picture in the layout, but is not necessarily the opening or first photo in the layout sequence.

White space is an important, often misunderstood, and frequently misused element of design. The two basic rules for use of white space:

1. Don't trap outsize areas (islands) of white space within the spread. It will destroy any layout effect the designer is after.

2. Excess white space should fall to the outside margins of the page or spread.

Alignment of elements in a layout can be overdone, as we all know. A conscious effort to line up everything results in dull, static, uninteresting layouts. A practice followed by some designers has two of the four sides aligned—perhaps the top and left side—and allows the edges of elements on the remaining two sides to fall where they may (within reason). Our preference is for a three-sided alignment, with excess white space falling off the fourth side.

The principle of internal consistency tells us that approximately equal amounts of white space should separate the prime elements of a layout— copy blocks and photos. A layout rule of thumb holds that photographs in a spread should number at least three and not more than seven. Some designers find it helps to begin a layout by placing the inside pictures first, working out from the gutter. This method almost guarantees you'll use white space properly.

## PHOTO CAPTIONS

Captions (or cutlines if you are a semantic purist in such matters) are for describing and explaining a picture to a reader, in an interesting and accurate way.

The Continuing Study Committee of the Associated Press Managing Editors has compiled "Ten Tests of a Good Caption." See if you agree with the editors.

1. Is it complete?
2. Does it identify fully and clearly?

3. Does it tell when?

4. Does it tell where?

5. Does it tell what's in the picture?

6. Does it have the names spelled correctly, with the proper name on the right person?

7. Is it specific?

8. Is it easy to read?

9. Have as many adjectives as possible been removed?

10. Does it suggest another picture?

And rule number 11, the Cardinal Rule never, never to be violated: NEVER WRITE A CAPTION WITHOUT SEEING THE PICTURE!

## MOTION PICTURES, VIDEOTAPE, HOLOGRAPHY, ET AL.

This is a kind of grab-bag section, highlighting other photographic media with which public relations practitioners should have at least a nodding acquaintance.

Motion picture films for public relations purposes date from 1897, when a whiskey firm and a bicycle manufacturer screened films outdoors in New York City. By 1912 several large corporations, including General Electric, AT&T, and U.S. Steel, were in the sponsored film business. Few are the companies in the current *Fortune* 500 list who do not have some investment in films—films for advertising, public relations, recruiting, training, and even reporting to stockholders and bankers.

Motion pictures and videotape are extremely effective audiovisual media because they can combine movement, language, drama, color, and sound— all of the elements of good communications.

Cost, obviously, is an important consideration of using films for any purpose. One of the first items of cost is the script, which, in turn, determines what most of the other costs will be. Allot 10 to 15 percent of the overall film budget for the script, with another 5 to 10 percent for script polish and production planning. Before a camera has turned, some 25 percent of the budget has been accounted for.

Other costs normally encountered in filmmaking include considerations of format (8-mm, 16-mm, 35-mm; wide or standard screen; in black and white or color), length, the amount of location shooting, graphics, talent fees (including a narrator), special effects, music, and distribution. Experienced producers can estimate total costs very accurately, based on a reading of the final, approved script.

Newcomers to the sponsored film arena often overlook the importance of budgeting for distribution of the finished product. Money must be available for purchasing multiple prints, to pay promotion costs, and to cover all distribution and circulation costs.

To those who feel a need for more knowledge about motion picture production, we'd recommend for first readers the Kodak pamphlet, *Movies With A Purpose* (VI-13). The booklet features single-concept, or "trigger," filmmaking, but the content generally applies to all types of motion pictures. A few tips from *Movies With A Purpose:*

- Variety in scene length is as important as variety in camera position and image size.
- Don't "zoom" if you can do it another way. Try to "cut" instead.
- Start shooting *before* the action begins and continue shooting a few seconds after it ends. (Helpful in editing.)
- Narration should *not* describe the action seen on the screen.

The proper use of optical and special effects (fades, wipes, swish pans, dissolves, superimpositions, and the like) is explained, as are lens and shot selection.

Approaching motion pictures in corporate popularity and ubiquitousness are videotape systems. Portable ½-inch video cassette recorder–playback units are available for well under $1000. A black-and-white television camera adds a few hundred dollars more—or a color camera can be included in the system for $1500 or less. Sixty-minute cassettes list for around $17 and actually sell for a few dollars less. Best of all, the cassettes are reusable, an advantage not offered by conventional motion picture film. The major fly in the videotape ointment is the present lack of compatibility among available systems.

Since, as of this writing, practical holographic applications to photographic processes are rather limited, we'll offer little more than an admonition to keep an eye on holography. There are presently at least two patented holographic processes for making three-dimensional movies. A few exhibits of three-dimensional static images from holographic projectors have caused occasional lay interest—and that's about the size of it to date.

## DOS AND DON'TS

Since a chapter on a subject such as photography is replete with implied DOs and DON'Ts, some readers may feel the inclusion of a separate section ranks with lily-gilding and Newcastle coaling operations. But it is a fast, relatively painless method of presenting a number of pointers and tips not otherwise covered. Some of the tips are based on a 1977 American Consulting Engineers Council memo to members about making color slides of projects in progress and in use.

- In areas where cloud cover is available from time to time, try to shoot on a thinly overcast day when shadows are soft. This yields greater detail in shadow and highlight areas. When cloud cover does not exist, shoot when sunlight spills into the area of detail.
- Always attempt to have the sun behind you, providing better color saturation and improved detail. (As we have seen, this rule should be violated occasionally, using the sun to sidelight or backlight the subject—but always with the use of a lens hood and compensating for exposure.)

- Shooting between 10 a.m. and 2 p.m. gives better color balance. (But shooting before 10 a.m. and after 2 p.m. gives more pleasing colors and fewer harsh shadows.)
- If you question the best exposure, try shooting two extra slides, the first a half-step underexposed and the second a half-step overexposed. (One should *always* bracket exposures, of course. A safer rule is two extra shots on either side of the exposure called for.)
- Try to show as many aspects of the subject as you can. Shoot from different sides and vary long, medium, and close-up shots, including extreme close-ups of various details. Show the project's (subject's) relationship to the environment and its proximity to related subjects.
- Keep shots simple. Get as close as possible and don't include anything in the picture which doesn't add useful detail.
- Get model release forms signed when people are recognizable in your pictures. (See Chapter 16 for suggested release forms.)
- For public relations purposes, furnish well-composed, professionally-taken high quality glossy photos.
- When sending individual photos (mug shots), furnish 5 × 7 or 4 × 5 inch glossies. These sizes can be reduced to halftones with one shot of most copy cameras; 8 × 10s often require two reductions to bring the picture down to halftone size for thumbnail or half-column photographs.
- Leave white borders on all four sides of the photo for the the editor to write instructions on.
- Write "TOP" in the top margin if there is any possibility an editor may be confused.
- Don't overprint identifying data on photos, unless it's in an area that is obviously cropable.
- Perfect balance—in anything—tends to be dull. Compose your shots so that natural dividing lines (horizons, flagpoles, a building edge) do not split the image equally, either horizontally or vertically.
- In group shots get heads of individuals on different levels, to add vitality and combat dullness.
- Avoid having subjects point at anything. There are better ways of directing the viewer's attention.

## References

[1]Egon E. Weck, "Photography's (Not So) Latent Image," *Public Relations Journal*, March 1975, p. 6.

[2]Gerald D. Hurley and Angus McDougall, *Visual Impact in Print*, Visual Impact, Inc., Chicago, 1971, pp. 158–161.

[3]Carol Lee, "The PR Role in Good Annual Report Photography," *Public Relations Journal*, September 1977, p. 41.

[1]Robert Baker, "The Layout of Singles and Spreads," *Impact*, no. 158, Chicago, 1974, p. 3.

[5]Ibid., p. 4.

From a graphics standpoint, the company external possibly has the greatest freedom of any contemporary journalism, even including the "underground" press. It does not have to compete with the graphics of advertisers saying other things inside its covers; it does not have to compete with hundreds of other periodicals on newsstands. Here, if anywhere, the publication can explore new graphic statements, discover new illustrators, examine new techniques, create, through this very exploration, the image of its company as being advanced, creative, alive.[1]

# CHAPTER 12
# Internal and External Publications

THIS, ADMITTEDLY, IS a catchall kind of chapter, in which we try to cover several public relations tools and techniques that seem to fall outside all other classifications. Up for discussion in this particular potpourri are newsletters (and their relation to other direct mail promotions), proposals, booklets, folders, annual reports, announcements, and corporate identity programs. Included under the last item are graphics standards programs and logos.

A rule of thumb: If it isn't a letter, personally typed and signed, you have to give it something extra to get it seen and read. That something must include good layout, and it should include good printing. Add in good illustrations (art and photographs), first-class writing, and perhaps color—and you are on the way to getting the printed product noticed and read. Visual appeal should at least equal content appeal.

A few quick ideas:

- One architect has his business cards printed on Roledex cards.
- Another architect has her photograph printed on her business cards. People are more likely to keep a card with a photo on it—*and* to remember you the next time.

Figure 12-1. Face of a postcard used by architect Edgar Tafel, showing his design for St. John's in the Village Episcopal Church.

• New York architect Edgar Tafel uses post cards for short messages, with line drawings of his projects on the front. (See Figure 12-1.)

• You may never find a way to use this bit of information, but we thought you should have it. When Bantam published the paperback version of *Passages,* by Gail Sheehy, four different colors of covers were used. The explanation by a representative of the publisher: "Blue sells best to over-40 readers; green to 35-year-old intellectuals; orange is picked up by 30-year-olds; and magenta by the 20- to 30-year old reader." (No clue as to the best cover color for 50-year-old, color-blind, self-effacing intellectuals who think young.)

• A (very) rough rule of thumb: One full-time staffer should produce the *equivalent* of one 16-page publication a month.

## NEWSLETTERS

Several points on the use of direct mail by design professionals were discussed in Chapter 5. Newsletters, with their potential for productive, continuing, professional direct mail contacts with past, present, and potential clients, have become one of the more popular public relations tools in many engineering and architectural firms.

Commercial newsletters—written, produced, and promoted in hopes of making a profit—have the basic ingredients of gossip and an appeal to greed. The information conveyed in such newsletters, according to one publisher, should be "useful, easy and fast to read, and without frills." Some, if not all, of the same considerations apply to most public relations newsletters.

Newsletters, with their unique journalistic format, began in the sixteenth century to serve commercial, social, and political interests. After a relatively long period of disuse, they came back from obscurity early in this century, primarily to fill in gaps left by business publications and newspapers. Variations on the newsletter format include mini-newspapers (tabloid size or smaller), magazines, special booklets, and updates to a general capabilities brochure on a fairly regular basis.

One advantage of a newsletter is its relatively low cost, compared to other types of publications. And as a marketing tool a newsletter is particularly well suited to specialized communication—the rifle, rather than the shotgun, approach. A newsletter can

• keep open a direct line of communication between a design firm and its clients and prospects. It also serves as a public relations device—showing the firm's concern for and interest in individual clients.

• interpret and analyze important factors and forces at work in the design profession and the construction field, alerting readers to significant developments now and for the future.

• guide reader decisions on what to do, how to do it, when to do it—based on sound, current advice from authorities in the field.

• soft sell. Newsletter experts say that once reader rapport is established, items about a service or a product produce a solid response. But a newsletter should never hard sell or even appear to sell directly; otherwise it becomes an obvious piece of self-serving promotion.

In the chapters on supplemental publications in *How to Produce Professional Design Brochures,* we pointed out that starting a newsletter closely parallels the customary early steps in designing and producing a new office brochure. Some thought should be given to the publics a firm wants to reach and to what the objectives of the newsletter are. Likely audiences, or publics, to zero in on include:

• past and present clients
• lost clients
• prospective clients
• financial community
• local and regional media
• staff and families
• libraries of nearby professional schools

- suppliers
- consultants

The objectives are usually a little more difficult to define. They might include:

- to explain new services offered by your firm.
- to reflect staff changes and added capabilities.
- to aid internal staff morale.
- to serve as a continuing contact (bridge) between your firm and its clients and prospects.
- to reflect your firm's experience and competence, through the use of case histories, letters from clients, and other means.

The first five audience groups are made up of people who, for the most part, are already bombarded by media messages almost every waking moment. So anything new to be added to their reading load *must* be good—well above average—to even get their attention.

Before going much farther with this subject, we should mention that the *ideal* situation is to have two newsletters—a purely internal one for executives, staff members, and families; and an external publication for the other publics listed above. Some larger firms have such twin newsletter publishing ventures, but it is not a very practical approach for small- to medium-size firms. So keep the content of your newsletter as client-oriented and unparochial as possible; otherwise it may become an early casualty to an overload of staff marriages, new babies, photographs of the principals, and bowling league scores.

Of potential interest to outsiders (particularly to lost, past, present, and prospective clients) are items about staff promotions, project case histories, new work, honors won by principals and staff, and the texts of speeches and technical articles by staff members. Occasional service articles about new trends in design and construction or a different (money-saving) approach to a specific project type usually get good readership.

Use plenty of photographs, drawings, diagrams, sketches, and charts. Such visuals, along with short, active headlines, allow busy executives to grasp the main thoughts more quickly—and help them decide whether or not to take time to read into the text. For an idea of what others think is important in a newsletter, get copies of some published by other design and construction firms.

The average newsletter is a monthly, four-page publication, typewritten or in simulated typewriter type, in one color of ink on white paper.

Two or three columns in a vertical 8½ × 11 inch format are preferred over a single wide column. There is a long-standing debate as to the optimum width of a line of type for achieving the best legibility. One rule of thumb calls for a line width 1½ times the point size of the type used; that is, a 15-pica width for 10-point type; 18 picas wide for 12-point type, and the like. Another rule limits the width to the equivalent of 1½ alphabets of the type used. A point in typography is 0.013837 inches—or approximately ¹/₇₂ of an

Figure 12-2. Newsletter of the Boston Museum of Science. Three folds convert the full 11 × 17 inch sheet into a mini-letter 5½ inches square.

inch; a pica is 12 points or 0.166 inch. Still another column width rule of thumb suggests 10 to 12 words as the maximum in one line for eye comfort, legibility, and comprehension.

Unfortunately, relatively little recent research has been done in this area. One study sometimes cited was written by M. A. Tinker and D. G. Patterson for the June 1929 *Journal of Applied Psychology*. Almost 50 years ago they determined the optimum line (column) width for 10-point type as 80 millimeters, or about 19 picas. There is little point in getting caught up in such esoteric debates. Use two columns to an 8½ × 11 inch page and set the column width between 18 and 20 picas, or roughly 3 to 3⅜ inches. Use at least 10-point type, with 2 points of spacing between lines. Remember that most of your readers will *not* be 19-year-olds with 20-20 vision.

There is nothing magic about the 8½ × 11 inch vertical format for a newsletter. The Boston Museum of Science Newsletter (Figure 12-2) uses the same 11 × 17 inch sheet as for an 8½ × 11 inch four-page format, but three-folds the paper into six 5¾ × 11 inch pages. A final fold for mailing makes it into a 5½-inch square. Each page has two 14-pica-wide columns, with ragged right margins.

This paragraph is set "ragged right" for illustration. The normal set for books and most other publications is "justified both sides" or "flush right and left"—which means that each line of type is spaced out to exactly so many picas in width. Tests have shown that most people are not aware of whether the right margin of something they have just read was ragged or justified. Text can also be set ragged left (difficult to read) or in a centered or midline format (each line symmetrically arranged, as in book title pages and some poetry).

Our recommendation is to begin a newsletter on a quarterly publication basis. Even four pages can get to be difficult to fill with interesting material when the editor is on a part-time basis. Some newsletters use a number instead of a date, avoiding any tie-in with the calendar. (One firm began its newsletter as number 100, to give it an instant publishing history. Fortunately, no one ever asked for back copies 1–99.)

Since there obviously is no consideration given by the receiver for a free newsletter, you are not legally bound to maintain any regularity in its publication. There is a certain amount of credibility and reader loyalty to be gained from regular publication schedules, however—whether it's on a monthly, quarterly, or semiannual basis.

Once the news and illustrations for an issue are in hand, the routine steps in publishing a newsletter are:

1. Prepare a dummy (usually a rough dummy).
2. Have the copy typeset—or type it on a typewriter.
3. Get photographs converted into halftone prints—called Velox prints. Get other artwork reduced to the proper size.
4. Paste up all of the elements (type, photos, illustrations) in their proper position on a "mechanical"—illustration board or heavy paper sheets—ready for the printer.
5. The printer makes paper or metal plates from your "camera-ready" art and runs the job.

Here we are considering only the offset printing process for the newsletter, since that is undoubtedly the method that will be used.

One other procedural matter is the method selected for getting the newsletter produced. Some firms opt to have an outside consultant take full responsibility for the job. Others manage to find the right people in-house. Still others use a combination of consultant and in-house staff. If yours is to be a quarterly publication it should not require more than a couple of days a month of some staff member's time.

Perhaps the best initial arrangement is to have a consultant work with the in-house person, doing the layout, editing, preparing mechanicals, and dogging the printer's heels. After the experience of preparing a few issues, the staffer should be able to do most of these things. Since *everyone* needs an editor, use the consultant or someone competent from the staff to do a final read of all copy before it goes to the printer.

The expense of a newsletter normally comes out of a firm's marketing budget. If the publication is produced entirely in-house, all costs should be identified and charged back to the proper budget item.

If the newsletter is to be set in phototype, with justified (even) right and left column margins, the type will cost between $1 and $1.50 a column inch, or $20 to $30 a page to set. Paper and printing costs for 400 copies will add another $150 to $200.

Most newsletters from design firms go by first-class mail. If you mail to at least 200 names you may want to check out third-class bulk mail costs. Third class requires a special annual permit, filling out forms for the post office for each mailing, zip-coding the pieces in order, and delivery of the newsletters to the post office. If you mail 300 to 400 copies each month any savings from third class will probably be eaten up in internal costs for the handling described above. The average eight-page newsletter, on 50- or 60-pound offset stock, will weigh 1 ounce or less, so the extra weight allowance in third class is not that important. To get a rough idea of total costs, figure a unit price of about $1 per newsletter. If the newsletter is well-written and represents or reinforces the image you want for your firm, it can be money well spent.

A few other tips:

- Use a different color stock for each issue.
- As newsletter themes, feature different client types (and their projects) your firm works with.
- Run letters of appreciation and satisfaction from clients (or excerpts from such letters).
- Don't underestimate the intelligence of your readers.
- Effective newsletters are consistent in writing, style, and design. Assigning publication responsibility to one person will help make this happen.
- Write succinctly, and to the point. Discard more news than you print.
- In your writing, use short sentences and paragraphs, strong nouns and verbs, and the active voice.
- Use actual examples and case histories; most readers relate to them better than to generalities and theoretical examples.
- Be sure your mailing list includes all commercial and association publications in your field.

Figure 12-3. Newsletters come in all forms and formats. The publications shown from DMJM, CH2M HILL, and C. F. Murphy are practically magazines. All of the above newsletters are issued quarterly.

• You might want to accompany the first issue of your newsletter with a well-designed distinctive folder for recipients to use in filing copies of the publication for future reference.

Newsletters from a variety of design firms are shown in Figure 12-3.

## PROPOSALS

It may seem strange to find a section on proposals in a book about public relations. But when proposals are considered as yet another marketing tool of professional service firms, the rationale for including a discussion of what goes into an effective proposal should be clear.

A proposal is simply a written submission of a firm's qualifications for a specific project. Occasionally a more general "qualifications proposal" is submitted to a client or another consultant as a kind of attention-getter, but our primary interest here is in proposals addressing a single, identified project—usually as the result of a request for a proposal (RFP) from the prospective client. When fee estimates are included the document becomes a fee proposal.

Formal proposals are required by more and more clients as an aid to cutting down the list of firms who express interest in a project. For some projects proposal submissions are required by law. The writing of a professional, productive proposal, either unsolicited or in response to a RFP, is an art involving planning, scheduling, judgment, research, coordination, layout, graphics, exposition, and quality control. Unresponsive, unimaginative, and irrelevant replies to RFPs waste the resources and time of the prospect as well as of the consultant.

A proposal must convince the prospective client that the proposing firm's methodology and organization is sound, and that the principals and project team have a clear and thorough understanding of the client's and the project's requirements. A guide for the preliminary steps in handling a proposal:

1. Analyze the project in detail.
2. Learn more about the project than the prospective client knows; then begin fitting the pieces together.
3. Decide whether or not it's a project your firm has any reason to pursue. Answer these questions:

> Do we have the capabilities (people, experience, and finances) and credibility in the required areas?
>
> Does the prospective client have the necessary funds to pay for our services?
>
> Do they really need *us?* How many (and of what quality) are our competitors? Where do we rank against the probable competition?
>
> Is the geographic area of the project of real interest to us?

The usual elements of a proposal include:

1. Cover
2. Letter of transmittal
3. Executive summary
4. Scope of services and work to be accomplished
5. Methodology
6. Time schedule
7. Organization
8. Experience of the firm(s)
9. Qualifications of its staff
10. Cost

The first three elements—cover, transmittal letter, and executive summary—should all be selling instruments. Everything in the proposal should be directed towards convincing the prospect that your firm is uniquely qualified to do the job, of course, but these three elements are particularly important. Many of those on the selection committee will read nothing else in the proposal package.

The transmittal letter should be brief (1 to 1½ pages), making reference to the RFP or other specifics that motivated the proposal. It is extremely important that the letter be addressed to the right person and be fully referenced. The one- to three-page executive summary follows the transmittal letter and is to give readers a quick overview of the total proposal contents. Making up the summary is one of the last steps in preparing a proposal. The proposal must do its part in setting your firm above all other respondents in clarity, graphics, attention to detail, and responsiveness to the RFP.

Proposals are normally group efforts, but someone must be in charge, serving as a kind of coordinator/project manager/editor. Without such single-point responsibility little of importance will be accomplished. A basic outline for the various sections and elements of a proposal and for developing the scope of service is usually worked out in a proposal conference. Individual assignments are given out by the coordinator and deadlines are established and agreed to.

It is not necessary to wait until all of the writing is finished before reviewing and editing copy for reproduction. For example, decisions regarding the exact wording on the proposal cover and the title page (if any) can be made at the proposal conference. These elements can then be processed through the graphics section, plates made, and the necessary quantity printed. Immediate attention to long lead items such as organization and bar charts and maps will help get these and similar items out of the way well before deadlines intrude.

For the final word on proposals we turn to a director of capital projects for the U.S. Agency for International Development (AID), Robert Bakley:

> We get proposals in here all the time with standard resumes of personnel. They may say that a man has bridge experience and often leave out the fact that he also has grain silo experience, which is what the project is about.
>
> Often we get a long list of personnel, and we can't figure out what they're going to be doing on the project. I got one proposal that didn't contain the name

of a single person to be used on the project. And later these people came in and complained because they had not been given the project. Our experience is that the larger the firm, the poorer the technical proposal. . . .

[A] technical proposal we received from one of the giants in the construction industry [was] just one page, covering how they plan to handle the project. No names, no bio data, nothing. What they are saying is: "Look, you know who we are, and we know we can do the job." This same company has been short-listed on three big projects here and each time it winds up at the bottom of the list—because its technical proposal is terrible.[2]

## BOOKLETS, FOLDERS, ANNUAL REPORTS

Part of the direct mail program of some firms consists of regular mailings of project folders, with each folder devoted to a single project—either in work or completed. Other firms concentrate on the production of special material for clients. Two such folders by the Pearce Corporation, St. Louis, are shown in Figure 12-4.

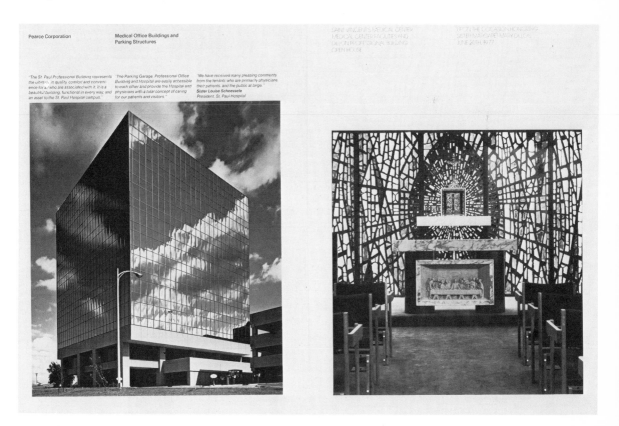

Figure 12-4. These handsome folders from the Pearce Corporation were prepared for clients and cover medical office buildings and parking structures, left, and commemorate open house ceremonies for several projects at St. Vincent's Medical Center. Excellent photographs and good quality stock are used for both publications.

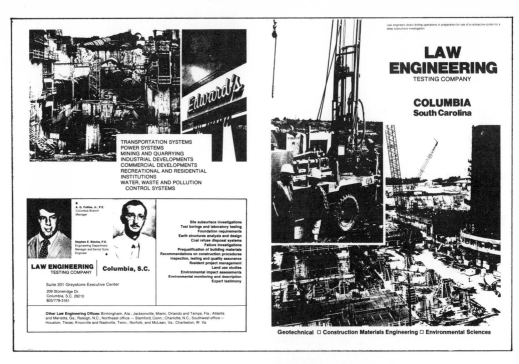

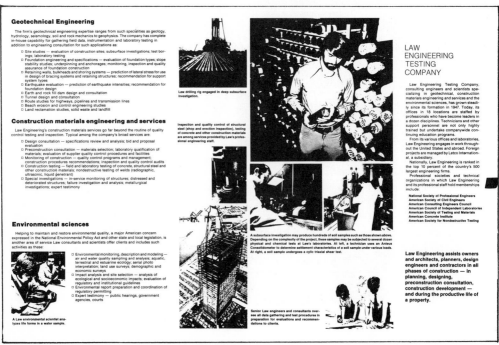

Figure 12-5. Top, the customized front and back pages of Law Engineering's folder for its Columbia, South Carolina, branch office. Bottom, the inside spread, which is the same for all of Law's branch offices.

Where a company has several branch offices, as is the case with many engineering firms, local managers may feel they have an identity problem when their promotional materials concentrate on personnel and qualifications of the home office. As a rule, the most a branch office can hope for is to have its address included somewhere in a listing of all branches—usually in small type on the back of a catchall folder.

Law Engineering Testing Company, among others, has helped its branch offices to maintain individual identities with separate four-page folders for each location. The two inside pages are the same for all offices, giving general information about the total operation. The outside pages are customized to a degree. (See Figure 12-5.)

The relatively small number of design firms that are publicly owned must, by law, produce annual reports for their stockholders. One such mandated report, for CRS Design Associates, Inc. (CRSDA), is shown in Figure 12-6.

Other design firms, with no legal requirement to give a public accounting of their annual operations and finances, put together a yearly report for

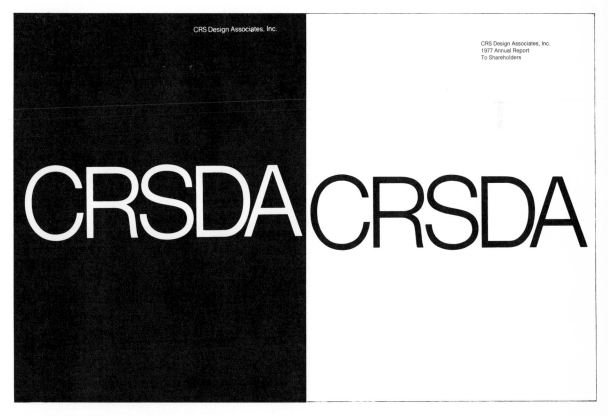

Figure 12-6. The two-part CRS Design Associates, Inc., annual report to stockholders for 1977. The interior of the booklet with the black cover, left, resembles a general capability brochure. The white covered booklet on the right contains only financial information required by the Securities Exchange Commission.

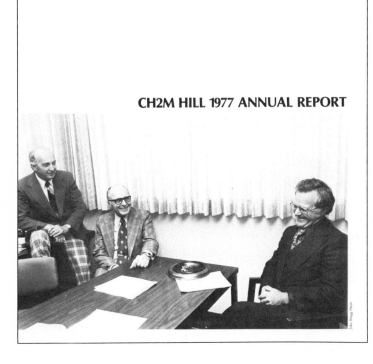

CH2M HILL 1977 ANNUAL REPORT

Figure 12-7. An example of a nonrequired annual report, from CH2M HILL. The firm has published annual reports for several years and makes good use of them in its public relations program.

distribution to their regular mailing list of clients and prospects (see Figure 12-7). These voluntary annual reports can be excellent public relations vehicles for larger offices—and another comfortable contact with their markets. Naturally, no financial or other proprietary information is included in reports from nonpublic firms.

In addition to their primary use as a mail-out piece at the time of publication, annual reports can be given to visitors and clients for the rest of the year. Some firms include the reports in recruiting packages.

Annual reporting for publicly held companies is a $120-million-a-year business, according to *Dun's Review*. Current estimates hold that some 15,000 such companies send out a total of at least 50 million reports each year—at an average cost of around $2.40 each. Depending on quality and quantity, the cost of an annual report ranges from 25 cents up to $5 per copy.

## MISCELLANEOUS ANNOUNCEMENTS

Under this classification the possibilities are limited only by a firm's collective imagination and ingenuity. A Toledo, Ohio, architectural firm once sent out a formal announcement to prospects and past and present clients announcing its incorporation. Nothing more earthshaking was involved than adding "Inc." to the name the principals had used for years, but the response to the mailing included several prospect leads and one certain job. Other possibilities:

- Opening of a new firm (Figure 12-8)
- Opening a branch office (Figure 12-9)
- Moving to a new location (Figure 12-10)
- Executive changes (Figure 12-11)
- Publication of a book (Figure 12-12)
- Christmas cards (Figure 12-13)
- Parties and receptions (Figure 12-14)

## CORPORATE IDENTITY PROGRAMS

A corporate image, or personality, is the total public perception of a company. This image results from the perceived quality of a company's services or products, its activities in the public and business communities (and policies affecting such activities), and how information about these factors is communicated through public relations and advertising.

Corporate identification programs, utilizing technical manuals and graphics standards guidelines, can bring wider, more immediate recognition of the desired corporate image. There should be a recognizable continuity throughout a company's graphic family. Visual identity programs can be established to cover:

Stationery supplies (letterheads, envelopes, memoranda forms)
Business cards
Mailing labels
Checks
Purchase orders
Statements
Decals
Press releases
Stock certificates
Brochures, newsletters, annual reports, and other publications
Title blocks in drawings
Covers for proposals and computer printouts
Office decorations (entrance door, walls, ashtrays)
Field equipment
Job signs
Vehicle identification
Product and package labeling

OPEN HOUSE

We would be pleased to have you share with us the beginning of our firm.

FRIDAY, JULY 11, 1975
4-7 p.m.

Helman Hurley Charvat Peacock/Architects, Inc.
1155 Louisiana Avenue, Suite 101, Winter Park, Florida 32789
(305) 644-2656

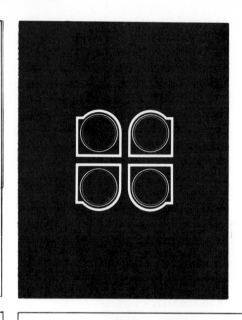

Helman Hurley Charvat Peacock/Architects, Inc.
1155 Louisiana Avenue, Suite 101, Winter Park, Florida 32789
(305) 644-2656

Alan C. Helman, AIA

William C. Charvat, AIA

Thomas R. Hurley, AIA

Thomas E. Peacock, AIA

...are pleased to announce the establishment of a new firm for the practice of architecture to be known as...

Helman Hurley Charvat Peacock/Architects, Inc.
1155 Louisiana Avenue, Suite 101, Winter Park, Florida 32789

Figure 12-8. Announcement of
the formation of a new firm
and invitation to an open
house. Location map for
the office is included.

## CHANGE OF ADDRESS
# ATHENS

HANSCOMB PARTNERSHIP are pleased to announce that, effective from 1st January 1976, our office is relocated at:

SYNGROU AVENUE 97/LAGOUMYTZI
ATHENS
Telephone 922 4975-6   Telex 219480 HAPAGR

The resident partner, George J. Gower, ARICS continues to provide international quantity surveying and project management services with special responsibility for projects in North Africa and the Eastern Mediterranean area.

OTHER WORLDWIDE OPERATIONS OF THE PRACTICE CONTINUE FROM OFFICES IN:
Anchorage Bahrain Calgary Cardiff Cheltenham Chicago Coleraine Coventry Deventer Edinburgh Greenwich Hamilton London Lilongwe Montreal New York Ottawa Quebec Rome Seattle Swansea Toronto Tunbridge Wells Vancouver Winnipeg

# HANSCOMB are now in BAHRAIN

RESIDENT PARTNER
EUGENE MORTER FRICS

PROVIDING A FIRM BASE FOR
QUANTITY SURVEYING AND PROJECT MANAGEMENT
OPERATIONS IN THE MIDDLE EAST AREA

"On a really fast camel you could be in the centre of Bahrain in twenty-four hours!"

Figure 12-9. Hanscomb Roy Associates announces a change of address for the firm's Athens office and the opening of a new office in Bahrain.

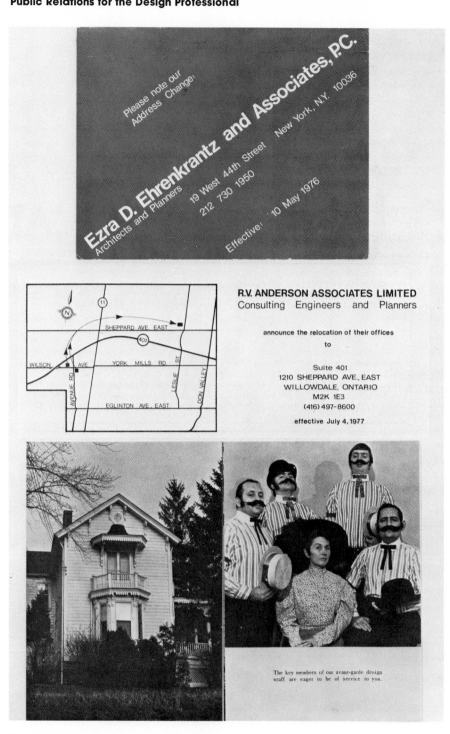

Figure 12-10. Announcements of office moves take many forms. The inclusion of a map is often helpful.

Figure 12-11. Some 8000 of
these cards were sent to
announce the selection of a
new president at CH2M HILL.

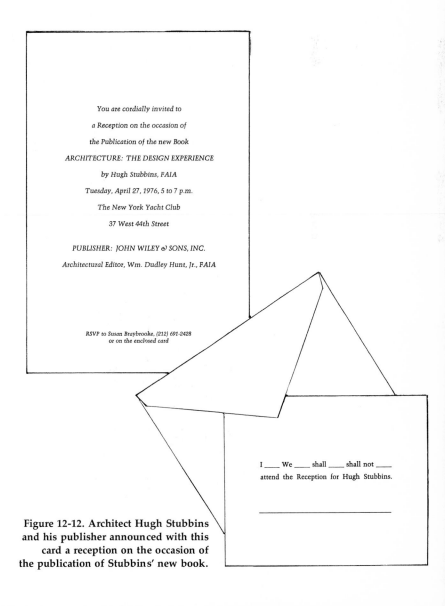

*You are cordially invited to*

*a Reception on the occasion of*

*the Publication of the new Book*

*ARCHITECTURE: THE DESIGN EXPERIENCE*

*by Hugh Stubbins, FAIA*

*Tuesday, April 27, 1976, 5 to 7 p.m.*

*The New York Yacht Club*

*37 West 44th Street*

*PUBLISHER: JOHN WILEY & SONS, INC.*

*Architectural Editor, Wm. Dudley Hunt, Jr., FAIA*

*RSVP to Susan Braybrooke, (212) 691-2428
or on the enclosed card*

I _____ We _____ shall _____ shall not _____
attend the Reception for Hugh Stubbins.

_____

Figure 12-12. Architect Hugh Stubbins
and his publisher announced with this
card a reception on the occasion of
the publication of Stubbins' new book.

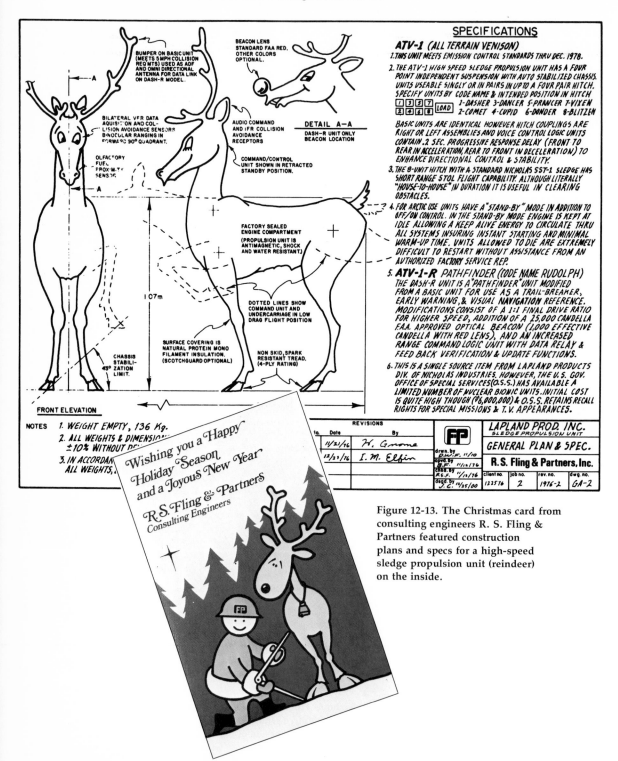

Figure 12-13. The Christmas card from consulting engineers R. S. Fling & Partners featured construction plans and specs for a high-speed sledge propulsion unit (reindeer) on the inside.

**GRUZEN & PARTNERS**
ARCHITECTS PLANNERS

CORDIALLY INVITES YOU
TO JOIN US FOR COCKTAILS
IN HONOR OF OUR
COLLABORATING FIRMS

TUESDAY EVENING
MAY 4, 1976
5:00—7:30 P.M.

THE WARWICK OF PHILADELPHIA
17TH AND LOCUST STREETS
ADAMS ROOM

LIST OF COLLABORATING FIRMS:
ANDERSON-NICHOLS, BOSTON, MASS.
BABER, CORT AND WOOD, ASHEVILLE, N.C.
BARNES, LANDIS, GOODMAN & YOUNGBLOOD, AUSTIN, TEX.
MARK BECK ASSOCIATES, INC., TOWSON, MD.
ANDREW BLACKMAN, NEW YORK, N.Y.
BLONDHEIM, WILLIAMS & CHANCY, EUFAULA, ALA
BRADLEY PARTNERSHIP OF ARCHONICS, FORT WAYNE, IND.
BUCHER-MYERS & ASSOCIATES, SILVER SPRINGS, MD.
CS DESIGNERS, INDIANAPOLIS, IND.
CASTRO-BLANCO, PISCIONERI & FEDER, NEW YORK, N.Y.
CONNELL/METCALF & EDDY, CORAL GABLES, FLA.
H. L. DANEMAN ASSOCIATES, NORTH WALES, PA.
DURRANT-DEININGER-DOMMER-KRAMER-GORDON. P.C., WATERTOWN, WISC.
ENVIRONMENTAL DESIGN GROUP, INC., WINTER PARK, FLA.
FELL, BRUSSO, BRUTON & KNOWLES, TULSA, OKLA.
FEREBEE WALTERS & ASSOCIATES, CHARLOTTE, N.C.
FREEDMAN/CLEMENTS/RUMPEL, JACKSONVILLE, FLA.
GLASER & MYERS AND ASSOCIATES, INC. ARCHITECTS, HYDE PARK, OHIO
HELMAN HURLEY CHARVAT PEACOCK/ARCHITECTS. INC., WINTER PARK, FLA.
HOFTGER, LAWRENCE. LAWRENCE & FLESHER, OKLAHOMA CITY, OKLA.
VICTORINE & SAMUEL HOMSEY, INC., WILMINGTON. DELA.
HOUGHTON-QUARTY-WARR, ARCHITECTS, NEWTON, N.J.
JONES/MAYER & ASSOCIATES/INC., ST. LOUIS. MO.
JOVA, DANIELS & BUSBY, ATLANTA. GA.
FENTON G. KEYES ASSOCIATES, PROVIDENCE. R.I.
KIRKMAN, MICHAEL AND ASSOCIATES, OMAHA, NEBR.
KORETSKY KING ASSOCIATES, SAN FRANCISCO, CALIF.
McELVY, JENNEWEIN, STEFANY & HOWARD, TAMPA, FLA.
McLEOD, FERRARA, ENSIGN, CHARTERED ARCHITECTS, CHEVY CHASE, MD.
WILLIAM MORGAN, ARCHITECTS, P.A., JACKSONVILLE, FLA.
MURPHY, HUNTON, SHIVERS, BRADY, ARCHITECTS, P.A., ORLANDO, FLA.
O'DELL, HEWLETT & LUCKENBACH, BIRMINGHAM, MICH
ORGANIC, TEHERAN, IRAN
PANCOAST ARCHITECTS, MIAMI, FLA.
PLANNING FEASIBILITY URBAN DESIGN ARCHITECTURE, BOSTON, MASS.
RAY ASSOCIATES, LEBANON, PA.
ROSE, BEATON & ROSE, WHITE PLAINS, N.Y.
ISADORE & ZACHARY ROSENFIELD, NEW YORK, N.Y.
SHERLOCK SMITH & ADAMS, INC., MONTGOMERY, ALA.
SKIDMORE, OWINGS & MERRILL, SAN FRANCISCO, CALIF.
JOHN STEVENS ASSOCIATES, INC., DETROIT, MICH
TISCHLER & COMERRO, PATERSON, N.J.
VAN BOURG, NAKAMURA, KATSURA, KARNEY, INC., OAKLAND, CALIF.
JASPER D. WARD, III AIA, LOUISVILLE, KY
JOE WASSERMAN, NEW YORK, N.Y.
F. CARTER WILLIAMS, ARCHITECTS. RALEIGH, N.C.
WOLD ASSOCIATES, ST. PAUL, MINN.

RSVP
GRUZEN & PARTNERS, 1700 BROADWAY, NEW YORK 10019

Figure 12-14. Two party invitations. Gruzen & Partners held a reception at the 1976 AIA convention in Philadelphia in honor of its collaborating firms—forty-seven of them! POD, of Orange, California, was celebrating its second year of operation.

The American Revolution Bicentennial Administration (ARBA) saw fit to issue a 48-page "official graphics standards manual" in advance of the 1976 Bicentennial year. From the introduction to the manual, which covered authorized use of the Bicentennial symbol:

> The standards set forth in this Manual are established to insure the integrity of the design in all media, color, and dimensions. All use must be in strict conformity with these standards and must incorporate the highest standards of design, dignity, and good taste.
>
> The symbol must never be altered in any way and must always appear in the configurations specified in this Manual.

Helvetica regular in all caps was the type style specified for printing around the five-pointed star symbol by designers Chermayeff and Geisman.

### Construction of Symbol

This guide to construction of the American Revolution Bicentennial symbol is intended for use when reproducing the symbol in extremely large sizes, as in the case of large signs, etc.

Photographic methods of reproduction should be used in all possible cases. Artwork suitable for photographic reproduction is included on pages 34-45 of this Manual.

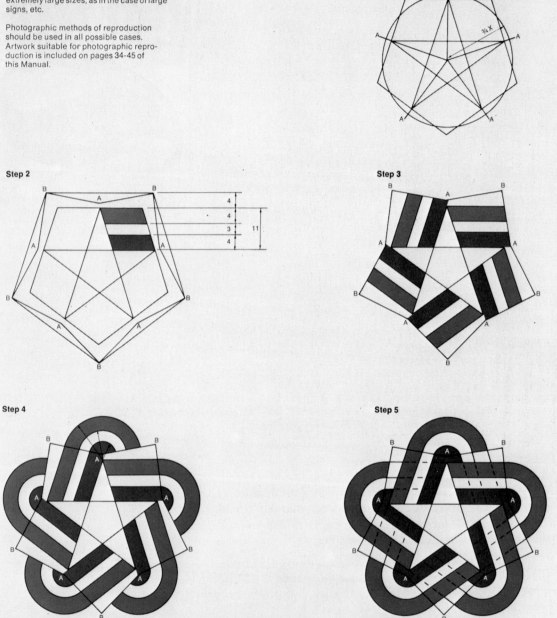

10

Figure 12-15. Constructing the Bicentennial star symbol, by the book.

Page 10 of the ARBA manual, reproduced in Figure 12-15, gives detailed instructions for construction of the symbol.

## LOGOTYPES

A major component of most successful corporate identity programs is a logotype (logo, for short)—known legally as service marks and otherwise as identity symbols. Logos have been characterized as a step in the visual unscrambling of a company's corporate or product line identity.

Logos are usually based on one or more of the following elements:

- Symbols—related to the company's operations, services, or products.
- Glyphs (from hieroglyphic)—essentially meaningless symbols.
- Signature or initials—(also known as logograms and logographs) in a contemporary typeface, either off the shelf or custom designed.

The best symbol has the fewest elements. It can be enlarged to 200 to 300 times normal size for use in highway signs, or reduced to ¼ inch in height for reproduction on business cards or in small advertisements—and be identifiable in all cases. A good logo works both in black and white and in color. It also reads in reverses (see Figure 12-16) and as a repetitive pattern background, as on a brochure cover.

Figure 12-16. Positive and reverse versions of a logo. This symbol was used in the 1977 *Report of the Task Force on Disorders and Terrorism.*

Many logos consist of a structurally related symbol and signature, either of which can be used separately for decorative or special purposes. For highest retention value under modern varied and often difficult viewing conditions, geometric forms are preferred over illustrations.

Good logos are unique, work in such adverse conditions as short exposure, competitive surroundings, and poor light; do not go out of style; and appropriately represent their companies. At best, logos are semipermanent symbols—the average life span of an unmodified logo is about 7 years.

The evolution of a specific logo and the rationale for the current version are often interesting exercises in corporate thinking. When Crown Controls Corporation changed its logo in 1974 (the fourth change in 15 years) a press release explained: "While our previous logotypes served well for many years, they represented a lightweight image carried over through the late fifties and

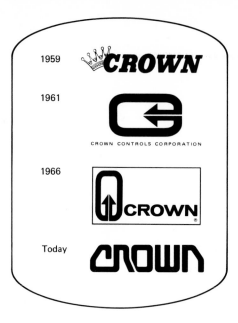

Figure 12-17. Fifteen-year
evolution of the logo
for Crown Controls Corporation.

sixties. The new design mirrors the true image of lift truck products we manufacture today." See Figure 12-17 for the changes in Crown's logo.

When Saul Bass created a new corporate logo for United Airlines several years ago the company marked the occasion with ten pages of press releases. Not only did the air carrier have a new symbol to unveil, United concurrently took the bold step of changing the "air lines" in its name to one word—"airlines."

United's president, Edward E. Carlson, interpreted his company's new logo: "The new symbol and color scheme were created to project an image of greater warmth and modernism and will signify the reliability and efficiency which traditionally have been United's hallmarks with the public. The new identification is calculated to express the innovative, forward-looking approaches and attitudes United is presenting in the marketplace. It is a constant expression of our outlook and our desire to provide outstanding services to our customers."

If you believe anyone really talks like that, then you may see all that Mr. Carlson professes to see in the United logo (Figure 12-18).

Figure 12-18. The Saul Bass logo for United Airlines—projecting "an image of greater warmth and modernism . . . signifying reliability and efficiency."

## References

[1]Don Fabun, "External Publications," *Handbook of Public Relations,* 2d ed., Howard Stephenson, editor, McGraw-Hill Book Company, New York, 1971, p. 619.

[2]"AID's Man in Cairo Critiques Consultants' Proposals," *Engineering News-Record,* Nov. 17, 1977, p. 37.

# PART
# 3

Ascertaining the results of a public relations effort is, for a number of reasons, the most neglected branch of the art. Such evaluation is difficult because it deals with that most difficult of things to measure—changes in human opinion. . . . Human thought takes place in a constantly changing environment in which not all the factors may be known. It is often extremely hard to say "this" caused "that," and yet some connection of cause and effect must be a goal of public relations activity evaluation.[1]

# CHAPTER 13
# Measuring Results

THE OBVIOUS IRONY in John Marston's statement, above, is the implication that public relations, while purporting to be able to *create* changes in human opinion, seems unable (or unwilling) to measure whatever changes have been wrought. Far too many practitioners have, for far too long, hidden ineptness and, perhaps, a lack of faith in their own efforts behind a claimed inability to demonstrate results any more tangibly than handsomely mounted displays of press clippings.

## PR IS NO EXCEPTION

In corporations the chief executives look to department and division heads for information on which to base immediate decisions and long-range planning. Manufacturing must furnish data on product output, sales reports on dollar volume, personnel on staff performance to meet production goals, finance on money raised for operations and expansion, and accounting on collections and cash flow. Public relations should be able to furnish data on a par with the output from similar disciplines in business and industry—in concrete terms, backed up by reasonable documentation.

In an earlier chapter we spoke of the importance of setting up a PR program of work—an annual corporate road map of goals and objectives. The more specific the program goals, the easier it is—or should be—to establish cause and effect and the cost/benefit ratio of public relations activities. One practitioner suggests "meaningful evaluation of PR's performance can only occur in an environment where PR itself is managed consciously as a rational function."[2]

Some of the items for which there may well be measurable results, comparing the situation today with at least a year ago:

> Press relations
> Client relations
> Staff attitudes
> Community attitudes
> Attitudes of thought leaders
> Government relations

Results measurement means finding out not only what has been accomplished, but what is still to be accomplished—with each of a firm's publics.

## CLIPPING BOOKS — ONLY PART OF THE STORY

Periodic reports on the number of news releases prepared and distributed, along with clippings to demonstrate use, is the traditional way of supplying tangible evidence to management of PR accomplishments. As we saw in the chapter on news releases, the percentage of releases actually used by editors and news directors is woefully small.

Since most executives are unable to relate raw press clippings to their understanding of corporate objectives, some public relations people use a news analysis approach to improve communications and perception at this level. More significant measurements than total inches of clippings include total circulation of the papers and magazines involved, markets penetrated by stories used, reader exposure (how many people may have seen one article), type of use (in straight news, case histories, features, mentions, or roundups), and the length of stories.

A few PR dinosaurs still insist on equating total print inches and broadcast minutes to the cost of the same space or air time on a paid basis. The Analytical Division of Burrelle's Press Clipping Bureau says, "[Advertising value] is the ultimate *qualitative* measure securable from a clip. Ad value has the advantage of being *the one measure* understood by all executives. It talks their language and is a convincing answer to the value of a communications performance . . . ad value provides the strongest verifiable measure of publicity worth."

Those who insist on correlating their publicity results with paid space or purchased air time do a disservice to themselves and the name of public relations. Advertising pages and commercial air time are open to anyone with the money to buy them. And for their dollars purchasers can convey practically any message they desire, subject to no editing, shortening, or considerations of style.

Earning one's way into news columns and air time on radio and television, on the other hand, is a true test of research and writing skills and of media relations—and is certainly not open to just anyone with a fat checkbook. In this sense, print or air publicity is worth many times the cost of paid advertising, and PR practitioners fail a basic professional responsibility by not making the point clear to their management.

An example of newsclip analysis by a public relations director for his chief executive officer might read like this:

### Press Release No. 2-8028 — XYZ International

On the basis of clippings received to date, this press release on our headquarters building for XYZ International was carried in 40 publications—newspapers, trade journals, and other consumer publications. The message had an estimated readership exposure of 10 million in our three major market areas [headquarters and branch office locations] of St. Louis, Kansas City, and Chicago. The equivalent of four newspaper pages, ten shelter magazine pages, and two news magazine pages were devoted to coverage of the material in the release. Cost of distribution was $490.

*Publications using the story were:* (a list of the forty publications and their circulations follows).
*Sample leads:* (Quote six or eight representative leads from the stories carried by larger publications).
*Highlights:* (Discuss significant or unusual uses of the release material—with illustrations [number and what type]; as part of a business page roundup on new corporate headquarters; accompanied with an interview with your president; and the like).

It should be evident that this type of presentation and documentation helps an outsider relate PR efforts to company interests and objectives—and is much more instructive than dumping forty clippings on the chief executive's desk with a comment that "we did OK this month."

News analysis reports as described above can be obtained from outside sources. Burrelle's Analytical Division, mentioned earlier in this section, provides such a service for a fee. While the analysis can be performed rather easily in-house, some might prefer the appearance of greater objectivity from an external evaluation. But don't let the consultant equate total results with advertising costs for the same editorial space and air time.

## OPINION RESEARCH

An obvious check on the effectiveness of individual public relations efforts and the total program is to conduct before-and-after public opinion research.

If the discipline of public relations—which is more art than science today—is to become an applied social and behavioral science, which some academicians maintain it is, then its practitioners must know how to measure, evaluate and interpret attitudes. Opinion research is the PR practitioner's primary means to tap the climate of opinion. It's that simple. It is a tool that gives the PR practitioner (who is competent and trained in its use) the power to convert the unknown into the known and to become a more knowledgeable decision maker.[3]

Measurement of opinions—individual judgments on objectives and issues—is quite a different task than measuring attitudes. People have opinions, views, beliefs, and conclusions on many, if not most, issues, and are usually very willing to talk about them. "ABC Architects, Inc., designs fine buildings" is an opinion. The Gallup Poll on presidential ratings by the public is an opinion poll. In 1978 respondents were asked, "Do you approve or disapprove of the way Carter is handling his job as President?" Answers were approve, disapprove, or no opinion. According to the Gallup organization, Carter's popularity (the approvals) dropped from 55 percent to 39 percent in the first quarter of 1978.

Attitude measurement is much more difficult and complex because of the many factors involved. As a general rule, surveys alone are used in opinion research. Attitude research, because it must measure the full range of mental positions and impressions (emotions, motivation, predisposition, and the like), uses many techniques in addition to surveys—and is correspondingly more expensive and time-consuming.

Mail questionnaires and personal interviews, either by telephone or face to face, are the most used techniques for opinion research. For a relatively simple example, let's say you are interested in a general reader evaluation of your firm's external newsletter. The questionnaire shown in Figure 13-1 might be used.

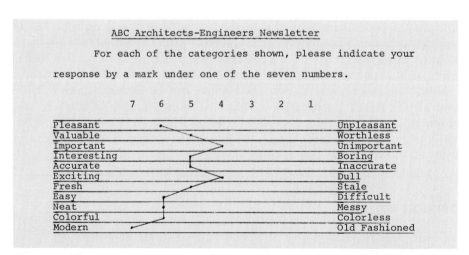

Figure 13-1. The newsletter evaluation profile as completed by a reader. A drawback to this type of questionnaire is that respondents may be primarily regular, interested readers—which could impart an automatic bias to the survey results.

For self-administered questionnaires complete directions must be included. The personal interview approach requires selection and training of interviewers. One study concluded that interviews can cost up to sixty times as much as questionnaires.

## QUESTIONNAIRES

Determining what information is required and how to get it are the first steps in conducting opinion research. A questionnaire will be required in the majority of cases, whether data is to be gathered by mail, by telephone, in one-on-one interviews, or in group interviews.

An important point to remember when setting up new research programs, or in expanding existing ones, is that all or part of the research may be repeated periodically to measure opinion or attitude changes in respondents to initial studies. Benchmarks must be established against which future results are tabulated and measured, and certain parts of the questionnaire should lend themselves to replication to give a basis for future comparisons.

In designing a questionnaire keep each question and the total questionnaire as short as possible. Begin with easy-to-answer, interesting questions. Other DOs and DON'Ts for questionnaire construction:

## DO

- Pretest questionnaires.
- Keep questions to twenty words or less.
- Avoid words with emotional connotations.
- Use language respondents can understand and relate to.
- Limit each question to one point.
- Make the questions easy to answer, by use of check marks, cross-throughs, circles, and the like.
- Use four, not three, answers in multiple choice questions. People tend to favor a middle choice.
- Keep questions in a logical sequence, unless sequencing may distort the answers.
- Enclose a self-addressed, postage-paid envelope for replies to mail questionnaires.
- Send a follow-up questionnaire to those who fail to respond to the original one.

## DON'T

- Compound two or more questions into one.
- Use ambiguous words.
- Ramble.
- Attempt to lead, influence, or bias responses.
- Mix up general and specific questions. Move from one into the other.

• Ask respondents to rank more than five items in order of their importance.
• Exceed five categories in scaling questions.
• Include too many questions.

The simplest questionnaire to answer and tabulate is built around closed-end, direct questions, of which there are six basic types.

1. Ranking
How would you rank these firms with respect to their experience with high-rise office structures?

|                                       | Rank  |
| ------------------------------------- | ----- |
| Edward Durrell Stone & Associates     | (　) |
| Helmuth, Obata & Kassabaum, Inc.      | (　) |
| CRS, Inc.                             | (　) |
| Perkins & Will                        | (　) |
| Ellerbe                               | (　) |

2. Preference
If you selected an engineering firm tomorrow, which of the following would you prefer?
(　)  Harza Engineering Company
(　)  CH2M HILL
(　)  Bovay Engineers, Inc.
(　)  Malcolm Pirnie, Inc.

3. Dichotomous
Smaller firms do better design.
(　)  True      (　)  False
Are you satisfied with your marketing program?
(　)  Yes      (　)  No

4. Closed response
A. What brand of drawing ink do you usually buy?

———————————————————————

B. List all light fixture manufacturers you are familiar with.

———————————————  ———————————————
———————————————  ———————————————
———————————————  ———————————————

5. Multiple choice
If you were entering architectural school today, which of the following would you select?
(　)  University of Virginia
(　)  Notre Dame University
(　)  Tulane University
(　)  Columbia University

6. Rating scales
How would you rate the quality of buildings designed by XYZ Architects & Engineers?
(　)  Excellent
(　)  Good

( ) Fair
( ) Don't know

Rate the on-time, on-budget performance of ABC Design, Inc.

| Bad | | | | Good | | | | Excellent | |
|---|---|---|---|---|---|---|---|---|---|
| 1 | 2 | 3 | 4 | 5 | 6 | 7 | 8 | 9 | 10 |

Another consideration in doing opinion research is whether the study is to be done as an in-house project or by outside consultants. Some design firms simply set up a dummy research company to handle mailing and tabulation of questionnaires.

An example of the latter approach is illustrated in Figure 13-2. A questionnaire was received from Civic Research, P.O. Box 34320, Dallas, Texas 75234.

Q: How would you rate CHICAGO as a place to hold business meetings? On each of the following attributes, please indicate whether you consider Chicago to be excellent, good, fair or poor.

| | CHICAGO | | | | |
|---|---|---|---|---|---|
| | Excellent | Good | Fair | Poor | No Opinion |
| Central location for attendees | ( ) | ( ) | ( ) | ( ) | ( ) |
| Meeting room facilities | ( ) | ( ) | ( ) | ( ) | ( ) |
| Hotel accomodations | ( ) | ( ) | ( ) | ( ) | ( ) |
| Restaurants | ( ) | ( ) | ( ) | ( ) | ( ) |
| Entertainment/night life | ( ) | ( ) | ( ) | ( ) | ( ) |
| Sports/recreational facilities | ( ) | ( ) | ( ) | ( ) | ( ) |
| Tourist/cultural attractions | ( ) | ( ) | ( ) | ( ) | ( ) |
| Travel time to get there | ( ) | ( ) | ( ) | ( ) | ( ) |
| Convenience of air schedules | ( ) | ( ) | ( ) | ( ) | ( ) |
| Transportation in and around town other than car rental | ( ) | ( ) | ( ) | ( ) | ( ) |
| Reasonableness of total cost | ( ) | ( ) | ( ) | ( ) | ( ) |
| Q: Overall, how would you rate Chicago as a meeting place? | ( ) | ( ) | ( ) | ( ) | ( ) |

Q: Have you been to Chicago in the past 12 months for a business meeting? That is to an executive conference, sales/marketing meeting, training seminar, convention, or any other kind of business meeting that is held away from your office of operation or corporate headquarters?

Yes ( )
No ( )

IF YES: What type of meeting(s) did you attend in Chicago?

Executive conference ( )
Sales/marketing meeting ( )
Training seminar ( )
Convention ( )
Other: ________________
(please describe)

Q: Were you in any way involved in a decision to schedule a meeting in Chicago this past year?

( ) Yes ( ) No

**Figure 13-2. The Civic Research questionnaire page on Chicago as a city for business meetings. Dummy research firms are occasionally used in surveying to conceal the identity of the real client.**

The transmittal letter was signed by a J. C. Plagens, Supervisor. The Dallas telephone company lists no telephone for Civic Research—an odd circumstance for a research organization.

The three pages of the research instrument cover three cities—Chicago, Dallas, and St. Louis (the Chicago page is shown). Since the mailing originated in Dallas, it seems fair to assume that the client is from Dallas.

The questionnaire appears to be innocuous enough. It is apparently designed to develop a mailing list of meeting planners on behalf of a Dallas organization, and in that respect violates one of the rules—a guarantee of anonymity to respondents.

### References

[1]John E. Marston, *The Nature of Public Relations,* McGraw-Hill Book Company, New York, 1963, p. 289.

[2]Robert S. Mason, "What's a PR Director For, Anyway?" *Harvard Business Review,* September–October 1974, p. 95.

[3]Leonard Snyder, "PR Professionals Must Practice Applied Research," *Public Relations Journal,* June 1975, p. 26.

Advertising gives you a freedom of choice.[1]

A business, advertising on the printed page, cannot be misunderstood unless it chooses to be. Short of a court of law, few other public arenas offer the opportunity to set the record straight, to speak for yourself and sign your name to it.[2]

Half my advertising goes to waste, but which half?[3]

# CHAPTER 14
# Advertising

**D**UE TO CONTINUING court rulings, proposed and adopted modifications to various professional ethical codes, and a gradually changing attitude on the subject among professionals, this proved to be one of the most difficult chapters to write. Since any printed product begins to go out of date the instant it comes off the press, it is reasonably certain subsequent events will date or render invalid some of the points covered here. The use of advertising by a variety of professional groups has been a breaking news story since at least June 16, 1975, when the U.S. Supreme Court ruled in favor of the plaintiff in *Goldfarb et ux. v. Virginia State Bar et al.*—and nothing we might say in these pages can freeze future developments or the professional ramifications bound to arise from that court decision. In the Goldfarb decision, as most design professionals will recall, the Supreme Court held unanimously that the learned professions are not immune to or exempt from price-fixing prohibitions of the antitrust provisions of Section 1 of the Act of Congress of July 21, 1890, as amended (15 U.S.C. Section 1), commonly known as the Sherman Act. A number of follow-on case findings have steadily widened the impact of Goldfarb on the professions.

Cheering from the sidelines, as the Department of Justice and the Federal Trade Commission attacked restrictions on advertising by professionals, has been the vast advertising and publishing industry—advertising agencies, public relations firms, and media in all their forms. The implication of well over a million well-paid professionals (doctors, lawyers, veterinarians, CPAs, architects, and engineers) coming into the advertising market would be bound to attract attention. One Washington, D.C., lawyer pointed out in 1976 that if all 21,000 attorneys in the Capitol area were each to place an eighth-page ad in the Yellow Pages, the Washington directory would increase by some 2500 pages. At that time the directory contained but 1650 pages, and one can imagine the interest of directory publisher R. H. Donnelley Corporation. In 1976 the annual gross income to Donnelley from 21,000 eighth-page ads in the Yellow Pages would have exceeded $16.5 million. The figure would be considerably higher today.

Design firms who decide to enter the world of advertising should be aware that there are both good and bad advertising consultants. Some ad agencies will make a great initial presentation of their staff, experience, abilities, and present client list—and do a miserable job once hired. Others (the majority, actually) will take the time to research and know their clients, service the account conscientiously, promptly, and professionally, and give advice upon which clients can generally rely. If design professionals need the reminder, there is often a vast difference between presentation promises and actual performance.

Advertising consultants and agencies expect to make presentations to potential clients—usually against several of their competitors—just as often happens when design firms are pursuing a prospect. One should not be shy about questioning an agency's background and experience in handling service-oriented accounts. Past work with contractors, building materials suppliers, package builders, and developers can be considered relevant experience in most cases.

The fewer than 5000 advertising agencies in the United States, generally concentrated in New York and Chicago, employ around 200,000 people. Most have staffs of ten or less.

As in any area of promotion, advertising efforts must have clearly defined objectives to be productive. Media selection, usually handled by an advertising agency, is critical to the success of any advertising campaign. The advertiser's target audiences may or may not be the ones a specific medium delivers. Reaching potential hospital clients, for example, is accomplished more effectively and economically through certain association and specialized medical publications than, say, by ads in *Time* or *Vogue*.

Once the proper media have been selected, the message must be right. Message planning, at its most elementary, usually involves:

1. Getting attention—the first job of an ad.
2. Holding interest. The layout must encourage gaze motion, insuring a natural flow through the elements of the ad.

3. Arousing desire on the part of the reader, listener, or viewer to buy the service or own the product. Key to this point is to sell benefits rather than features.

4. Getting action—and reinforcing decisions to buy. The obvious payoff for all advertising.

According to a study attributed to Yale University the twelve most persuasive words in the English language are

| | | |
|---|---|---|
| Money | Results | Guarantee |
| Save | Health | Discovery |
| New | Safety | Proven |
| You | Easy | Love |

Some public relations practitioners and advertising copywriters wondered how the Yale researchers overlooked "free." "Free" and "new" have always been considered two of the best words for selling.

If one accepts the study results, then this advertising headline should sell practically anything to practically anyone:

> If you love to save money safely, use PLORG—the new proven health discovery for guaranteed, easy results!

Some years ago Rosser Reeves, a veteran of advertising wars, developed a pretty good definition of advertising: "Advertising is the art of getting a unique selling proposition into the heads of the most people at the lowest possible cost." A unique selling proposition (USP) is comparable to the "competitive differential" approach to marketing espoused by Paul Kennon of Caudill, Rowlett, and Scott (CRS) and others. Under the heading of "Marketing Your Uniqueness," Kennon states flatly, "Without a distinction in the marketplace architectural firms will not survive."

Rosser Reeves's definition of advertising is just as valid for services as it is for products, but working such words as *new* and *free* into ads for professional design services presents a few problems. There are, however, a few rules of thumb which do apply:

- Use ad space for informing, persuading, and selling—not for puffery, ego trips, or lectures.
- Select the media for your advertising messages as carefully as you'd spec a steel frame for a high-rise structure. Decide on the publics or audiences you want to reach; then rely on your consultant or ad agency to advise on size, colors, placement, frequency, and the like.
- Consider advertising as just one of the tools in your total marketing effort. Be sure that all elements of the overall sales program are coordinated and work as an entity.
- Keep copy, art, and layout simple and oriented to the reader (and potential clients).

Interspace, a Philadelphia and Washington, D.C., interior design and

# We moved a railroad.

When the tough Conrail management team began operations in Philadelphia they turned to Interspace for help. They needed enough space for 80 executives planned, constructed and furnished in a matter of weeks. It had to be fast, and it couldn't be expensive.

Interspace welcomed the challenge. It required fast-track planning and design. It meant locating suitable used furniture and using the entire inventory of a chair manufacturer. It meant close coordination with the realtor, building owner, interior contractor, telephone company, city authorities, as well as Conrail officials. It meant moving furniture one weekend until midnight. But, we did it.

What did Conrail think of our job? A Conrail official wrote us the following:

"Interspace did exactly what we wanted and it was a job well done in a timely manner. If you ever have need to use me as a reference, please feel free to do so and rest assured that I will give a very positive one"

 **INTERSPACE**
PHILADELPHIA          WASHINGTON

**Figure 14-1. One of a series of print ads for Interspace, an interior design and planning firm. The headline could have been a little punchier, perhaps, but the body copy is relatively free of puffery and ego-tripping.**

and planning firm, sends advertising flyers to a select mailing list (see Figure 14-1). Copy in the Interspace ad is client-oriented, with a minimum of executive salve and ego-tripping. The last paragraph is a third-party endorsement from a satisfied customer.

Just as many design firms make it a practice to obtain and distribute reprints of supplier ads featuring their projects, your own ads can be reprinted and mailed to important prospects and clients—moving the message transmission from shotgunning to the rifle approach.

## PROFESSIONAL ADVERTISING

In its June 27, 1977, ruling in favor of the plaintiffs in *Bates et al. v. State Bar of Arizona,* the Supreme Court of the United States gave a slightly qualified blessing to advertising by professionals. Two young Arizona lawyers, John R. Bates and Van O'Steen, had placed an ad 16 months earlier in the *Arizona Republic,* a Phoenix newspaper. After the ad appeared the two men were suspended from practice by the Arizona State Bar, and the case began to make its way upward through the courts. (See Figure 14-2.)

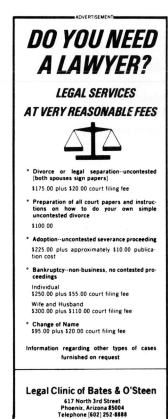

Figure 14-2. The Bates and O'Steen advertisement for legal services, as it appeared in the *Arizona Republic.* The ad turned out to have far-reaching consequences for all professionals.

# Richard Sanders, Attorney.

### Why you've never seen an advertisement like this before

Attorneys don't advertise because the State, through the Courts and the Bar Association, threatens to put them out of business if they communicate with the public in this direct way.

I think the State is wrong to restrict my freedom to speak, and your freedom to listen.

### Times have changed — back

Today, there is a growing realization that, when restrictions are placed on communications of any kind, for whatever 'good' reasons, the result is *not* good. This is not a new idea.

200 years ago, Thomas Jefferson, himself a lawyer, thought our Constitution would not be complete without a Bill of Rights. The Bill of Rights was later adopted as the first ten amendments to the Constitution. And the very *First* Amendment provides that "Congress shall make no law . . . abridging the freedom of speech, or of the press . . ."

Despite this clear Constitutional mandate, a labyrinth of law *does* exactly what Jefferson feared, restricting the free flow of information. On the surface, these laws are supposed to 'protect' you. Actually, they prevent you from having access to facts and opinions you need to make informed decisions.

I hope times have changed — back to the basic idea that freedom of speech is the *first* right of the American people.

### Caveat emptor

Let the buyer beware is good advice. But you can't 'beware' without information. And, up to now, your sources of information about attorneys and their services have been extremely limited. Try the yellow pages. Ask a friend. Lack of information about what an attorney does, how much it costs, and why and when you need legal advice doesn't 'protect' you. But it may well keep you from getting the help you need at reasonable cost — before you have a serious, and usually expensive, legal problem.

I believe attorneys — and other professionals — *should* advertise, and that you, and the public at large, will be better served when we do.

### Information you can use

When you mail the coupon below, I will send you a brochure about legal services, and additional information about subjects you check, without cost or obligation. Or give me a call. MA 3-6042 There is no charge for a brief consultation about your needs.

Would Thomas Jefferson approve? He staked his "life, property and sacred honor" on my right to freedom of speech. Freedom isn't for just a few. It's for you and me, too.

---

*Mail to:* **Richard Sanders, Attorney** • **224 Dexter Ave. N., Seattle, 98109**

**Please send me free information about legal services, and the subject(s) I've checked below.**

☐ Family Law

☐ Wills and Probate

☐ Personal Injury

☐ Business & Commercial (Incorporation, Collections, Contracts, Advisory Services)

☐ Other _____

NAME _____ PHONE _____

ADDRESS _____ CITY _____ ZIP _____

Figure 14-3. The phenomenally successful ad (in terms of response) placed by Seattle attorney Richard Sanders a few days before the Bates and O'Steen ad appeared in Phoenix.

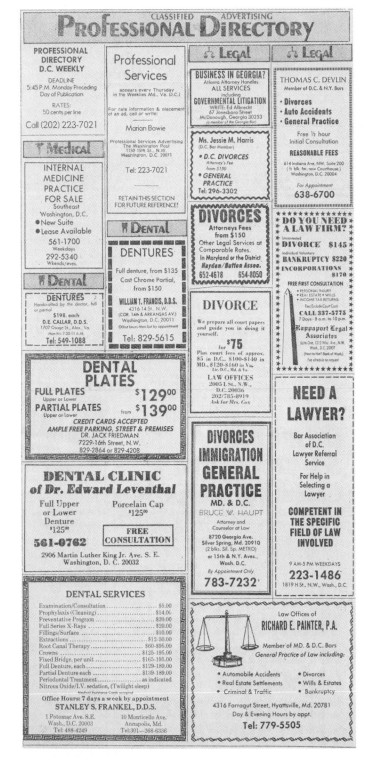

Figure 14-4. The *Washington Post*'s "Professional Directory" for May 4, 1978, carries ads from dentists and lawyers. Prices for full dentures (upper or lower) range from $125 to $198.

Eleven days before the appearance of Bates and O'Steen's one-column by 5-inch ad, Seattle attorney Richard Sanders ran a four-column by 10-inch display ad in the *Seattle Post-Intelligencer,* which resulted in the return of more than 400 reply coupons asking for more information. No charges were filed against attorney Sanders. (See Figure 14-3.)

As of this writing the American Bar Association and the fifty state bar associations have done little to lift anti-advertising restrictions for their members, as mandated by the 1977 Supreme Court decision. The Maryland Court of Appeals approved liberal advertising regulations in March 1978, allowing lawyers in that state to advertise freely in any media. Banned is false, fraudulent, misleading, or deceptive advertising, and attorneys are made personally responsible for the content of their ads.

With most of the bans against lawyers in the process of being overturned or modified, physicians appear to be the next group up to bat in the continuing controversy over professional advertising. Virginia and Maryland dentists got the green light to advertise their services in late 1977. A Silver Spring, Maryland, dentist, who advertises "full dentures with a money-back guarantee for $129" in local newspapers, attracts patients from as far away as West Virginia and New Jersey. His ad points out that these are "the same exact dentures" he sold for $300 in 1973.

The May 4, 1978, *Washington Post* "Professional Directory" of classified ads for dental and legal services is an example of the changes that are occurring in professional advertising. Ads for five dentists and nine law firms were carried. (See Figure 14-4.)

Actually, advertising by doctors is not particularly novel. The program for the 1909 New York City Grand Opera House production of "A Fool There Was" carried an ad for plastic surgeon Pratt—"Open evenings. Consultation free." (See Figure 14-5.)

In at least some areas of a depression-stricken America doctors ran paid ads in the 1930s. Some of the ads, according to one American Medical Association executive, featured "outrageous specials."

According to the American Hospital Association (AHA), at least 10 percent of its 7000 member hospitals were running conventional display ads in newspapers and magazines by 1978. AHA, expecting the paid advertisement trend to increase, published guidelines on the subject.

The 484-bed Sunrise Hospital in Las Vegas advertises to fill its empty rooms on weekends. Elective surgery patients who enter on Friday or Saturday automatically qualify for a drawing for a trip, valued at up to $4000, to wherever the winner wants to go. In a little over a year the free trip promotion had increased weekend admissions by 60 percent. Advertised rebates of 5 percent or more on hospital bills have also helped some hospitals fill empty weekend beds.

David Brandsness, the Sunrise Hospital administrator who developed the free trip lottery, challenges the traditional belief that advertising is unnecessary for the health care industry. "The function of advertising is either to increase volume or to change buying habits," Brandsness points out. "In our

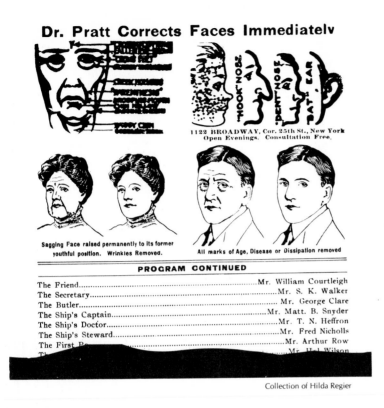

Collection of Hilda Regier

Figure 14-5. This advertisement appeared in the program for the 1909 play, "A Fool There Was." It might be characterized as a fairly hard-sell ad for its plastic surgeon sponsor.

particular case it's the redistribution of the patient load. It allows us to operate more efficiently."

## ADVERTISING FOR DESIGN PROFESSIONALS

After several years of soul-searching debate and a number of not so gentle nudges from the Justice Department, the American Institute of Architects finally approved the use of advertising by its members on May 24, 1978. The vote, taken during the organization's annual meeting in Dallas, was 82 percent in favor of changing the AIA code of ethics to allow advertising. Member architects are allowed to purchase dignified advertisements and listings only in newspapers, periodicals, directories, or other publications indicating firm name, address, telephone number, staff descriptions, and the fields of practice in which they are qualified. No testimonials, photographs, or comparative references to other architects—and, for now, no billboards, television, radio, skywriting, or advertising throwaways.

The question of whether design professionals, including architects, can advertise had already been largely decided. Some firms began advertising several years ago (see sample ads in Figure 14-6). In July 1977 the New York

## Your plant was designed when energy was cheap.

Your manufacturing plant was designed for plentiful, low-cost energy. Now there isn't enough to go around. Costs have doubled. Energy is no longer cheap.

## Weston can save you 10-30% now that it isn't.

Over the past 20 years, Weston has specialized in solving energy and environmental management problems for a wide variety of industries.

For immediate action on your energy costs or documentation on Weston's extensive experience in energy conservation and management. call or write:

Brian J. Lewis, Vice President—Client Services.
ROY F. WESTON, INC., Weston Way, West Chester, Pa. 19380.
215/692-3030.

West Chester, Pa.
Atlanta
Chicago
Cleveland
Houston

ROY F. WESTON, INC
**WESTON**
ENVIRONMENTAL CONSULTANTS-DESIGNERS

Reply to Dept. WSJ-1

**PAE** | **PACIFIC ARCHITECTS AND ENGINEERS INC.**
**PAE INTERNATIONAL**
600 S. Harvard Boulevard, Los Angeles, California 90005
Tel. (213) 381-5731  Cable PACARCHS Telex 677282

SEATTLE
ANCHORAGE
WASHINGTON, D.C.
FRANKFURT
GUAM
TOKYO
BANGKOK
JAKARTA
SINGAPORE
ATHENS

- PLANNING
- ENGINEERING AND ECONOMIC FEASIBILITY STUDIES
- ARCHITECTURE
- ENGINEERING
- SYSTEMS ENGINEERING
- CONSTRUCTION MANAGEMENT
- FACILITY ENGINEERING
- PLANT OPERATION AND MAINTENANCE
- EDUCATION AND TRAINING

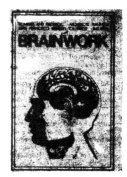

PACIFIC ARCHITECTS AND ENGINEERS INC.
PAE INTERNATIONAL
600 S. Harvard Boulevard, Los Angeles, California 90005
Tel. (213) 381-5731  Cable PACARCHS  Telex 677282

**PAE**
PLANNING
DESIGN
SYSTEMS
CONSTRUCTION MANAGEMENT
OPERATIONS & MAINTENANCE
TRAINING

SEATTLE
ANCHORAGE
WASHINGTON, D.C.
FRANKFURT
GUAM
TOKYO
BANGKOK
JAKARTA
SINGAPORE
ATHENS

SERVICES
ARCHITECTS EXPERIENCED IN home site selection/home design and additions or remodeling.
Dommer and Frederick 845-8998

Figure 14-6. Examples of ads from the mid-seventies by design firms. Clockwise, from upper right, Pacific Architects and Engineers ad from *Southern California Business* (July 28, 1976); Pacific Architects and Engineers ad from *The Wall Street Journal* of April 22, 1976; two ads from the Berkeley, California, architectural firm of Dommer and Frederick; three ads from other California design firms (the smaller ads appeared in local neighborhood papers in 1975–1976); and an energy-related ad by Roy F. Weston, Inc., in *The Wall Street Journal* of May 20, 1975.

State Board of Regents, which oversees architects, engineers, and twenty-seven other licensed professions, ruled that professionals could advertise in all print and broadcast media. Price advertising is not allowed in radio or television ads. False, fraudulent, deceptive, misleading, sensational, and flamboyant ads are banned, as are those containing testimonials or guarantees.

As more design firms add advertising to their mix of sales tools and techniques, these facts about print advertising should be kept in mind.

- Perhaps 5 percent of the audience you pay to reach with an ad will take time to read any of it.
- For everyone who reads the text or copy message, four will not get past the headline.
- On the average, half of the text will be read by the one in four who read beyond the headline.
- The ad that can tell its story in 100 words or less, and is comprehensible in 15 seconds or less, has the best chance of being remembered. (The most successful billboard messages do not run over five words.)
- The attention value of an ad is twice as important as the power of the text to convince readers.
- Ads should generally appeal to basic human emotions—and have specific appeal to identified markets.
- An ad has about 2.5 seconds to stop the reader of a printed page.

Applying the above statistics to the 9000 claimed circulation of *Modern Schools*, for example, tells us that 450 readers may notice your ad and 112 of them may read up to half the text message. On this basis the cost per thousand readers—a standard index in the advertising business—of a full page ad in *Modern Schools* ($690 in 1977) is not $76.67 per thousand, but a whopping $6160.71 per thousand actual readers!

Applying a realistic ratio of direct responses to readership tells us that the cost of getting a lead from an ad in *Modern Schools*—or any other publication—is going to be pretty high. If all one seeks from an ad is immediate, direct, and measurable response, in the form of an inquiry or the return of a postage-paid reply card, there obviously are more cost-effective ways of accomplishing the job. Direct mail, for one. But if the cumulative effect on a firm's marketing position is considered (as it should be), then the success or failure of advertising cannot realistically be measured by tangible returns.

## POSITIONING

Positioning in a market is no more and no less than your firm's image, as perceived by your publics—including prospects, clients, staff, and competitors. The basic principle behind positioning is demonstrated by your answers to such questions as these:

- What is the tallest building in the United States? Most design professionals know it's the Sears Tower in Chicago; at 110 stories and 1454 feet, it's the tallest in the world. Now, what is the second tallest? The fourth tallest? (Second place in the United States is held by the World Trade Center in New York; fourth place currently goes to the Standard Oil of Indiana Building in Chicago.)

- Who was the first person to make a solo flight across the Atlantic Ocean? Even today, more than 50 years after the event, most people can answer Charles Lindbergh. But who was the second solo flyer across the Atlantic?
- Who was the first man to set foot on the moon? Neil Armstrong, of course, but relatively few will remember the names of the third and fourth astronauts to stand on the moon. (Charles Conrad, Jr., and Alan L. Bean.)
- What is the name of the highest mountain in the world? Few would not know that it is Mount Everest at 29,028 feet. Now, name the world's second highest mountain. (K2 in Kashmir.)

The first (tallest) building, the first person on the moon or to fly solo across the Atlantic, the first mountain—and the design firm perceived as first in a prospect's mind—are all positioned to a degree that makes them difficult to supplant or dislodge.

Successful positioning in a market is deliberate, planned, persuasive, and pervasive. If your firm is not positioned among clients and prospects as are General Motors for automobiles, Coca-Cola for soft drinks, IBM for typewriters and computers, and Johnson & Johnson for first-aid supplies, you have an obvious positioning problem.

Be realistic in your positioning goals. If you have operated in an international market, your efforts obviously must be worldwide in scope. But if yours is an area practice—three counties, or the northeast section of a state—don't aim initially at a national position.

Some marketing theorists have suggested that positioning should reverse the traditional roles of advertising and public relations in the development of marketing strategy. The rule, often violated, should be: publicity first, advertising second.[4]

In a linear approach to programming advertising and public relations, goes the theory, the elements are designed to unfold in a planned sequence, work together, and reinforce each other. The spatial approach to programming tends to unleash all promotion elements simultaneously—on various levels and essentially uncoordinated. Results are spotty and inconsistent—and consistency is the keystone of successful positioning.

Any position sought by a design firm should be based on objective research. Whatever the research costs, buy it. Supplement outside research by talking to a few clients and several prospects. A good position, properly supported and reinforced, can last for many years, and is as much an asset as a reference library, typewriters, and drafting equipment.

After determining the single position you want to occupy in the market, convince everyone in the firm to concentrate on the one positioning approach. Don't get trapped into pursuing generalized positions—aim for positive, attainable, specific positions.

Your total marketing program should be created to support and reinforce a chosen position. If no service category exists in which your firm can logically and profitably take a position, then you must position your company and services against competing service categories. Positioning is normally an "against" stance in the market.

## INTERNATIONAL ADVERTISING

Now that so many design and construction firms are active in markets beyond the borders of the United States, a few words on certain pitfalls to be avoided in advertising overseas are in order.

Unfamiliarity with current spoken and written usage in foreign languages is the main downfall of most U.S. firms breaking into print or broadcast media in other countries for the first time. A story—possibly apocryphal—about the wife of a prominent California judge is illustrious of the point. Fascinated by the characters on the menu in a San Francisco Chinatown restaurant, she copied them carefully on a scrap of paper and later worked them into a monogram for a knitted sweater.

The finished sweater was attractive and she wore it often, the object of pleasant and appreciative smiles wherever she went. And especially in Chinatown, for the characters she had so carefully worked into the wool translated as, "This dish is cheap, somewhat hot, but very good."

Not all such errors have so innocent an explanation. In the Italian-Ethiopian war of 1935–1936 the Italian army commanders constantly complained about Ethiopian shelling of their aid stations and field hospitals—all clearly marked with large red crosses. One neutral observer came up with a three-point explanation.

1. In the sparsely settled African terrain, the Italians invariably located their aid stations and hospitals within military encampments.

2. The Italian gunners and bombers had a considerably less than 100 percent accuracy rating in their own bombardments.

3. In Ethiopia red crosses had for centuries been used to designate brothels. Apparently, every time an Ethiopian gun crew scored a direct hit on an Italian medical facility flying the red cross the soldiers assumed they'd contributed to undermining enemy morale.

When advertising in any foreign country the safest procedure is to get the copy translated by a national of the country, who lives in the country where the ad will appear and who understands English and most technical terms. Have all symbols (logos) and slogans carefully checked for unwanted meanings in the other country. (In Flemish, General Motors' old slogan, "Body by Fisher," could only be translated as "Corpse by Fisher.")

Write original copy in as simple a style and English as possible, avoiding Americanisms such as "input," "high-performance," and "optimize." As is the case in many foreign languages, there are some English words that defy intelligible translation in certain languages. It's worthwhile, as a final check, to get the foreign version translated back into English by a second translator. Occasionally some weird versions of the original result.

In summarizing this chapter—admittedly a broad overview of a complex subject—remember that all promotional efforts are (or should be) aimed at informing, persuading, and reminding a company's target publics about the services or products offered by the company. Since any prospect for design services has thousands of firms from which to choose, your company must inform prospects about its consulting services and related activities, while persuading them to select you from among the many. And, as we all know, reselling of clients can never stop. Persuasion, reminding, reinforcement of previous promotional messages must operate continuously.

For additional information and background on the subject of advertising, we recommend *How to Advertise*, by Kenneth Roman and Jane Maas (St. Martin's Press, New York, 1975, 156 pages). The authors are vice presidents of the New York City advertising firm of Ogilvy & Mather.

### References

[1]Michael E. G. Kirby, "Tell the Story As It Is," *The Washington Post*, Nov. 30, 1975.
[2]Reginald Brack, Jr., "In Defense of Advertising," *Public Relations Journal*, March 1976, p. 17.
[3]Anonymous advertiser.
[4]Howard Geitzer and Al Ross, "Positioning," *Public Relations Journal*, November 1975, pp. 40–43.

The line between public relations and lobbying is a thin one; lobbying might be defined as the practice of public relations directed toward one very specific and important group.[1]

## CHAPTER 15

# Lobbying and Washington Representation

**M**UCH AS THE case with "public relations," definitions of "lobbying" and speculation about the term's origin abound. *Webster's Third New International Dictionary* (1971) defines lobbyists as "persons who frequent the lobbies of a legislative house to do business with the members; specifically, persons not members of a legislative body and not holding government office who attempt to influence legislators or other public officials through personal contact."

In *Reminiscences of Sixty Years in the National Metropolis*, newspaper correspondent and indefatigable recorder of the Washington scene Benjamin Perley Poore discussed an interesting adjunct to the federal lobby of the mid-1800s.

> One of the neutral grounds, where men of both parties met in peace, was the superbly furnished gambling house of Pendleton, on Pennsylvania Avenue. . . . Pendleton belonged to one of the first families of Virginia, and his wife, a most estimable lady, was the daughter of Robert Mills, the architect of the Treasury. . . .
>
> The people who assembled nightly to see and take part in the entertainments

of the house consisted of candidates for the presidency, senators and representatives, members of the Cabinet, editors and journalists, and the masters of the third house, the lobby. *Pendleton's in its palmiest days might have been called the vestibule of the lobby. . . .* Pendleton himself was an operator in the lobby.[2] [Emphasis added]

In another section of his reminiscences Poore suggests that lobbying techniques under President Cleveland's administration were not all that different from those used by some modern-day lobbyists.

> The lobby is a quiet but efficient part of congressional machinery. . . . An occasional investigation reveals the work of ex-congressmen, who hover about the Capitol like birds of prey, and of correspondents so scantily paid by the journals with which they are connected that they are forced to prostitute their pens. But the most adroit lobbyists belong to the gentler sex.
>
> Some of them are widows of officers of the army or navy, others the daughters of congressmen of a past generation, and others have drifted from home localities where they found themselves the subjects of scandalous comments. They are retained with instructions to exert their influence with designated congressmen. Sometimes the congressmen are induced to vote aye on a certain measure; sometimes to vote no, and it often occurs that where the lobbyist cannot make an impression on them one way or the other, they will endeavor to keep them away from the House when the roll is called.
>
> To enable them to do their work well they have pleasant parlors, with works of art and bric-a-brac donated by admirers. Every evening they receive and in the winter their blazing wood fires are often surrounded by a distinguished circle. Some treat favored guests to a game of euchre and as midnight approaches there is always an adjournment to the dining room, where a choice supper is served. A cold game pie, boiled oysters, charmingly mixed salad, and one or two light dishes generally constitute the repast, with iced champagne or Burgundy at blood heat.
>
> Who can blame a congressman for leaving the bad cooking at his hotel or boarding house, with the absence of all home comforts, to walk into the parlor web which the cunning spider-lobbyist weaves for him?

So much for the good old days, about which someone has pointed out we call them "good" because we were bad; "old" because we were young; and "days" in spite of the fact that it's the nights we really remember.

Not all lobbyists are Washington representatives, of course, since much lobbying goes on in state capitals, county courthouses, and city halls. But practically all Washington reps consider at least some degree of lobbying on behalf of clients as part of their job.

Just as an increasing number of national organizations are moving their headquarters to Washington, D.C., more and more design and construction firms have established some kind of base in the District of Columbia. The concentration of power, federal money, influence, and international contacts between the Potomac and Anacostia Rivers makes the city difficult to ignore in matters of marketing and public relations. More on the pros and cons of Washington representation later.

## FORMS OF LOBBYING

In view of constitutionally guaranteed rights of free speech and to petition, there can be no question of the basic legality of ethical lobbying activities by business, special interest groups, and individuals on behalf of almost any subject.

### Personal

Since constant commuting to state capitals and to Washington is expensive and time-consuming, most of us must be content with expressing our views on legislation and issues from a distance. After voting, communicating with elected officials is the most important form of citizen participation in our system of government. Communication can take many modes—telephone calls, letters, petitions, telegrams, postcards, personal visits—but letters are by far the most popular method. And the correspondence record engendered is difficult for a senator, representative, president, governor, or mayor to disavow.

Letters written to members of Congress should normally go only to the writer's own senators and representatives—not to those from other states or other districts. The exceptions to this rule are when nonlocal members of Congress sit on committees considering legislation of particular concern to the writer, or when they have announced for a higher elective office, such as the presidency.

Here are fifteen tips for getting maximum effectiveness from a letter to Washington. Most of these points also apply to letters to state legislators.

• Keep letters as brief and to the point as possible. Confine them to a single issue. One page is best; never exceed two pages.

• Letters should be an individual creation—not form letters signed by the sender or a letter whose style and wording were obviously directed or inspired by some other individual or special interest group.

• Write on personal or business letterhead, typed if possible, with the sender's name and address shown on the letter itself as well as on the envelope. Sign the letter over your typed name at the end. Don't follow business letter usage of showing your initials, followed by the typist's initials (GLJ:cmr) at the end of the letter.

• Be specific about the subject. Give the name and bill number of legislation if you can.

• Be explicit about your reason for writing. Explain how the legislation or the issue would affect you, your family, your business, your profession, your community—whatever is applicable and can be supported by the facts. Give examples.

• An effective letter is carefully reasoned, clearly stated, natural in its phrasing. It should not be stereotyped, stiff, tendentious, affected, argumentative, extravagant in its demands, threatening in tone, or suggest that it was written at the direction or urging of an organization. Most organized pressure campaigns have little impact on Congress.

• Don't enclose petitions, copies of your letter, or reams of documentation of your position.

• Avoid name-calling and innuendo.

• If you have some personal connection with the member of Congress you are writing, mention it in the letter.

• When you've made your point ask your senators or representatives to state their position on the issue when they reply. Include your telephone number and invite them to call you when they are near your home.

• Be careful of timing. Don't fire off a letter detailing your position on a bill 6 months after it was enacted into law. Try to write when the bill is in committee.

• Don't always write on negative matters. Let legislators know when their vote pleased you or has helped you. And when you get a reply to a letter about pending legislation, write again to thank the elected official for his or her interest and for taking time from a busy schedule to answer you.

• As a general rule, don't send copies of your letter to local media. It can put legislators on the spot and is not a recommended way to initiate or cultivate productive, long-term relationships.

• Don't be discouraged when the reply is obviously a form letter. Too many writers give up when they receive the "Thank you for your comments" answer. If your letter asked specific questions which demand a definitive reply, write again and refer to the questions in the original letter. The various forms of stock replies will eventually be exhausted and you will finally get a personal, individual answer.

• Above all, never write in real anger—about something or someone. Such letters generally serve no useful purpose. Sometimes it helps to write a letter when you're angry, without mailing it. Write it again the next day after you've cooled off.

Letters to senators should be addressed:
The Honorable John P. Doe
United States Senate
Washington, DC 20510

Dear Senator Doe:

And to representatives:
The Honorable Jane F. Doe
House of Representatives
Washington, DC 20515

Dear Congresswoman Doe:

A suggested close is "Sincerely yours," but if you know the member of Congress or other elected official personally, he or she may be addressed by first name or nickname—and the close can be as warm as you feel is appropriate.

Recommended address forms for other public officials:
The President
The White House
Washington, DC 20500

Dear Mr. President:

Cabinet Secretary:
The Honorable John G. Doe
Secretary of Commerce
U.S. Department of Commerce
Washington, DC 20230

Dear Mr. Secretary:

State Governor:
The Honorable John X. Doe
Governor of New Jersey
State House (or State Capitol)
Trenton, New Jersey

Dear Governor Doe:

State Legislator:
The Honorable Jane B. Doe
Missouri House of Representatives
State House (or State Capitol)
Jefferson City, Missouri

Dear Representative Doe:

Mayor:
The Honorable John M. Doe
Mayor of Chicago
City Hall
Chicago, Illinois

Dear Mayor Doe:

Since 1972 the volume of incoming mail for U.S. representatives has more than tripled; an annual total of well over 100 million pieces is received. The Senate postmaster estimated the 1977 mail to that body increased by some 8 million letters over the 33 million pieces logged in 1976. All of this works out to an average of more than 1000 letters every working day for each of the 535 members of Congress.

That averages can be misleading is pointed out by the fact that in early 1978 California's two senators averaged 25,000 letters a week, or around 1.3 million a year. More than half their office operating budgets went for staff and the computerized machines used to answer the mail avalanche. Some of the older automatic typing machines can crank out individually addressed letters (the same letter) at the rate of one every 90 seconds. Newer machines can produce a letter every 20 seconds.

With sophisticated computers generating much of the incoming mail, we've now achieved a technological breakthrough of sorts, in which our computers are writing their computers. One of the most important aspects of the American political system—voters communicating with their top elected officials—has become a two-way computerized monster.

The real impact of mass mailings to Congress is in dispute. Some members maintain the thousands of "me-too" letters that can be generated almost overnight by well-financed organizations have little effect on their thinking and voting. But the more astute organizations, such as the National Rifle Association, motivate only the act of letter writing by their members. Content and phrasing are those of the individual letter writers—and the messages thus command greater attention in congressional offices. Occasionally the sheer tonnage of even sound-alike letters will command attention on Capitol Hill.

Thomas J. Donohue, executive vice-president of Citizens Choice, a conservative Washington-based lobbying organization, was quoted on the front page of *The New York Times* for April 17, 1978: "Congressmen first learn how to count and then to think."

Counting, incidentally, is also very important in lobbying circles. Potential votes of senators and representatives are usually recorded on a 1 to 5 scale:

1. Firmly committed
2. Leaning toward
3. Iffy
4. Leaning against
5. Firmly against

A senator might tell a lobbyist, "You can put me down as a 1." Happiness in Washington is having enough 1s and 2s to ensure a favorable vote on your bill.


## Pressure Groups

Out of the total number of bills introduced during a session of almost any state legislature, from 5 to 15 percent can have a direct effect on the design profession. The figure is at least as high for legislation coming out of Washington, D.C. The fact is that an increasing percentage of the population is affected by more and more of the proposed laws and regulations—and those most apt to be affected are often not able to pass intelligent judgment on the legislation.

For each interested group or profession someone must act as a legislative watchdog—to monitor, recommend action, and present the consensus position. The alternative is to leave the legislative arena to chance or to other, more vocal pressure groups. The (usually) paid watchdog is more properly known as a lobbyist. His or her profession is lobbying.

> In any matter of importance involving the continuing interest of government, someone has to be hired to watch changes, or to introduce them, and to make it his business to know the ropes—who legislators are, where they come from, what their beliefs and interests are, what the nature of their legislation is, and what they are responsive to. Such a representative also has to know what the group that he works for really wants, what the opposing interests are up to, and what the general public's reaction may be.[3]

> It's no secret that lobbying is the silent service of the political scene and that campaign contributions are the mother's milk that makes it work. Everybody plays the game—Chamber of Commerce, American Bar Association, American Farm Bureau Federation, American Magazine Publisher's Association, big labor, big business.[4]

An example of low-key, low-pressure lobbying is shown in Figure 15-1. On July 14, 1975, the president of the McGraw-Hill Book Company wrote to McGraw-Hill authors, asking them to write or wire their representatives in support of Education Appropriations Bill H.R. 5091, which contained $51 million for public and college libraries. In this case the appropriations bill had been passed, but the President was expected to veto it because it exceeded the White House budget request. Similar letters were sent authors when legislation affecting the copyright laws was pending in Congress a few years ago.

The most successful lobbyists on the national scene might have been cloned from the elected officials and appointed administrators they work with—generally young, with better-than-average educations, and willing to work 15- to 18-hour days to accomplish their objectives. Their advice is to get to know the people in government who control your individual or company's or association's destiny.

Make friends early in the game by inviting *all* candidates in *all* elections to visit your firm. Make small personal contributions ($25 or so) to every candidate. Give one early in the primaries and another just before the election. Be sure to send a letter of congratulations to the winner, mentioning your support in general terms.

Now you have a friend in government—comparable to the "sponsor" you must identify within the prospect organization before you can count any marketing effort successful. Just as you depend on the sponsor to represent your firm to the client organization and to supply you with information as it's needed, you can call on your friend in the government for guidance and help through the complex legislative and bureaucratic mazes. As *Engineering News-Record* points out, "Politics, like poker, is not a game for kibitzers. One must spend some chips to get into the game. Individually, and through their professional associations, engineers [and architects] will fight their frustra-

McGraw-Hill Book Company

1221 Avenue of the Americas
New York, New York 10020
Telephone 212/997-1221

Alexander J. Burke, Jr.
President

July 14, 1975

To McGraw-Hill Authors:

I am writing you to ask your support for federal legislation in
which you may share our interest - Education Appropriations Bill H.R. 5091.

Because the current bill exceeds the President's budget, it is
generally expected that the bill will be vetoed by the President, and
unless Congress overrides this veto, educational and library programs
will be reduced to levels below prior years.  In addition, in order to
achieve even these lower levels of expenditures, a complete recycling
of this legislation through both houses of Congress will be necessary,
creating a delay in authorizations as well as planning difficulties for
educational institutions and agencies whose activities are partially
funded by the federal government.

The congressional bill exceeds the President's budget in the following major areas:

$100 million more in assistance for disadvantaged children

$ 41 million more for public libraries

$ 10 million more for college libraries

In spite of its stated resolve, Congress has been conspicuously weak
in overriding Presidential vetoes, and it is for this reason we are seeking your help.

It is expected that the key vote will occur in the House during the
last week in July.  If you are in favor of maintaining or increasing
federal aid to education and libraries, please write or wire your representative today expressing your support for their bill, and asking that
they override the anticipated veto.

If you do so, I would appreciate your sending me a copy of your
communication so that we can have some measure of the support that is
being generated on behalf of this program.

Sincerely yours,

Alexander J. Burke Jr.

Alexander J. Burke, Jr.

AJB:mm

**Figure 15-1.** Letter sent to all McGraw-Hill authors, soliciting support for a 1975 education
appropriations bill. Recipients were asked to write or wire their representatives asking for an
override vote of an anticipated presidential veto of the bill.

tions about public policies only by forcing themselves into the decision-making process."[5]

The legislative program of the California Council of the American Institute of Architects (CCAIA) is widely recognized as a model for state activity by design professionals. In a discussion of the chapter's approach a few years ago, C. Day Woodford, Fellow, American Institute of Architects (FAIA), made these points.

> Legislators favorably inclined are influenced by one or more of the following factors:
> • Personal friendship and respect for architects they know in their community.
> • Respect for representatives of the profession whom they meet in the capitol or city hall.
> • Political support by architects as individuals at the time of their candidacy.
> • Opportunities to meet their home town architects through AIA chapter meetings and civic affairs.
> • Favorable reports on architects' work from their local school districts, city councils, and county supervisors.
> • Favorable attitudes of other people whom they know; friends, contractors, engineers, material dealers, and the like.
> Legislators unfavorably inclined toward architects are influenced by one or more of the following factors:
> • Poor personal experience with architects they have retained or have had bad business dealings with.
> • Political expedience; pressure from other groups.
> • Unfavorable reports on experiences with architects from school boards, local government, or private clients.
> • Unfavorable attitudes toward architects of other people they know, i.e., contractors and subcontractors, building designers, engineers.
> Work with your AIA chapter to put a "Know Your Legislator" plan into effect for the benefit of all the legislators in your chapter area. Remember, too, that you can't just "know your legislator" and expect things to happen. Developing respect goes along with the effort. An example of what we're talking about occurred in a recent campaign for city councilman in Los Angeles. Two men running for office asked an architect to write a statement for them on physical environment. Both were elected and both are now strong supporters of AIA projects. That architect, incidentally, had 14 more requests to write statements for politicians. One of the best ways to develop respect is to do good work for your client and take credit for your good work.
> Consider whether there are certain legislators whom your chapter members should make an extra effort to support at election time. Let your chapter members know which legislators have done an outstanding job, from the profession's viewpoint, and, conversely, which legislators seem weak in their understanding of the problems of the architectural profession.
> Some suggestions for establishing a friendly relationship with your legislator:
> • Call for an appointment at the legislator's office when he is in his own home town. A personal contact is the only way to start.
> • Introduce yourself as one of his constituents interested in public affairs and good government.

- Explain to him that you understand how difficult it is for a legislator, required to vote on hundreds of bills in a short time, to obtain the facts about any particular bill.
- Offer to help him. Explain that as an architect your knowledge and information about the construction industry can be helpful to him in gathering facts about bills affecting the public health and safety, as related to this industry.
- Tell him that each year many bills are proposed which affect the public health, safety, and economy; that are directly related to our profession and the construction industry.
- Ask him if he understands the role and function of an architect in this regard. Be prepared to explain the architect's role and, if he is willing and interested, take him through your office. Be objective in this approach—and *never* defensive.
- Ask him if he would be interested in your opinions or in facts you could obtain in matters in which you are well versed.
- You should thank him for his time and interest. Make your visit warm, personal, and brief.
- When he is running for election, contribute to his campaign fund. The amount is not as important as the contribution. Be sure to use your office letterhead when making contributions.

## THE FIFTH ESTATE

In *How to Market Professional Design Services* I noted that around Washington, D.C., one top congressional administrative assistant (AA) may be worth three run-of-the-mill members of Congress when it comes to getting answers and actions. I advised: "Get acquainted with the AAs and other staff people in the office of your representatives and senators."[6]

In view of the parade of new faces to Congress in the last few years, that advice is even more important now. AAs and LAs (legislative assistants) are the nonelected power on Capitol Hill. One veteran Washington attorney calls the behind-the-scene aides the "invisible fifth estate. You don't know who they are, you can't touch them, you can't identify them. They just operate."

The Washington press corps recently rated their most valuable sources of information. The ranking:

1. Congressional staffs
2. *Congressional Record*
3. Members of Congress
4. Disgruntled employees
5. Lobbyists
6. Press releases

North Carolina Senator Robert Morgan put it: "This country is basically run by the legislative staffs. They are the ones who give us advice as to how to vote, and then we vote on their recommendations."

And congressional aides sometimes topple the great from power, as in the case of former Representative Wayne Hays of Ohio and other, less publicized, incidents. Hays's friend, Elizabeth Ray, was a $14,000-a-year clerk on the House Administration Committee, chaired by Hays.

Some who came to Congress are unable to stand the pressures and the pace—or grow old in the office in somewhat ungraceful ways. General ineptness afflicts a few, but that can be camouflaged to a startling degree. Senility, satyriasis, alcoholism, and other diseases of the mind and body are routinely covered for by aides. Even where no disability is involved, senators and representatives find they must depend more and more on their aides and other legislative specialists.

Contrary to the Washington lawyer's comments, the fifth estate *can* be identified. The effort is worth it.

## THE WASHINGTON REP

The number of people who classify themselves as Washington reps has grown by quantum leaps over the past 10 years. Some work almost entirely on Capitol Hill, sitting in on committee hearings and markup sessions, or prowling the halls of the Senate and House office buildings in hopes of collaring members on the way to their offices or to answer a roll call.

Still others make the rounds of federal departments, agencies, and bureaus in search of work for their clients. A growing number are specialists in narrow fields of expertise—maintaining contact with foreign embassy personnel, for example.

A 1977 study of business representation in Washington showed the following percentages of time spent among various legislative and administrative liaison functions by Washington reps of major U.S. corporations:

| | |
|---|---|
| Service to government | 24 percent |
| Lobbying | 23 percent |
| Regulatory agency liaison | 19 percent |
| Public relations | 19 percent |
| Embassy liaison | 8 percent |
| Other | 7 percent |

The study also found that in addition to their own Washington offices, most companies are represented in some other way by one or more organizations or individuals: 82 percent are represented by trade associations, 56 percent are represented by lawyers, 18 percent by professional lobbyists, 13 percent by public relations professionals, and 9 percent by research organizations.[7]

Education and career backgrounds of Washington reps are diverse, to say the least. Not a few have immigrated to the lobbyist centers of K Street and Connecticut Avenue from Capitol Hill. These include former senators, representatives, staff members of congressional committees, and many congressional aides.

Retired civil servants and military officers help swell the ranks. There are many more colonels and Navy captains operating as consultants than admirals and generals. Presumably this is because flag rank officers are able to move more easily into appropriate levels of corporate management. In some cases the general or admiral cum business executive is quick to retain former high-ranking, now retired, aides and executive officers as their firm's Washington representative. At times, these relationships border on the incestuous, particularly when the major client of the firm is the Department of Defense. But without all these actual and potential conflicts of interest some Washington news reporters and columnists would be hard put to fill their weekly news quotas.

Other lobbyists/reps come from journalism, law, advertising, the White House, public relations, and jail. Not a few of those caught up in recent Washington scandals have hung up a consultant's sign on their release from various federal and state penitentiaries.

Two former aides to Connecticut Senator Abraham Ribicoff made local headlines in April 1978, when it was revealed they had circulated a memo to several corporations offering their services for a $200,000 retainer—in connection with a tax relief bill for Americans working overseas the senator was sponsoring. They planned to keep their client group small—not more than ten companies would be allowed in ($200,000 × 10 = $2 million).

The five-page memo of solicitation suggested the firm, operating as Malmgren, Inc., was "in an unusually good position to influence the outcome of the debate, and move it in a good direction." To avoid any room for confusion on the part of the corporate recipients, the memo spelled it out: ". . . Salzman [one of the former staffers] has been the principle [sic] drafter of [the bill]. He was, of course, formerly Legislative Assistant to the Senator."

Senator Ribicoff was properly outraged and issued a statement denying any special relationship between him and the aides. "They are completely out of line to make such a representation," huffed the Senator.

Although the incident does not say a great deal for the native intelligence of the principals, the fact that it occurred at all may give some insight into contemporary Washington mores and morality.

On the same day the Malmgren, Inc., story broke, United Press International distributed an equally weird tale to its subscribers. Ambassador to Saudi Arabia John C. West signed off on a highly flattering report on Adnan Khashoggi, in effect recommending him as a sales agent U.S. business firms might hire to represent them in the Middle East. Khashoggi is the Arab agent accused of payoffs and bribery for such U.S. corporations as Northrop, Raytheon, and Litton Industries.

According to UPI, Ambassador West signed the report "shortly before the Saudi government hired an American public relations firm whose officials include the ambassador's son and a former close political associate."

The best-paid Washington reps are such lawyers as Clark Clifford, Richard Kleindienst, former Senator J. William Fulbright, John Connally, and William D. Ruckelshaus. They and their law firms increasingly represent foreign interests and governments. One reason lawyers are so popular as Washington reps and fixers is the traditional confidentiality of all matters between clients and attorneys.

If you believe your interests might be better served through a full- or part-time Washington representative, there are several avenues to explore before hiring one. Check with the Washington staff of your professional associations—The American Institute of Architects, American Consulting Engineers Council (ACEC), National Society of Professional Engineers, and the like. The ACEC sponsors a monthly breakfast meeting of those who represent design and construction firms in Washington, D.C. From forty to seventy real live Washington reps can be surveyed and evaluated at these sessions.

Ask disinterested consultants who operate in other fields—management, marketing, or public relations, for example—for suggestions and recommendations. And check with your congressional delegation. They see the gamut from bad to excellent reps constantly.

Be prepared to pay fees of $1000 a month and up. Mostly up. Most Washington reps, concerned with potential conflicts of interest, will not represent more than one design firm. Others work with a kind of national network of design firms, divided by geography and in-house disciplines.

A few Washington reps should be put out of business, if not in jail. Those, obviously, are the ones you want to avoid by your preliminary investigation.

## POLITICAL ACTION

Much of the foregoing has touched on various aspects of political action. The truth of the oft-repeated adage that "your vote counts" is proved by examples such as these:

• Alaska, 1966. Republican Walter Hickel defeated incumbent Democrat William Egan by 1080 votes—a margin of less than 3 votes per precinct.

• Colorado, 1972. Three-term incumbent U.S. Senator Gordon Allott was turned out of office by Democrat Floyd Haskell by a margin of 9588 votes—out of more than 925,000 cast.

• Delaware, 1972. Joseph Biden, Jr., became the youngest member of the U.S. Senate when he defeated two-term incumbent Republican J. Caleb Boggs by 3162 votes.

• Maryland, 1970. Parren J. Mitchell won the Democratic primary in the Seventh Congressional District by only 38 votes. Mitchell went on to win his first term in Congress in the general election.

• Oregon, 1968. Republican Robert Packwood defeated veteran incumbent Wayne Morse for the U.S. Senate by an average of 1.2 votes per precinct.

• South Dakota, 1962. George McGovern won his first term in the U.S. Senate by 597 votes; an average of ⅓ additional vote per precinct for his opponent would have changed the outcome.

• Texas, 1968. Richard Nixon lost the state of Texas by less than two votes per precinct.

An interesting sidelight on the 1960 presidential race is found in *Judith Exner—My Story* (Grove Press, New York, 1977). Author Ovid DeMaris points out that Richard Nixon lost Illinois to John F. Kennedy by 8858 votes; a switch of 4500 votes in Cook County's 5199 precincts would have given Nixon the state's 27 electoral votes. A net gain of 4539 votes for Nixon was found in a GOP check of 699 paper ballot precincts, but an official recount was not allowed and the original election figures remain on the books.

The Illinois electoral votes would not have given the election to the Republicans, of course, since Kennedy won Texas by 28,000 votes. No official claims of miscounts were made in Texas, either, but election night fast counts are not unknown in the Lone Star State. Nixon would have needed both states to gain a narrow electoral college majority of two. Camelot thus began on a slightly tarnished note—not helped much by the fact that John Kennedy's entire popular vote margin was $\frac{1}{10}$ of 1 percent.

Election chicanery is not limited to Illinois and Texas, or to the United States—or even to modern times. One of the earliest bought elections on record—to select a new emperor of the Holy Roman Empire—took place more than 4½ centuries ago. The electorate for the 1519 election was relatively small; four princes and three archbishops. Charles V, the 19-year-old Spanish king, was able to buy five of the electors and ensure his victory for an estimated total outlay of around $40 million. At $8 million a vote the young monarch far outclassed the usual payouts by ward heelers in our larger metropolitan areas.

Election irregularities are not unknown in such European countries as France and Italy, where campaign funding laws are nonexistent or not enforced. One of the most unusual Italian campaigns was that of Corrado Tedeschi in 1953. Candidate Tedeschi promised to deliver a beefsteak a day to every adult on his election. Caught passing out samples of his pledge in Florence, he was arrested for bribing voters.

Participation in campaigns by a much larger percentage of the electorate than is now the case is one answer to corruption, bribery, and false ballot counts. Political action committees (PACs) for that purpose are growing in popularity. Even though PACs offer a relatively passive type of involvement, they are better than zero participation.

PACs can be set up by business and professional groups to channel political contributions to selected candidates. Direct corporate contributions are prohibited by law, of course, but executives and employees of companies in a given industry, profession, or area can band together to raise and distribute meaningful contributions.

It's illegal to tie a raise in salary or a bonus to a political contribution to a certain candidate—but it's entirely within the law to encourage private political action, with pay levels set high enough so that executives can afford to make personal contributions. PACs can sponsor fund-raising events and make direct solicitations. The PAC's directors then apportion contributions to candidates of their choosing.

## PROFESSIONAL MISCONDUCT

In February 1974 architect John G. Paulson was committed for trial on charges of bribing a union official to obtain a design contract for the union's new headquarters and for corrupting a government railway official in connection with the award of a terminal project. Paulson had already been found guilty on thirteen separate charges of corruption and sentenced to 5 years in prison.

An under secretary of the Department of Agriculture, found guilty of accepting more than $70,000 in payments from Paulson, also faced 5 years in prison for using his office and influence to direct design awards to Paulson's office.

Do these sentences and charges seem unduly harsh in view of Paulson's offenses? Perhaps it is because Paulson was an English architect—and his illegal activities were conducted in Scotland and England, rather than in one of the score or more U.S. states where similar antisocial actions have come under the scrutiny of prosecutors, grand juries, and the general public. Paulson's fall from grace brought down several high-ranking English officials, including a former Home Secretary.

Since 1970 scandal has touched a number of architectural and engineering firms. Strangely enough, no one and no professional organization seems to have been keeping score. The AIA set up a National Inquiry Committee in May 1974 to investigate alleged ethical and legal violations by its members. In the first 18 months of its operation some thirty investigations were undertaken, but interest, activity, and funding soon declined and the group passed quietly out of existence in late 1977. No fanfare, no public announcements or obituaries—not even a graveside service.

In what now sounds very much like a cynical cop-out—but may have been just fatuous understatement—the 1974 AIA president was possibly predicting an early death for the investigating committee when he said, " . . . the few [architect offenders] may have been victimized by a political system that encourages corruption!" This is surely a novel, if patently unsupportable, theory of systemic "immaculate conception."

One unfortunate result of the publicized activities of a few corrupt and corrupting design firms has been a drawing away by many honest, competent professionals from all involvement with public projects at any level of government—a form of compounding the felony, so to speak.

It hardly makes sense to sit idly by—or attempt to blanket the existing situation with massive, studied indifference—while a handful of bad apples work away at rotting the reputation of the design profession, secure in the knowledge that most people do not want to get involved; will *not* get involved. Walter Wagner editorialized in the November 1973 *Architectural Record:* "[The corruption] could stop. Now. Today . . . if every architect and engineer simply refused ever again to take part in this kind of extortion. Not everyone will. So it now becomes the responsibility of every architect . . . to blow the whistle long and hard at dishonest practices that he becomes aware of."

Get involved. If, as we suggested in Chapter 3, adherence to an ethical code of conduct is truly one of the factors that differentiates professionals from used car salespersons and shell-game operators, then we must act like professionals.

## References

[1]John E. Marston, *The Nature of Public Relations,* McGraw-Hill Book Company, New York, 1963, p. 61.

[2]Benjamin Perley Poore (1820–1887), *Perley's Reminiscences of Sixty Years in the National Metropolis,* 2 vols., Hubbard Brothers, Philadelphia, 1886.

[3]Marston, loc. cit.

[4]Stuart Auerbach, "'Sore Throat' Gives AMA High Fever," *The Washington Post,* July 13, 1975.

[5]"Key to Influence: Participation," *Engineering News-Record,* Oct. 16, 1975, p. 100.

[6]Gerre Jones, *How to Market Professional Design Services,* McGraw-Hill Book Company, New York, 1973, p. 188.

[7]*The Information Report,* Spring 1977, Washington Researchers, p. 2. Study conducted by Washington Researchers.

For value received, I hereby grant to [photographer's name] and his assigns permission to use my photograph and/or statement for advertising, trade or similar purposes.[1]

# CHAPTER 16
# Legal Considerations

IN *HOW TO Prepare Professional Design Brochures* we told the story of the Midwestern design firm that decided to use its internal newsletter as an educational vehicle for staff members. A series of articles about major problems of the firm's recent buildings was outlined by the public relations department and approved by the principals.

The initial installment described in great and candid detail how design errors and faulty construction supervision had contributed to a wall collapse in one of their buildings. All in all, a splendid idea for staff continuing education—right?

Wrong.

Copies of the supposedly internal publication got into external hands. The client was in the process of suing the design firm and the contractor, naturally, and plaintiff's attorneys suddenly began smiling a lot. One was found giggling into a brief. The attorneys for the design firm resigned from the case in a huff, while the contractor booked passage on an around-the-world cruise.

Engineers and architects are hardly novices in litigious matters these days, but with clients, governments, and plain citizens suing everyone in sight at the drop of a hat (or pane of glass), it behooves us to control what can be controlled. In recent years, according to one insurance source, lawsuits for faulty design and construction have increased around 20 percent a year. In 1960 one out of eight design firms was sued; in 1976 the figure had risen to three out of ten, and the average claim had tripled. While figures were not available as of this writing, the 1978 ratio was certainly approaching four out of ten firms.

Legal review of anything going public—even news releases—has always been desirable from most points of view. Pressures of deadlines and a general reluctance to submit material to review by attorneys are among the reasons this step is often omitted. Lawyers are notoriously turgid writers and when they feel they must edit for style as well as content the result is usually dull, deadly, and demeaning to the original author.

Regulatory agencies, such as the Federal Trade Commission (FTC), have become much more stringent in recent years, especially in the area of advertising claims. In recent months the FTC has enforced its "corrective advertising" rule against such products as Listerine and the oil additive STP. The STP Corporation agreed to place $700,000 worth of advertising in various media, carrying the explanation that certain past claims for its product were made in error (see Figure 16-1).

In May 1978 the FTC announced that celebrities who appear in advertisements would be held personally liable for false claims made in the ads. Any penalties that might be assessed would be borne partially by the star salesperson, the FTC said.

## SUBLIMINAL ADVERTISING

From a Federal Communications Commission (FCC) Public Notice dated November 27, 1957:

> Deep concern has been expressed by members of the public, the broadcast industry and leaders in public life with respect to the use of "subliminal perception" advertising by television stations. That this concern has a firm basis is evidenced by the action of the NARTB [National Association of Radio and Television Broadcasters; now the National Association of Broadcasters (NAB)] and the caution with which television licensees have approached the technique. Obviously, it is a matter which vitally concerns the public interest. Accordingly, the Commission's study is being directed toward determining what appropriate steps, if any, should be taken by the Commission with respect to the possible use of the above technique by the television licensees. The posture of the problem is such that the public interest is not in immediate danger of being adversely affected. Ample proof has been given of the recognition by television licensees of their responsibilities and obligation to operate their stations in the public interest.

Since the FCC, at that time, had no knowledge that any television station had used subliminal perception techniques, the notice was cautionary only. In late 1973 the Commission received complaints that some TV stations were using a commercial containing the subliminal message "Get it!" referring to the product advertised. Another warning was issued, in which the FCC

ADVERTISEMENT

# FTC NOTICE

As a result of an investigation by the
Federal Trade Commission into certain allegedly
inaccurate past advertisements
for STP's oil additive, STP Corporation
has agreed to a $700,000 settlement.
With regard to that settlement,
STP is making the following statement:

It is the policy of STP to support its advertising with objective information and test data. In 1974 and 1975 an independent laboratory ran tests of the company's oil additive which led to claims of reduced oil consumption. However, these tests cannot be relied on to support the oil consumption reduction claim made by STP.

The FTC has taken the position that, in making that claim, the company violated the terms of a consent order. When STP learned that the test data did not support the claim, it stopped advertising containing that claim. New tests have been undertaken to determine the extent to which the oil additive affects oil consumption. Agreement to this settlement does not constitute an admission by STP that the law has been violated. Rather, STP has agreed to resolve the dispute with the FTC to avoid protracted and prohibitively expensive litigation.

February 13, 1978

**Figure 16-1. A STP advertisement from the March–April 1978** *Harvard Business Review,* **published as part of the company's settlement with the Federal Trade Commission.**

pointed out that "such broadcasts are contrary to the public interest. Whether effective or not, such broadcasts clearly are intended to be deceptive."

The National Association of Broadcasters Television Code prohibits use of "any technique whereby an attempt is made to convey information to the viewer by transmitting messages below the threshold of normal awareness."

Things were quiet on the subliminal front until 1978, when the FCC gave a Midwestern television station emergency authorization to insert a subliminal message, "Contact the chief," in news accounts of a mass murderer's victims. The police had hoped to reestablish contact with the killer by the use of the technique.

In the late 1960s a few theater owners admitted to occasional insertions of subliminal message frames in films. A desert scene—so brief it could be perceived by the mind but not the eye—was supposed to make movie patrons thirsty enough to head for the refreshment stand.

## COPYRIGHT

The concept of copyrighting literary works had its origin among the royalty of Renaissance Italy. The first copyright law in this country was passed in 1783 by the Connecticut legislature—primarily, according to historians, at the behest of Noah Webster, who wanted to protect a spelling book he had written.

The first U.S. copyright law was enacted by Congress in 1790, with comprehensive revisions made in 1831, 1870, and 1909. The 1909 statute, which governed copyrights in this country until January 1, 1978, obviously did not cover conditions brought about through such technological advances as radio, jukeboxes, television, instant copiers, computers, tape recorders, and, more recently, home videotape recorders. After a 10-year effort to update horse-and-buggy-era copyright statutes, Congress finally passed and President Gerald Ford signed a new copyright law (Public Law 94-553) on October 19, 1976.

The new statute became effective on January 1, 1978, superseding the 1909 copyright act. Changes were many and significant. Highlights of the new act:

• For works created after January 1, 1978, the duration of copyrights granted is for the author's life, plus 50 years, bringing the U.S. into line with the seventy-four other countries who follow the Berne copyright convention. For works done for hire (a book written under contract to and copyrighted by McGraw-Hill Book Company, for example) the protection is for 75 years from the date of first publication or 100 years from the original creation, whichever is shorter.

• Under the 1909 copyright law, as amended, authors could protect their works for 28 years from first publication and renew the copyright for another 28 years. After that, the work went into the public domain. Copyrights in their first term on January 1, 1978, under the old law, will run for the standard 28-year period, but the renewal will be for 47 years.

• Prohibitions against copyrighting most government publications are continued in the new law.

• Five new classes of copyrights are substituted for the old law's fifteen. The new classification system:

1. Class TX—nondramatic literary works. Includes all types of published and unpublished works written in words or other verbal or numerical symbols; fiction, nonfiction, poetry, periodicals, textbooks, directories, catalogs, advertising copy, and the like.

2. Class PA—works of the performing arts. All works prepared to be performed directly before an audience or indirectly by means of any device or process. Examples: musical works (and accompanying lyrics), dramatic works, motion pictures, and other audiovisual works.

3. Class VA—works of the visual arts. Pictorial, graphic, and sculptural works, including photographs, prints, maps, charts, technical drawings, advertisements, and models.

4. Class SR—sound recordings. Works that result from the fixation of a series of musical, spoken, or other sounds—with the exception of motion picture soundtracks and audio cassettes accompanying a filmstrip; these are considered integral parts of the audiovisual work and come under Class PA.

5. Class RE—renewal registration. Since this covers only renewals of copyrights that were in their first term on January 1, 1978 (works originally copyrighted between January 1, 1950 and December 31, 1977), Class RE will eventually fall into disuse, leaving but four copyright classes to deal with.

Application forms for all classes are available from the Copyright Office, Library of Congress, Washington, D.C. 20559. Each application is subject to a $10 fee, and two complete works must accompany the application. Many people are under the mistaken impression that the Library of Congress keeps and files all of the thousands of books and other works submitted annually through the Copyright Office. If this were the case, a third of Washington's buildings might be required to house all copyrighted materials received. The Library retains for its permanent collections only those works which meet the Library's selection standards. About half of all materials now copyrighted are selected. The remainder go uncataloged into warehouse storage. Eventually, the warehouse stocks are made available to members of Congress and libraries. At least a few representatives and senators have built up sizable personal libraries from Library of Congress discards.

The 1978 copyright law retains the three traditional elements of a copyright notice—the word "Copyright," the abbreviation "Copr.," or the symbol ©; the year of first publication; and the name of the copyright owner. For example:

Copyright 1979 Gerre Jones

The notice should appear in a place where it can be easily seen and in type large enough to be read comfortably.

## THE FAIR USE DOCTRINE

A copyright prevents others from copying all or substantial sections of a work verbatim—it doesn't protect ideas expressed in the work. On "fair use" (how much of a work can be copied or reproduced without infringing on the original owner's copyright), the new law says:

> The fair use of a copyrighted work, including such use by reproduction in copies or photorecords . . . for purposes such as criticism, comment, news reporting, teaching (including multiple copies for classroom use), scholarship or research, is not an infringement of copyright. In determining whether the use of a work in any particular case is a fair use the factors to be considered shall include
>
> 1. The purpose and character of the use, including whether such is of a commercial nature or is for nonprofit educational puposes;
>
> 2. The nature of the copyrighted work;
>
> 3. The amount and substantiality of the portion used in relation to the copyrighted work as a whole; and
>
> 4. The effect of the use upon potential market for or value of the copyrighted work.

Piracy (using the copyrighted literary work of another without permission) and plagiarism (passing another's ideas or writings off as one's own) are forms of stealing and thus punishable under the law. The safe procedure is to request permission from the copyright holder to use *anything* from a protected work. In my writing I use the letter shown in Figure 16-2 to request permission to quote from a copyrighted work.

You can obtain a copy of Public Law 94-553 and a general summary of its provisions from the Copyright Office. Circular R21, *Reproduction of Copyrighted Works by Educators and Librarians*, is also helpful to a better understanding of the statute.

## LIBEL, SLANDER, AND DEFAMATION

Since it is both impossible and imprudent to try to cover such important legal points as these in a few paragraphs, we will give a few definitions, some general ground rules for avoiding libel actions, and a sincere admonition to work closely with an attorney whenever the going is sticky.

*Defamation* is injuring a person's reputation, fame, or character by false, unjust, and malicious statements. One court made this distinction between justified criticism and defamation:

> Criticism deals only with such things as invite public attention or call for public comment, and does not follow a man into his private life, or pry into his domestic concerns, and it never attacks the individual, but only his work.[2]

*Libel* has been defined by the courts as "written defamation" and "false and malicious publication." There is a form of permanency to libel. *Slander*, as you might imagine, is oral defamation. "Libel and slander are both

Jane R. Doe, Manager
Rights and Permissions
Blank Book Company
124 Main Street
New York, N.Y. 10000

                              Re: Public Relations - A to Z

Dear Ms. Doe:

I am preparing a book tentatively titled Public Relations for
the Design Professional, to be published by McGraw-Hill Book
Company in 1979.  It is intended for use by architects, engineers, and other design professionals.

I should like permission to reproduce in my book, and in any
of its future editions, the material indicated below:

          Author:  M. N. Creel
          Title and publication date: Public Relations -- A to Z,
                              1973.
          Selection 1: "Think in terms...public relations results."
             Page 20
             Approximate number of words: 220

          Selection 2: "PR practice...hard-headed clients."
             Page 35
             Approximate number of words: 45

It is understood, of course, that full credit will be given to
the author and publisher, either in a footnote or as a reference
within the text, or both.

A release form is given below for your convenience.  The duplicate copy of this request is for your files.

Sincerely,


Gerre Jones
  .   .   .   .   .   .   .   .   .   .   .   .   .   .   .

Permission is granted for use of the material as stipulated.


_____          _____
Date                         Signature

                             _____
                             Title

Figure 16-2. Sample form letter for requesting permission to use copyrighted material.

methods of defamation; the former being expressed by print, writing, pictures, or signs; the latter by oral expressions."[3]

Dick Schmidt, a Washington communications attorney, advised reporters attending a 1978 conference on media law to follow Scripps-Howard's nine rules for avoiding libel:

1. Tell the truth.
2. Report arrests in a fair and impartial manner.
3. Get the other side of a story.
4. Watch quotations.
5. Never railroad a story through.
6. Observe the privacy law.
7. Avoid gossip.
8. Make retractions and corrections only with the advice of counsel.
9. Never indulge in careless reporting.

On the subject of truth, which is not all that absolute a defense in libel and slander actions given the varied opinions as to what "truth" is, Thomas Jefferson had his own opinion on the matter. As the American Minister to Paris in 1787, Jefferson made a statement often quoted by the press: "Were it left to me to decide whether we should have a government without newspapers, or newspapers without a government, I should not hesitate a moment to prefer the latter."

By the end of his second term as President, Jefferson had reached the conclusion that "nothing can now be believed which is seen in a newspaper. Truth itself becomes suspicious by being put into that polluted vehicle." Few news people quote the latter statement.

## PHOTO RELEASES

The safest procedure with photographs is to get a signed release from everyone recognizable if there is *any* possibility you'll ever use the picture for *any* commercial purpose. A photo made for news purposes—to be distributed with a news release or for use in a television news program, for example—normally would not require a release. But if later you want to use that picture in a general capabilities brochure, then a release would be necessary.

The purpose of a release is to protect you and your firm against future claims of violations of individual privacy rights. People have the right *not* to have their likenesses used for commercial purposes without their specific consent. Libel, slander, and invasion of privacy rights are torts—and liability generally extends to all parties in a tort.

In engineering and architectural firms, staff members' pictures are often used in promotional material. Any time this is done without a signed release on file, the design firm risks a future lawsuit. Employees can get fired or leave for other reasons. If disgruntlement sets in later, they may have an excellent cause of action against a former employer if their photographs are still in use in a brochure.

The ideal way to handle this situation is to include a model release in all of the other forms to be signed when a new employee comes to work for you. Everyone on staff up to at least the associate level should sign a model release.

This chapter opened with a brief form model release. Dated, signed, and properly witnessed, it gives a reasonable amount of protection to the photographer and ultimate user. There are more complicated release forms, of course, and some are reproduced later in this section. Usually, the more complicated and involved the form, the more protection it provides the user—but many people will refuse to sign a broad form release.

Minors may not legally sign away their rights in a photo release. Further protection is afforded the user by asking signers to warrant that they are over 21 years of age (or over the age of consent). When underage subjects are involved, a parent or guardian must sign the release.

So far, the discussion has been about personnel releases. If you want to use a picture of someone's property—pet, house, car, and the like—get a release signed by the legal owner of the property. Property releases are often more difficult to get; most people do not understand them and some undoubtedly fear that they may be signing away their ownership rights.

There is an interesting, supposedly true, story about property releases and a television commercial being shot to advertise an automobile. The car was placed in front of an attractive private home in the suburbs and photographed. The photographer's assistant asked the woman in the house to sign a property release, explaining that her house would be seen in a TV special the auto manufacturer was sponsoring.

The lady took the release and said her husband would have to sign it. Everyone involved in the filming forgot about the release. Except the owners of the house. After the special appeared the sponsor received a brief letter from the couple, pointing out that the release somehow had never gotten signed—and expressing their disappointment at not being able to see their home in color; they did not own a color receiver.

Within a week the homeowners were the proud owners of a new color TV set, and the automobile company was the not-so-happy owner of a signed property release for the house.

Property releases are seldom, if ever, obtained for well-known, landmark-type buildings such as office structures. Technically, the owners of the Empire State Building could have sued the makers of the original *King Kong* film.

Crowd scenes for commercial use can be tricky to photograph, especially when people in the foreground are identifiable. The only safe practice is to get them to sign model releases. Some advertising and public relations practitioners use crowd shots made in other countries to avoid this problem. The odds are that people in a crowd shot made in Marienplatz or Stachus in Munich will never see their images in an architectural brochure distributed in the United States. In the unlikely event they should see the picture, chances of them suing are remote.

Here is one version of the long form model release, covering adults and minors, and waiving all rights to inspect the finished photographs or the printed form in which they will be published.

MODEL RELEASE

For and in consideration of my engagement as a model by (<u>photogapher</u>), hereafter referred to as the photographer, on terms or fee hereinafter stated, I hereby give the photographer, his legal representatives and assigns, those for whom the photographer is acting, and those acting with his permission, or his employees, the right and permission to copyright and/or use, reuse and/or publish, and republish photographic pictures or portraits of me, or in which I may be distorted in character, or form, in conjunction with my own or fictitious name, on reproduction thereof in color, or black and white made through any media by the photographer at his studio or elsewhere, for any purpose whatsoever; including the use of any printed matter in conjunction therewith.

I hereby waive any right to inspect or approve the finished photograph or advertising copy or printed matter that may be used in conjunction therewith or to the eventual use that it might be applied.

I hereby release, discharge and agree to save harmless the photographer, his representatives, assigns, employees or any person or persons, corporation or corporations, acting under his permission or authority, or any person, persons, corporation or corporations, for whom he might be acting, including any firm publishing and/or distributing the finished product, in whole or in part, from and against any liability as a result of any distortion, blurring, or alteration, optical illusion, or use in composite form, either intentionally or otherwise, that may occur or be produced in the taking, processing or reproduction of the finished product, its publication or distribution of same, even should the same subject me to ridicule, scandal, reproach, scorn or indignity.

I hereby warrant that I am over the age of consent, and competent to contract in my own name insofar as the above is concerned.

The above release applies to all photographic sessions and photographs taken of me prior to this date and all photographic sessions and photographs taken of

me from this date forth. Compensation, if any, will
be agreed upon prior to each photographic session.
    I have read the foregoing release, authorization and
agreement, before affixing my signature below, and
warrant that I fully understand the contents thereof.

Dated _____

_____          _____
    Name                                      Witness


_____          _____
    Address                                   Address
.............................................................
    I hereby certify that I am the parent and/or guardian
of _____, an infant under
the age of twenty-one years, and in consideration of
value received, the receipt of which is hereby
acknowledged, I hereby consent that any photographs
which have been, or are about to be taken by the
photographer, may be used by him for the purposes set
forth in the original release hereinabove, signed by
the infant model, with the same force and effect as if
executed by me.


_____
    Parent or Guardian


_____
    Address


The consideration or fee paid to nonprofessionals is usually $1 or a copy of
the picture, or both. Professional modeling fees are set according to individual or union scales.

Keep in mind that, by definition, a defamatory photograph is always libel.
An otherwise innocent photograph can be made libelous through errors in
names or a defaming cutline. Newspapers occasionally get into trouble by
using a photograph to illustrate a story on some criminal or unsavory subject.
The picture subject, by implication, becomes associated with the article,
whether or not there is any real connection.

Since this chapter dealt with several areas of law which have been subject
to varying judicial interpretations in the past, we again caution readers to
check with their attorneys at the first signs of trouble. And keep a pad of
model releases handy.

## References

[1]Short form of a model release.
[2]*Schwimmer v. Commercial Newspaper Company*, 131 Misc. 552, 228 N.Y.S. 220, 221.
[3]*Ajouelo v. Auto-Soler Co.*, 61 Ga.App. 216, 6 S.E. 2d 415, 418.

If we take the word and consider it a product that the public relations industry produces, the purpose for which the word is conceived is in a pure sense the objective of public relations. Its dissemination is the technique of publicity. Public relations is the formulation of policy in the use of communication, whereas the business of publicity is its widest possible circulation.[1]

# CHAPTER 17
# Conclusion

**O**LD-TIME REVIVAL preachers used to admonish young pastors: "Tell 'em what you're gonna tell 'em; tell 'em; then tell 'em what you told 'em!" That advice might serve as a fitting topic sentence for this final chapter, except that our method of "telling 'em what we told 'em" will be more by example and extended comment than by reiteration.

Kenneth Henry, reviewing several books about public relations in the *Harvard Business Review* for November–December 1974, observed, "A PR book that uses well under 10 percent of the text for how-to-do-it instruction is welcome indeed." Although it hasn't been checked, I have a feeling that Henry's arbitrary 10 percent limit on how-to-do-it information has been considerably exceeded in this book. I am not certain what the penalty is in such cases, other than not being welcome at the offices of the *Harvard Business Review*.

Another Henryism: "External publicity, including press releases, accounts for as little as 10 percent of [the public relations practitioner's] time and thought." An interesting, if doubtful, statistic, proving, if nothing else, that its author has a strange fascination with the number 10. Henry, who is the director of public relations for a large association, knows better.

More than 50 percent of the membership of the Public Relations Society of America responded to a 1978 survey covering attitudes, opinions, and personal data. The respondent practitioners ranked the time spent in various activities as follows:

1. Media relations
2. PR management and administration
3. Publicity
4. Community relations
5. PR counseling
6. Editor of publications
7. Employee relations
8. Government relations
9. Investor relations
10. Consumer affairs
11. PR teaching
12. Advertising and sales promotion

Note that numbers 1 and 3 encompass external publicity; some aspects of external publicity are certainly involved in numbers 4, 6, 8, 9, and 10—and possibly in numbers 2, 5, and 12.

The survey also showed the typical PRSA member to be 45 years old, earning $26,000 a year, and in public relations more than 15 years. Just under 39 percent of the respondents had formal education in their field. Almost 10 percent of those reporting had annual salaries in excess of $50,000.

Those who expected to find a lot of discussion about issue-oriented, socially conscious, morally uplifting public relations techniques and practices have undoubtedly been disappointed. For this I offer no apology. Those familiar with my personal philosophy of writing and teaching know it to be more how-to-do-it than theoretical; more nuts-and-bolts than elevating. This wrapup chapter, then, will be eclectic and practical, and—as promised in the preface—will attempt to position the role, function, and place of public relations in today's scheme of things.

Frank Wylie, 1978 president of the Public Relations Society of America, underscored the importance of the practical approach to public relations in his inaugural address:

> A public relations professional has the ability to understand and anticipate the direction and impact of trends; the ability to provide creative and sound counsel to clients; and the ability to communicate with equal facility to clients and the public.
>
> He or she is a person for all seasons, and a person of all interests.
>
> The public relations person does not exist or work in a vacuum, but rather enjoys the opportunity of being involved in all types and levels of client activities. As a result, the PR person must know far more than the professionals who work at the more restrictive disciplines. The PR person must be a well-informed generalist with a thorough knowledge of several specific fields. And he or she must have the judgement to place events, trends and encounters in a proper perspective.

Wylie also pointed out we are creating so much data that the information industry will be the fastest growing industry in America during the last quarter of this century. A recent Department of Commerce report tells us our economy is no longer based on manufacturing, but on the transfer of knowledge. Almost half (46 percent) of the Gross National Product (GNP) is now linked to producing, processing, and distributing information. And half of the U.S. labor force works in information-related fields—and earns 53 percent of all wages.

As we noted in Chapter 1, this flood of information has been building up for a long time. "One of the diseases of this age is the multiplicity of books," wrote one observer of the ever-growing body of knowledge—in 1613.

The information deluge is accompanied by a full-fledged media revolution. More on that shortly. The fact that we spend fewer hours at work and have more leisure time impacts on our national capacity to absorb information. In the decade 1965–1975 leisure time for the average American increased by some 4 hours a week. And the amount of time spent with media increased from 14.7 hours a week in 1965 to 18.2 hours in 1975. By 1980, the experts assure us, Americans will be eating every other meal away from home. Fast-food chains, for better or for worse, will get two-thirds of the eating-out dollars.

## THE MEDIA REVOLUTION

Some feeling for the parameters of the present media revolution can be gotten from the report of a Western Union investigating committee, appointed to look into Alexander Graham Bell's offer to sell his telephone patent. The 1876 committee found: "This idea is idiotic on the face of it. Furthermore, why would any person want to use this ungainly and impractical device when he can send a messenger to the local telegraph office and have a clearly written message sent to any large city in the United States?"

The fate of the telegram (now "delivered" by telephone) is well-known— as is the importance accorded Bell's "ungainly and impractical device" in today's communications matrix. National and international conferences and seminars are routinely held through elaborate telephone networks. Cut-in devices and table mikes enable participants to make comments and ask questions at will. In some areas the Picturephone adds another dimension to such sessions.

Computers, electro-optics (the physics of lasers), and electronics are some of the major contributors to the massive changes in communications technology. If you are not now familiar with such terms as "teletext" and "viewdata," get ready. These information systems, using current television, telephone, and computer technology, make the regular transmission of magazines and newspapers into homes a reality—along with accessing complete libraries and other major information sources. The systems were operational in late 1977 in parts of England, Germany, and Japan.

Electronic production and home delivery of news publications—from the reporter entering a story on a video-display terminal to the home viewer pushing a button to receive a printed copy of the TV screen display—is no longer a futuristic idea. It's here. Now.

You may recall the advice of the late mayor of Chicago, Richard Daley, to "look with nostalgia at the future." In that vein, I recall the operational facsimile printer in Missouri University's School of Journalism during my student days. Capable of delivering printed pages, it was a wonder machine at the time—1948. If you wonder why, more than three decades later, the average American home does not boast such a machine, consider the enormous capital investment in printing plants and machinery of the publishing industry. And, of at least equal importance, the power of the printing unions to hold back any technology that threatens their members. In New York, Washington, and Las Vegas, to name a few cities, presses have been smashed and pressrooms trashed in disputes involving installations of labor-saving equipment.

For now, the action is in other countries. In England teletext magazines ride on regular transmissions, decoded and displayed on home screens by a black box resembling a pocket calculator. (Texas Instruments supplies the decoder.) The teletext system uses scan lines which normally carry no signal. A limitation of teletext, in its present form, is that pages must be broadcast in sequence, at about four pages a second. Some viewers get impatient at having to view a lot of unwanted information.

Viewdata will answer most of the problems of teletext, in that it is transmitted by a telephone line connected to the TV set and offers two-way communication. Viewers can select the information they want from among some 60,000 pages of data now available to subscribers.

Meanwhile, the print media is going through its own revolution. Publishing flourishes in spite of its competition from television, radio, microfilm, and the like, because it is the only medium from which one can get material to mark, clip, store, and refer to at will. This monopoly on substance of its product is changing, as we have seen. Even though Gutenberg could probably find his way around pretty easily in most printing rooms today, the technology rolls on.

Laser photo transmission is here; laser typesetting is knocking at the door. Electrostatic printing can operate at up to 12,000 lines a minute—six times the speed of the best impact printers. Jet printing, a practical process for several years now, can handle up to 70,000 lines of type a minute—or 150,000 characters per second!

Micropublishing offers low cost information distribution and storage in miniaturized form. It has been said that all of the books on the Library of Congress's 270 miles of shelves could be stored on microforms in six standard four-drawer filing cabinets.

It is a safe bet that books such as this one will, in the near future, be typed on a video-display terminal by the author, edited and proofed on a publisher's remote television screen, passed along their computerized way to a jet or electrostatic printing plant, and be printed, bound, inspected, and packed for shipping untouched by human hands. People will intrude into the process in only the first and final stages—an author and an editor will still be required for the original creation (it is fondly hoped), and distribution and sales will still involve humans for the immediate future. Ultimately, some form of teletext will probably take over the final stages. A practical consideration, at that point, will be the collection and distribution of royalty payments to the human author.

## CORPORATE CONSCIOUSNESS RAISING

Public relations, as *Dun's Review* points out, is "now a function concerned with corporate survival."

Management at top and upper-middle levels are increasingly emerging from their protected corporate environments and stepping, with varying degrees of enthusiasm and success, into the world of public debate and confrontation. Some executives have been in the public arena for many years, but the average chief executive officer has tended to view it as a jungle and leave the firing line to others.

Successful public relations executives find it necessary to spend from one to several days a month in Washington, supplementing their company's established lobbyists. "In public relations now, all roads lead to the Hill," suggests a New York bank officer. High-profile government leaders find it increasingly easy to lay down the reins of government and pick up corporation presidencies and vice-presidencies.

In a corporate version of *Star Wars* celebrities and personalities are serving as spokespeople for some companies. Personality Bess Myerson now fronts for Citibank and Bristol-Myers. Ronald Reagan's long-time service on behalf of General Electric and conservative groups is well-known. As television continues to create overnight celebrities, this trend will no doubt grow among certain corporations.

Hill and Knowlton and J. Walter Thompson are among the public relations and advertising firms profiting from short-course TV training programs for executives. Some large companies now consider a person's public performance abilities at promotion time.

In all of this rush to go public, speech writers occasionally fail to keep up with current events. It is not unheard of for one to even rewrite a little history. In October 1976 Harold Geneen, International Telephone and Telegraph's outspoken chairman and chief executive officer, gave a talk, "Communications . . . and the Quality of Life." Copies of his speech were distributed to ITT's list of thought leaders around the country.

On pages 3 to 5 of the printed version are these remarks:

> And it so happens that tonight we stand on the threshold of three very new technological developments which of themselves are sufficient to create a whole new knowledge explosion. . . . These developments are the LSI (large scale integrated circuits) and the microprocessors that they make possible. These are fiber optics and PCM (pulse code modulations). . . . Incidentally, ITT did the basic development work for [optical fibers and PCM].

This all sounded naggingly familiar to at least one of the recipients. A quick scan of *Beyond Babel,* by Brenda Maddox, turned up the following:

> The digital code made it possible to wring the maximum advantage from another *discovery of the 1930s, pulse code modulations.* A. W. Reeves, working at the laboratories of Standard Telephone and Cables Ltd in Harlow, outside London, worked out a method of interleaving telephone conversations so that twenty-four calls could be carried on a line designed for one. . . . [Emphasis added.]

> By 1958 it was possible to make transistors so tiny that enough of them could be combined on a small chip of silicon to make a complete electrical circuit. That compact package is called an integrated circuit. To have, as is now possible, hundreds of such complete circuits pressed together in a chip of material as insignificant in size as a shirt button (and not much more expensive) is called large scale integration.[2]

That kind of coincidence has been known to shake people's faith.

I'm not exactly sure where this fits in, but a 1977 survey placed public relations people sixth in a list of 130 possibly stress-producing occupations. Ahead of PR people were health technicians,waiters and waitresses, practical nurses, quality control inspectors, and musicians. Numbers forty-five through fifty (the tail end of the top fifty most stressful jobs) were office managers, reporters and editors, teachers, sales representatives, press operators, and building painters. Photographers ranked sixteenth, while secretaries were in twenty-sixth place. There's a lesson in there somewhere.

## POP-TOP PR

Public relations campaigns sometimes are mounted on behalf of what many might view as negative—even antisocial—causes. In this section we'll look at two PR campaigns—one involving an antilitter vote in Dade County, Florida, the other a controversial groundbreaking a continent away. Any definitive characterizations are left up to the reader.

Occasionally a practitioner who has just finished a successful campaign for a client is moved to write it up in detail—as a way of passing along the techniques used to PR posterity. Richard G. Rundell wrote an account for the *Public Relations Journal* of his efforts in 1974 on behalf of canners, brewers, bottlers, retailers, and related industries in defeating an anti-litter bottle deposit law in Dade County, Florida.

The proposed law, calling for mandatory deposits on all beverage bottles and cans, was modeled after a similar measure passed in Oregon by the state legislature. Those opposing the Dade County ordinance (Rundell's clients) banded together as the Dade Consumers Information Committee (DCIC). DCIC, according to Rundell, was well financed by contributions from all over Florida and other parts of the country.

A quickie survey by two Ph.D.s from the University of Miami's political science department, commissioned by Rundell and the DCIC, showed the public favored the deposit law by a two-to-one margin. Rundell explained that the DCIC campaign against the ordinance was aimed at carefully selected minority groups—male fishermen aged 18 to 42, blacks (who were told they didn't have much of an environment to protect, anyway), Republican voters, shoppers in supermarkets, and the like. Each of Dade County's 116,000 Republicans received a mailing attacking the proposed law as an infringement on personal liberty and an attack on free enterprise.

A speakers' bureau was organized around representatives of the Chamber of Commerce, the Better Business Bureau, and some local and state politicians. Throughout the campaign, according to Rundell, they "made every effort to dispel the idea that this was a fight of industry versus idealists, of big industry versus little people."

The DCIC forces for personal liberty and free enterprise defeated the ordinance with 58 percent of the vote, in spite of all-out editorial support for passage of the law from the media. Happiness in Dade County is pop-top cans and throwaway bottles.

We're indebted to another public relations executive, John Krizek, for the story of how Transamerica Corporation built its high-rise, pyramid-shaped building in San Francisco, in spite of citizen and government opposition. That is the structure which moved a former *Los Angeles Times* architectural critic to comment: "The Transamerica Building ends in a dunce cap that adds 35 percent to its height. . . . Fun-loving San Francisco, 'everybody's favorite city,' is in the process of becoming the home of the world's largest architectural folly." Whether or not you agree with critic John Pastier, the cloak-and-dagger beginnings of its construction should be of interest.

Krizek, then public relations manager for Transamerica, claims a major role for public relations in moving the project from plans to reality—fighting off local and national press criticism, unsympathetic city officials, and opposition citizen groups all the way. Krizek explains some of his tactics:

> We learned indirectly that the opposition groups planned to meet one evening in a nearby nightclub. We attended, surreptitiously, to observe and listen. Out of this rally, attended by 100 or so, came a letter-writing campaign directed to the Board of Supervisors. We thereupon accelerated a letter-writing campaign of our own, including support from several neighbors who supposedly were to be "overwhelmed" by the project.
>
> A second rally was called by the opposition. This rally was attended by perhaps 125 people, but included in that total were at least 15 people, including wives, who were there representing the corporate staff, the architect's office, and other friends of the project—all incognito.[3]

At a sidewalk rally of the groups in opposition to the building, demonstrators were met by "a covey of attractive corporate secretaries" who "served iced tea to the demonstrators, with news cameras as witnesses." At a later rally, fortune cookies with pro-Transamerica messages were served with the iced tea.

The pyramid saga is a lengthy one. Not to keep you guessing as to the outcome, on a bleak day in mid-December 1969, the contractor checked with city hall to be sure all was in order for the site permit. We'll let Krizek take it from here:

> [A corporate vice president] flashed the message to the construction supervisor and public relations manager, lurking in a restaurant across the street from the site: "Have permits in hand. Get ready to move in 20 minutes."
>
> Photographers who had been waiting in phone booths appeared on signal. The small group converged casually on the site. Out of a basement excavation, where they had been hidden all morning from street view, crawled a tractor and a truck. And to the cheers of the smallest crowd ever to conduct a major building groundbreaking in San Francisco, the tractor bit through the surface of the parking lot, and the Transamerica Pyramid was safely under construction.[4]

Happiness in San Francisco is a pyramid twice as tall as the Egyptian originals.

## POP-TOP ARCHITECTURE

In marketing workshops for design professionals the discussion usually gets around to methods for handling a firm's marketing "constraints." Constraints can take many forms, including geography, size, experience, and problems encountered during construction. An example of the last-named constraint would be the discovery that a concrete parapet in the Montreal Olympics stadium was some 20 inches too tall—blocking the view from about a third of the seats on the stadium's third level. A similar problem in sight lines was encountered in the new Madison Square Garden arena in New York.

Possibly the best-known construction constraint, for everyone concerned, is the famous Boston window regurgitator—the John Hancock Mutual Life Company's 60-story home office tower.

Boston's tallest building—Hancock's corporate snook cocking at arch-rival Prudential across the way—was topped out in September 1971, enclosed by January of 1972—and began showering various of its 10,334 glass panes on the streets and pedestrians below a short time later. By September 1973, more than 3000 of the glass panels had been replaced by plywood.

Eventually, all of the glass was replaced by thicker panes, at an estimated additional cost of $7.7 million. Even the new glass caused trouble, as panes continued to break. At one point security guards on the sidewalk were detailed to watch the windows for signs of fracturing. At the first sign of trouble the guards alerted maintenance people inside by walkie-talkie to reverse the building's ventilation fans, sucking the breaking windows inward.

There is much more to the story, which will continue to unfold over future years as the many lawsuits come to trial or are settled. The point of this recital is that the designers, I. M. Pei & Partners, were able to meet the constraints imposed on their marketing efforts by this ill-fated project. Not only does the Pei firm continue to get significant commissions in Boston, but the Hancock Tower has received design awards from such groups as the American Institute of Architects.

An outstanding publicity campaign was mounted on architect Pei's behalf on the occasion of the opening of his National Gallery East Building in Washington, D.C., in the summer of 1978. Only a few reporters were crass enough to inquire about the Hancock building. The *Washington Post*'s reportorial gadfly, Sally Quinn, wrote a full page, unmarred by a Hancock reference, about the National Gallery building and its designer. Another *Post* reporter, who wrote a feature on Pei for the Sunday *Post Magazine,* dismissed the incident with: "All those windows crashed down from his John Hancock Tower in Boston, but these things happen."

The winter of 1977–1978 saw the collapse of several snow-laden arenas in the northeast part of the country, including the two-year-old Hartford Civic Center. It is too early to tell, as of this writing, whether those, too, will be resolved as "things that happen."

## WHERE DID WE GO WRONG?

Design professionals have every reason to ask the question. It is a well-established fact that more structures are built without benefit of professional architectural and engineering input than with it. The increasing number of lawsuits against design consultants was discussed in a previous chapter. Median earnings in most other professions consistently are 50 to 100 percent higher than those of engineers and architects. In the summer of 1978 some newspapers featured a picture of a sign on a Washington, D.C., building project: "Bricklayers wanted—$13.75 an hour." A 1977 survey of the profession showed the average hourly pay for *principals* of architectural firms to be $16.62.

A little-noted 1977 study by the School of Architecture of the University of Maryland, *An Assessment of Architectural Practice,* contains some of the answers. Funded by Maryland's School of Architecture and the Baltimore Chapter of the American Institute of Architects, the study's 41 pages of findings apply generally to all design consultants. If space were available we'd reprint the entire report here—it is that significant. Lacking space to carry it all, we'll have to be content with some excerpts and paraphrasings.

Perceptions of architects held by owners, contractors, and others in the building industry:

1. The *assumption* that most architects are equally talented and possess some technical knowledge.
2. The *notion* that most architects' fees are too high.
3. The *feeling* that many architects are impractical and unrealistic, and tend toward ephemeral and "kooky" designs.
4. The *belief* that the architect is an unavoidable necessity, the person from whom one buys a set of "blueprints" to build a building.
5. The *conviction* that most architects have no understanding or appreciation of construction costs.
6. The *assumption* that most architects' drawings and specifications will be rife with errors, omissions, discrepancies, and unbuildable details.[5]

The study concludes that the more negative attitudes listed have been generated essentially by actions of professionals themselves. We have identified the enemy—guess who it is.

In a lengthy section on how clients select architects, the study discusses the growing role of government at all levels—especially at the federal level.

> [Government] agencies tend to consider architectural firms' track record of projects, technical expertise, cost control methods, size, office organization, geographic location, and, occasionally, proposed fees as the critical parameters. *In addition, a firm's "image," as conveyed through its brochures, presentations, and public relations efforts is often implicitly crucial to selection.* However, it should be clear that all of these evaluation criteria tend to favor larger, more established, high-overhead, well-financed architectural firms. [Emphasis added.]
>
> Our survey questionnaire focused on this area of competition. On the issue of firm size, over 95 percent of the architects queried believed that "small firms are often unable to compete with large firms for prestige projects even though qualified." Almost 80 percent agreed that "large architectural firms have a decided advantage over small firms . . . because of their marketing efforts and capabilities . . . built into their overhead structure." Over half felt that "small firms would become unviable" except for very small projects. Ironically, four out of five said that, individually, they would prefer working in a small firm, mainly because of "flexibility" and "variety of experience."[6]

Survey respondents were asked to identify the most important considerations in designer selection. The ranking:

1. Design talent and creativity.
2. Prior experience in similar work.
3. Organization and management skills.
4. Knowledge of practical aspects of building (time scheduling, economics, construction).
5. Fees (the cost of services).
6. Reputation.

Compare the above-listed criteria from the 1977 University of Maryland study with the list of thirteen criteria corporate buyers of design services say they use to select AE firms for interviews. In order of importance:

1. Firm's past experience related to the project.
2. Staff size.
3. Staff background (education, experience, honors, and the like).
4. Firm's location (proximity to project).
5. Accuracy of cost-estimating procedures.
6. Postconstruction follow-up.
7. Engineering experience.
8. Satisfaction of past and present clients.
9. In-house specialties and disciplines offered.
10. Design awards won by the firm.
11. Firm's prestige (regional or national).
12. Articles about the firm and its work in the architectural and engineering press.
13. Articles about the firm in the general press.

Two additional considerations were given, but not ranked, by the corporate respondents:

> Present workload for all clients.
> Firm's record for meeting schedules.[7]

On marketing efforts, the University of Maryland study points out:

> To cope with the realities of the marketplace, architects have begun to change their ways of approaching clients. More accurately, they have been *forced* to make changes. Approximately 80 percent of the architects interviewed agreed that "the marketing of architectural services is becoming a major and indispensable part of a firm's activities and overhead," while only half felt that it *should* be a major part. One fifth indicated that they had actually "hired personnel specifically for marketing purposes."[8]

The study's conclusions on the role of marketing:

> 1. Getting work is becoming an ever-larger and rapidly expanding part of the architect's efforts.
> 2. Getting work is becoming *increasingly* costly for architects.
> 3. The chances of being selected for any given project are *decreasing* as the competition quantitatively increases.
> 4. The process of selecting architects is frequently inequitable, tending to favor certain kinds of firms over others, irrespective of inherent and potential capability to perform.
> 5. To keep ahead, architectural firms are offering non-architectural services, are entering fields clearly outside the field of architecture (in which they may ultimately be unable to compete) and are often attempting to play roles for which they may or may not be prepared in order to survive.
> 6. Marketing services is becoming less "professional" and more "commercial" in nature, with paid advertising just around the corner.[9]

After a penetrating look into the state of modern architectural education (Sample comment: "The schools have been slow in acknowledging the growing importance of non-design aspects of architectural practice, such as management, economics, cost analysis, marketing, and legal concerns."), the survey assesses the role of the American Institute of Architects (AIA):

> 1. The AIA, despite its lobbying and public relations efforts, does not seem to have significantly influenced or shaped public attitudes about architecture or about architects.
> 2. The AIA membership is often too introspective and spends much of its time talking only to itself
> 3. The AIA has been quite unsuccessful and unclear in defining and enforcing standards of professional practice.
> 4. The AIA has not adequately addressed the needs and standards of professional education in architecture.
> 5. The AIA is tending to blur and compromise the architect's role as designer by unreasonably expanding the definition of architectural services as a short-term, business remedy.
> 6. The AIA's most valuable service to the individual practitioner may well be

the provision of documents, publications and information which are *useful* to him in practice.[10]

This objective assessment is perhaps the primary reason the study has not been publicized within the profession. A final excerpt, from the study's conclusions:

> The profession, if it is to become what it could be—influential, respected, financially stable, effective, and, let us say it, indispensable, must move squarely into the mainstream of American life and culture. Architects must communicate with, guide, and serve their constituents. They must further sharpen their knowledge and skills, elevate their standards of practice, and apply their expertise with confidence and commitment to every design problem, especially those which they have traditionally shunned or treated as step-children. Architects must convince the *whole* public that they unquestionably provide valuable, useful, and unique services. They must make known what those services are, what they cost, and insist on fair compensation. They must then render services which live up to their promise and potential of quality, which more than justify their cost. Ultimately, they effect the lives of every citizen who sees, uses, or thinks about architecture.[11]

My personal feeling is that this study should be required reading in schools of architecture and engineering and among the staffs and officers of professional design organizations. It has many of the answers to where we've gone wrong—and contains several good suggestions for remedying the situation. Design professionals could do worse than to adopt "communication, guidance, and service" as a triple-threat approach to their own public relations. No responsible PR practitioner would hold out public relations as a panacea for all of the problems of the design profession—and, indeed, of the human race—as set out in this book. But if there is no beginning, there is no creation; and no light.

And since communication depends so heavily on choice of words, plus the medium used, we conclude with quotations from a couple of anonymous third-century-BC writers.

"A word fitly spoken is like apples of gold in pictures of silver." (Proverbs XXV, 11)

"How forcible are right words!" (Job VI, 25)

### References

[1]L. Roy Blumenthal, *The Practice of Public Relations,* The Macmillan Company, New York, 1972, p. 2.

[2]Brenda Maddox, *Beyond Babel,* Simon and Schuster, New York, 1972, pp. 29–31.

[3]John Krizek, "How to Build A Pyramid," *Public Relations Journal,* December 1970, p. 17.

[4]Ibid., p. 21.

[5]Roger K. Lewis, *An Assessment of Architectural Practice,* no. 3-77, School of Architecture, University of Maryland, August 1977, p. 11.

[6]Ibid., p. 20.

[7]Gerre Jones, *How to Prepare Professional Design Brochures,* McGraw-Hill Book Company, New York, 1976, pp. 17–18.
[8]Roger K. Lewis, op. cit., p. 23.
[9]Ibid., p. 26.
[10]Ibid., p. 34.
[11]Ibid., p. 41.

# Bibliography

THIS BIBLIOGRAPHY CONSISTS of twelve sections covering:

| | |
|---|---|
| Advertising | Newsletters |
| Bibliographies | Photography |
| Directories | Public Relations—General |
| Exhibits and Meetings | Speeches |
| Layout and Graphics | Stylebooks |
| Lobbying and Politics | Writing |

Obviously, no bibliography covers *everything* in a field—and no claims are made that this one is more than a sampling of the more than 1000 books currently listed in the Library of Congress card catalog under "Public Relations."

No prices are given for any of the books or periodicals listed. My experience has been that prices change at least annually—inexorably upward—and my advice is to check the current price for any of the publications you are interested in buying. Some are quite expensive—certain of the directories, for example—and your local public or university library would be a good place to check first.

Addresses are given for some of the publishers who might be difficult to find in standard lists. Books from major publishers do not show addresses, on the premise readers would probably order those books through local book dealers. Otherwise, there are several guides, such as Bowker's, to publishing firms.

Comments and explanations appear after some listings.

When a publication is available from the U.S. Government Printing Office, that is the only publication information shown. The full address:

Superintendent of Documents
U.S. Government Printing Office
Washington, DC 20402

### Advertising

Kleppner, Otto: *Advertising Procedure,* Prentice-Hall, Inc., Englewood Cliffs, N.J., 1973.

Ramond, Charles: *Advertising Research: The State of the Art,* Association of National Advertisers, Inc., 155 E. 44th St., New York, NY 10017, 1976.

Roman, Kenneth, and Jane Maas: *How to Advertise,* St. Martin's Press, New York, 1975.

Seiden, Hank: *Advertising Pure and Simple,* Amacon, New York, 1977.

### Bibliographies

Bishop, Robert L.: *Public Relations, A Comprehensive Bibliography,* University of Michigan Press, Ann Arbor, 1974. Articles and books on public relations, communication theory, public opinion, and propaganda, 1964–1974.

Cutlip, Scott M.: *A Public Relations Bibliography,* 2d ed., University of Wisconsin Press, Madison, 1965. Articles and books on public relations, 1900s–1963.

### Directories

*Ayer Directory of Publications,* Ayer Press, 210 Washington Square, Philadelphia, PA 19106. Published annually. The 1978 edition lists 22,700 publications.

*Bacon's International Publicity Checker,* Bacon's Publishing Company, 14 E. Jackson Blvd., Chicago, IL 60604. Lists over 8000 publications in fifteen countries. Published annually.

*Bacon's Publicity Checker: Magazines and Newspapers.* See address above. Published annually in 2 volumes, with quarterly revisions. The 1978 edition had information about more than 13,000 publications in the United States and Canada, arranged for public relations use.

Barbour, Robert L. (ed.): *Who's Who in Public Relations (International),* 5th ed., PR Publishing Company, Inc., Meriden, N.H., 1976.

*Editor and Publisher Yearbook,* Editor and Publisher, 850 Third Avenue, New York, NY 10022. Published annually.

*Encyclopedia of Associations,* 12th ed., Gale Research Company, Gale Book Tower, Detroit, MI 48226, 1978. In 3 volumes. Volume I, *National Organizations of the U.S.,* with almost 15,000 entries, is the basic volume.

*Guide to American Directories,* 10th ed., B. Klein Publications, P.O. Box 8503, Coral Springs, FL 33065. Information about 6000 directories on all subjects is arranged under 300 major classifications.

*National Trade and Professional Associations of the United States & Canada & Labor Unions,* Washington Monitor, Inc., 499 National Press Building, Washington, DC 20045. Published annually; includes some 6000 organizations.

*Newsletter Directory,* Gale Research Company. See address above. About 3000 listings of newsletters and reporting services.

*Newsletter Yearbook Directory,* The Newsletter Clearinghouse, P.O. Box 311, Rhinebeck, NY 12572. Published annually. About all anyone needs to know about newsletters.

*O'Dwyer's Directory of Public Relations Firms,* Jack O'Dwyer, 271 Madison Ave., New York, NY 10016. Published annually.

*Professional's Guide to Public Relations Services,* Richard Weiner, Inc., 888 7th Ave., New York, NY 10019, 1975.

*Public Relations Register,* Public Relations Society of America, 845 3d Ave., New York, NY 10022. Published annually; cross-indexed listing of PRSA members.

*Society of American Travel Writers Roster,* Society of American Travel Writers, 1120 Connecticut Ave., N.W., Washington, DC 20036. U.S. and Canadian travel writers, photographers, editors, and broadcasters, plus PR executives in the travel business.

*Standard Periodical Directory,* Oxbridge Publications, 1345 Avenue of the Americas, New York, NY 10019. Complete guide to U.S. and Canadian periodicals—more than 62,500 listings.

Standard Rate & Data Service, Inc., 5201 Old Orchard Road, Skokie, IL 60077, publishes a number of directories, including:
*Business Publication Rates and Data* (monthly)

*Consumer Magazine and Farm Publication Rates and Data* (monthly)

*Direct Mail Lists Rates and Data* (semiannually)

*Newspaper Rates and Data* (monthly)

*Weekly Newspaper and Shopping Guide Rates and Data* (semiannually)

*U.S. Publicity Directory,* Norback & Norback, 353 Nassau St., Princeton, NJ 08540. Published annually in 2 volumes: business and finance editors in one and radio and TV program and news directors in the other. Regional editions of the radio and TV directory are available.

Wasserman, Paul, ed.: *Encyclopedia of Business Information Sources,* Gale Research Company, 1976. See address above. For finding out where to find out about everything in business; 17,000 entries in 1280 subject areas.

*Working Press of the Nation,* 29th ed., National Research Bureau, Inc., 424 N. Third St., Burlington, IA 52601. Published annually in 5 volumes: 1, Newspapers; 2, Magazines; 3, TV and Radio Stations; 4, Feature Writers, Photographers and Syndicates; 5, International Publications.

*Writers Directory,* Washington Independent Writers, 1010 Vermont Ave., N.W., Washington, DC 20005. Leads on D.C.-based writers and editors for free-lance assignments.

### Exhibits and Meetings

*The Exhibit Medium,* Successful Meetings Book Division, 633 3d Ave., New York, NY 10017, 1978. Tells how to design, fabricate, show, and staff more productive exhibits.

Finkel, C.: *Professional Guide to Successful Meetings,* Successful Meetings Book Division, 1976. See address above.

*Hotel-Motel Facilities Directory,* Hotel Sales Management Association International, 362 Fifth Ave., New York, NY 10001. Published annually; a worldwide listing of meeting and convention facilities.

### Layout and Graphics

Ballinger, Raymond A.: *Layout and Graphic Design,* Van Nostrand–Reinhold, New York, 1970.

Biggs, John R.: *Basic Typography,* Watson-Guptill Publications, New York, 1968.

Burns, Aaron: *Typography,* Reinhold Publishing Corporation, New York, 1961.

Craig, James: *Designing With Type,* Watson-Guptill Publications, New York, 1971.

———: *Production for the Graphic Designer,* Watson-Guptill Publications, New York, 1974.

Croy, Peter: *Graphic Design and Reproduction Techniques,* Hastings House Publishers, Inc., New York, 1972.

Felton, Charles J.: *Layout,* 3d ed., Appleton-Century-Crofts, Inc., New York, 1954.

Garland, Ken: *Graphics Handbook,* D. Van Nostrand Company, New York, 1966.

Graham, Walter B.: *Complete Guide to Pasteup,* North American Publishing Company, Philadelphia, 1975.

*Graphics Master,* Dean Lem Associates, P.O. Box 46086, Los Angeles, 1977.

Jones, Gerre: *How to Prepare Professional Design Brochures,* McGraw-Hill Book Company, New York, 1976.

Maurello, Ralph S.: *How to Do Paste-ups and Mechanicals,* Tudor Publishing Company, New York, 1960.

Morison, Stanley: *Typographic Arts,* Harvard University Press, Cambridge, Mass., 1950.

*Pocket Pal,* 11th ed., International Paper Company, 220 E. 42d St., New York, NY 10017, 1974.

Ruder, Emil: *Typography: A Manual of Design,* Hastings House Publishers, Inc., New York, 1967.

Stevenson, George A.: *Graphic Arts Encyclopedia,* McGraw-Hill Book Company, New York, 1968.

Swann, Cal: *Techniques of Typography,* Watson-Guptill Publications, New York, 1969.

Turnbull, Arthur T., and Russell N. Baird: *The Graphics of Communication,* Holt, Rinehart and Winston, Inc., New York, 1964.

### Lobbying and Politics

*Almanac of American Politics,* Fund for Constitutional Government, 515 Madison Ave., New York, NY 10022. Published annually. Possibly more information about Congress and state governments than you want to know, but a useful reference.

Brownson, Charles B.: *Congressional Staff Directory,* P.O. Box 62, Mount Vernon, VA 22121. Issued annually. Companion books are the *Advance Locator* and *Election Index,* which update the *Staff Directory.*

*Congress in Print,* Washington Monitor, 499 National Press Building, Washington, DC 20045. Weekly alert on publications released for public distribution by congressional committees. Committee publications are usually printed in limited quantities and most are not available through the Government Printing Office. This publication tells what's available where and how to get copies.

*Congressional Directory,* U. S. Government Printing Office. Handy reference source published for each Congress.

*Congressional Sourcebook Series,* 3 vols. Compiled by the U.S. General Accounting Office; available from the U.S. Government Printing Office.

1. *Recurring Reports to the Congress.* A description of some 800 recurring reports required of executive branch agencies by Congress.

2. *Federal Program Evaluations.* Describes almost 1700 evaluation reports produced by

and for 18 selected federal agencies.

3. *Federal Information Sources and Systems.* An index of 1000 federal information sources and systems maintained by 63 executive agencies.

*Directory of Washington Representatives of American Associations and Industry,* Columbia Books, Inc., 734 15th St., N.W., Washington, DC 20005, 1978. All you wanted to know about lobbyists and whom they represent.

*Federal Yellow Book,* Washington Monitor, Inc. See above for address. Looseleaf directory of federal agencies and departments, fully updated through the year.

*Hudson's Washington News Media Directory,* Hudson's Directory, 2626 Pennsylvania Ave., N.W., Washington, DC 20037. Published annually, listing editors and correspondents for some 2500 print and broadcast media represented in Washington.

*Key Government Personnel,* Hill & Knowlton, 1425 K St., N.W., Washington, DC 20005. Excellent free guide from a major PR agency to almost 2000 key people in the federal establishment.

Lipsen, Charles B., with Stephan Lesher: *Vested Interest,* Washington Monitor, Inc., 1977. See above for address.

*United States Government Manual,* U.S. Government Printing office. Published for each new Congress. Contains much useful information.

## Newsletters

Jones, Gerre: "How to Start a Newsletter," *Professional Marketing Report,* P.O. Box 32387, Washington, DC 20007, January 1977.

Nagan, Peter S.: *How to Put Out a Newsletter,* Newsletter Services, Inc., 1120 19th St., N.W., Washington, DC 20036, 1978. The basics for association and nonprofit newsletters. Free.

Reid, Gerene: *How to Write Company Newsletters,* Rubicon Press, P.O. Box 144, Deming, WA 98244, 1977.

## Photography

Evans, Ralph M.: *Eye, Film and Camera in Color Photography,* John Wiley & Sons, Inc., New York, 1948.

Hicks, Wilson: *Words and Pictures,* Harper & Brothers, New York, 1952.

Hurley, Gerald D., and Angus McDougall: *Visual Impact in Print,* Visual Impact, Inc., Chicago, 1971.

Kalish, Stanley, and Clifton C. Edom: *Picture Editing,* Rinehart & Company, Inc., New York, 1951.

Kemp, Weston D.: *Photography for Visual Communications,* Prentice-Hall, Inc., Englewood Cliffs, N.J., 1973.

Molitor, Joseph W.: *Architectural Photography,* John Wiley & Sons, Inc., New York, 1976.

## Public Relations—General

Adams, A. B.: *Handbook of Practical Public Relations,* Thomas Y. Crowell Company, New York, 1970.

Bernays, Edward L.: *Public Relations,* University of Oklahoma Press, Norman, 1970.

Black, Sam: *Practical Public Relations,* Pitman, London, 1976.

Blumenthal, L. R.: *The Practice of Public Relations,* The Macmillan Company, New York, 1972.

Boettinger, H. M.: *Moving Mountains: The Art and Craft of Letting Others See Things Your Way,* The Macmillan Company, New York, 1969.

Budd, J. F., Jr.: *Executive's Primer on Public Relations,* Chilton Book Company, Radnor, Pa., 1969.

Canfield, B. R., and H. F. Moore: *Public Relations: Principles, Cases, Problems,* Richard D. Irwin, Inc., Homewood, Ill., 1977.

Carlson, Robert O.: *Communications and Public Opinion,* Praeger, New York, 1975.

Center, Allen: *Public Relations Practices: Case Studies,* Prentice-Hall, Inc., Englewood Cliffs, N.J., 1975.

Coffin, Royce A.: *The Communicator,* Amacon (The American Management Associations), New York, 1975.

*Critical Issues in Public Relations,* Hill & Knowlton, 633 3d Ave., New York, NY 10017, 1975.

Cutlip, Scott, and Allen Center: *Effective Public Relations,* 4th ed., Prentice-Hall, Inc., Englewood Cliffs, N.J., 1971.

Darrow, R. W., D. J.Forrestal, and A. O. Cookman: *Dartnell Public Relations Handbook,* The Dartnell Corporation, Chicago, 1969.

Gold, Vic: *I Don't Need You When I'm Right,* William Morrow and Company, Inc., New York, 1975.

Golden, L. L. L.: *Only by Public Consent: American Corporations Search for Favorable Opinion,* Hawthorn Books, Inc., New York, 1968.

Fischer, Heinz-Dietrich, and John C. Merrill, eds.: *International Communication,* Hastings House, New York, 1970.

Hall, Babette: *Public Relations, Publicity, Promotion,* Ives Washburn, Inc., New York, 1970.

Hill, John W.: *The Making of a Public Relations Man,* David McKay Company, Inc., New York, 1963.

Jefkins, Frank: *Planned Public Relations,* Intertext, London, 1969.

Jones, Gerre: *How to Market Professional Design Services,* McGraw-Hill Book Company, New York, 1973.

Klein, Ted, and Frank Danzig: *How to be Heard: Making the Media Work for You,* The Macmillan Company, New York, 1974.

Lerbinger, Otto: *Designs for Persuasive Communications,* Prentice-Hall, Inc., Englewood Cliffs, N.J., 1972.

Lesly, Philip: *Lesly's Public Relations Handbook,* Prentice-Hall, Inc., Englewood Cliffs, N. J.,

1971.

Lewis, H. Gordon: *How to Handle Your Own Public Relations*, Nelson-Hall, Inc., Chicago, 1976.

Marston, John: *The Nature of Public Relations*, McGraw-Hill Book Company, New York, 1963.

Newson, D. and Scott A.: *This is PR: The Realities of Public Relations*, Wadsworth Publishing Company, Inc., Belmont, Calif., 1976.

Nolte, L. W.: *Fundamentals of Public Relations*, Pergamon Press, Inc., Elmsford, N.Y., 1974.

*Public Relations Guide for Consulting Engineers*, American Consulting Engineers Council, 1155 15th St., N.W., Washington, DC 20005, 1977.

Roalman, A. R.: *Profitable Public Relations*, Dow Jones–Irwin, Inc., Homewood, Ill., 1968.

Rodes, Toby E.: *Public Relations—A Short Introduction*, Typo AG, Basel, Switzerland, 1977.

Simon, Morton: *Public Relations Law*, Appleton-Century-Crofts, New York, 1969.

Simon, Raymond: *Public Relations: Concepts and Practice*, Grid, Inc., Columbus, Ohio, 1976.

Steinberg, Charles S.: *The Creation of Consent: Public Relations in Practice*, Hastings House, New York, 1975.

Stephenson, Howard: *Handbook of Public Relations*, 2d ed., McGraw-Hill Book Company, New York, 1971.

Weiner, Richard: *Professional's Guide to Publicity*, Richard Weiner, Inc., 888 7th Ave., New York, NY 10019, 1975.

**Public Relations—Newsletters**

*Jack O'Dwyer's Newsletter*, 271 Madison Ave., New York, NY 10016. Weekly.

*PR Aids' Party Line*, 221 Park Avenue South, New York, NY 10003. Weekly.

*PR Reporter*, Box 600, Exeter, NH 03833, Weekly.

*Practical Public Relations*, Box 3861, Rochester, NY 14610. Twice monthly.

*Public Relations News*, 127 E. 80th St., New York, NY 10021. The original and the best. Weekly.

*Public Relations Quarterly*, 44 W. Market St., Rhinebeck, NY 12572.

*Publicist*, 221 Park Avenue South, New York, NY 10003. Bimonthly.

**Speeches**

Amram, Fred M., and Frank T. Benson: *Creating a Speech*, Charles Scribner's Sons, New York, 1968.

Bradley, Bert E.: *Fundamentals of Speech Communication: The Credibility of Ideas*, William C. Brown, Dubuque, Iowa, 1974.

Brooks, William D.: *Speech Communications*, 2d ed., William C. Brown, Dubuque, Iowa, 1974.

Campbell, John Angus: *An Overview of Speech Preparation*, Science Research Associates, Inc., Chicago, 1976.

Chase, Stuart: *Power of Words*, Harcourt, Brace & World, New York, 1954.

Droke, Maxwell: *The Speaker's Handbook of Humor*, Harper & Row, New York, 1956.

Friedman, Edward L.: *Speechmaker's Complete Handbook*, Harper & Row, New York, 1955.

———: *Toastmaster's Treasury*, Harper & Row, New York, 1960.

Hegarty, Edward J.: *How to Write a Speech*, McGraw-Hill Book Company, New York, 1951.

Howell, William S., and Ernest G. Borman: *Presentation Speaking for Business and the Professions*, Harper & Row, New York, 1971.

Humes, James C.: *Instant Eloquence*, Harper & Row, New York, 1973.

———: *Podium Humor*, Harper & Row, New York, 1975.

———: *Roles Speakers Play*, Harper & Row, New York, 1976.

Reid, Loren: *Speaking Well*, 3d ed., McGraw-Hill Book Company, New York, 1977.

Ross, Raymond S.: *Speech Communication: Fundamentals and Practice*, 3d ed., Prentice-Hall, Inc., Englewood Cliffs, N.J., 1974.

Shannon, Louis P.: *Speakers, Beware!*, Script Master, 271 Dallam Rd., Newark, DE 19711, 1975.

Stedman, William: *A Guide to Public Speaking*, Prentice-Hall, Inc., Englewood Cliffs, N.J., 1971.

Tacey, William S.: *Business and Professional Speaking*, William C. Brown, Dubuque, Iowa, 1975.

Vardaman, George T.: *Effective Communication of Ideas*, Van Nostrand–Reinhold Company, New York, 1970.

Vohs, John L., and G. P. Mohrmann: *Audiences Messages Speakers*, Harcourt Brace Jovanovich, New York, 1975.

Welsh, James J.: *The Speech Writing Guide*, John Wiley & Sons, New York, 1968.

Zimbardo, Philip, and Ebbe B. Ebbesen: *Influencing Attitudes and Changing Behavior*, Addison-Wesley Publishing Company, Reading, Mass., 1969.

**Speech Writing—Newsletter**

Tarver, Jerry, ed.: *Speech Writer's Newsletter*, Box 444, University of Richmond, Richmond, VA 27173. Bimonthly tip sheet on writing and giving speeches.

**Stylebooks**

Angione, Howard, ed.: *The Associated Press Style Book and Libel Manual*, Associated Press, 50 Rockefeller Plaza, New York, NY 10020, 1977.

*Ayer Public Relations and Publicity Style Book*, Ayer Press, 210 W. Washington Square, Philadelphia, PA 19106, 1974.

Flesch, Rudolf, *Look it Up*, Harper & Row, New York, 1977.

*A Manual of Style*, 12th ed., The University of Chicago Press, Chicago, 1969.

*New York Times Manual of Style and Usage*, Quadrangle Books, New York, 1976.

*U.S. Government Printing Office Style Manual*, rev.

ed., U.S. Government Printing office, 1973.

### Writing

Baker, Sheridan: *The Complete Stylist,* 2d ed., Thomas Y. Crowell Company, New York, 1972.

Bartlett, John: *Familiar Quotations,* 14th ed., Emily Morison Beck (ed.), Little Brown and Company, Boston, 1968.

Barzun, Jacques: *Simple & Direct: A Rhetoric for Writers,* Harper & Row, New York, 1975.

Bernstein, Theodore M.: *Watch Your Language,* Atheneum Publishers, New York, 1958.

———: *The Careful Writer: A Modern Guide to English Usage,* Atheneum Publishers, New York, 1965.

———: *Dos, Don'ts & Maybes of English Usage,* Quadrangle Books, New York, 1977.

Brown, Leland: *Effective Business Report Writing,* Prentice-Hall, Inc., Englewood Cliffs, N.J., 1973.

Burack, A. S., ed.: *The Writer's Handbook,* The Writer, Inc., Boston, 1970.

Ewing, David W.: *Writing for Results in Business, Government, and the Professions,* John Wiley & Sons, New York, 1974.

Flesch, Rudolf: *The Art of Plain Talk,* Harper & Brothers, New York, 1946.

———: *The Way to Write,* Harper & Brothers, New York, 1946.

———: *The Art of Readable Writing,* Harper & Brothers, New York, 1949.

———: *How to Test Readability,* Harper & Brothers, New York, 1951.

Fowler, H. W.: *A Dictionary of Modern English Usage,* 2d ed., Clarendon Press, Oxford, 1965.

Gunning, Robert: *How to Take the Fog Out of Writing,* Dartnell Corporation, Chicago, 1964.

*The McGraw-Hill Author's Book,* McGraw-Hill Book Company, New York, 1968.

O'Hayre, John: *Gobbledygook Has Gotta Go,* U.S. Government Printing Office, n.d.

Perrin, Porter G.: *Writer's Guide and Index to English,* 4th ed., Scott, Foresman and Company, Glenview, Ill., 1968.

Reid, Gerene: *How to Write News Releases That Sell,* Rubicon Press, P.O. Box 144, Deming, WA 98244, 1977.

Strunk, W., Jr., and E. B. White: *The Elements of Style,* The Macmillan Company, New York, 1959.

*Webster's Third New International Dictionary of the English Language, Unabridged,* G. & C. Merriam Company, Springfield, Mass., 1964.

### Writing—Newsletters

*The Editorial Eye,* 5909 Pratt St., Alexandria, VA 22310. Twice-monthly; well written.

*Editor's Newsletter,* P. O. Box 243, Lenox Hill Station, New York, NY 10021. Monthly.

*Impact,* Venture Publications, 203 N. Wabash Avenue, Chicago, IL 60601. Monthly and good.

# Appendix

IN 1976 THE Code of Professional Standards of the Public Relations Society of America (PRSA) came under Federal Trade Commission (FTC) scrutiny. The FTC charged that PRSA restrictions against encroachment and contingency fees violated antitrust provisions of Section 5 of the FTC Act. The ban against solicitation was said to be in restraint of competition and the contingency fee ban was seen as a form of price restriction.

In April 1977 the PRSA Assembly amended the Code by deleting the two FTC-questioned articles. Certain other language in the code was clarified. In August 1977 the FTC accepted a consent order and agreement to remove the offending articles. This is the present PRSA Code of Professional Standards for the Practice of Public Relations, as adopted April 29, 1977.

## Declaration of Principles

Members of the Public Relations Society of America base their professional principles on the fundamental value and dignity of the individual, holding that the free exercise of human rights, especially freedom of speech, freedom of assembly and freedom of the press, is essential to the practice of public relations.

In serving the interests of clients and employers, we dedicate ourselves to the goals of better communication, understanding and cooperation among the diverse individuals, groups and institutions of society.

We pledge:

To conduct ourselves professionally, with truth, accuracy, fairness and responsibility to the public;

To improve our individual competence and

advance the knowledge and proficiency of the profession through continuing research and education;

And to adhere to the articles of the Code of Professional Standards for the Practice of Public Relations as adopted by the governing Assembly of the Society.

## Articles of the Code

These articles have been adopted by the Public Relations Society of America to promote and maintain high standards of public service and ethical conduct among its members.

1. A member shall deal fairly with clients or employers, past and present, with fellow practitioners and the general public.

2. A member shall conduct his or her professional life in accord with the public interest.

3. A member shall adhere to truth and accuracy and to generally accepted standards of good taste.

4. A member shall not represent conflicting or competing interests without the express consent of those involved, given after a full disclosure of the facts; nor place himself or herself in a position where the member's interest is or may be in conflict with a duty to a client, or others, without a full disclosure of such interests to all involved.

5. A member shall safeguard the confidences of both present and former clients or employers and shall not accept retainers or employment which may involve the disclosure or use of these confidences to the disadvantage or prejudice of such clients or employers.

6. A member shall not engage in any practice which tends to corrupt the integrity of channels of communication or the processes of government.

7. A member shall not intentionally communicate false or misleading information and is obligated to use care to avoid communication of false or misleading information.

8. A member shall be prepared to identify publicly the name of the client or employer on whose behalf any public communication is made.

9. A member shall not make use of any individual or organization purporting to serve or represent an announced case, or purporting to be independent or unbiased, but actually serving an undisclosed special or private interest of a member, client or employer.

10. A member shall not intentionally injure the professional reputation or practice of another practitioner.

However, if a member has evidence that another member has been guilty of unethical, illegal or unfair practices, including those in violation of this Code, the member shall present the information promptly to the proper authorities of the Society for action in accordance with the procedure set forth in Article XIII of the Bylaws.

11. A member called as a witness in a proceeding for the enforcement of this Code shall be bound to appear, unless excused for sufficient reason by the Judicial Panel.

12. A member, in performing services for a client or employer, shall not accept fees, commissions or any other valuable consideration from anyone other than the client or employer in connection with those services without the express consent of the client or employer, given after a full disclosure of the facts.

13. A member shall not guarantee the achievement of specified results beyond the member's direct control.

14. A member shall, as soon as possible, sever relations with any organization or individual if such relationship requires conduct contrary to the articles of this Code.

# INDEX